Damaged

A Survivor's Story of the Damage Done by Sexual and Physical Abuse

The Unbelievable Story about My Truth

Volume 1

Lorina Pyle

I would like to dedicate this book to my incredible husband and beautiful children for their never ending love and support. Thank you for the forgiveness you have given me for the pain I brought into your lives and know that I love you beyond any words available to me.

Rev. Jean, without you, none of this would have been possible. Thank you for being the incredible spiritual instrument in my healing process and helping me to come into the light from the deepest, darkest places in which I was trapped for decades.

To my amazing and dear friend Marti, thank you for having the courage and dedication over these past few years to collaborate with me to bring to these pages my painful journey back in time so I could share my story with others. I could never have accomplished this effort without you.

To Tara Bernal, Marc Ameel, Samuel Scaife, III, Linda and David Neumann, and Cheryl White, your council and contributions to the final draft are so very much appreciated. And to Mara Peters, your final touch was icing on the cake to this whole process.

Detectives Norman Squire, Dan Covault, and Rick Castro, I must personally thank you for your steadfast dedication and commitment to pursuing these heinous predators for those of us seeking justice.

Table of Contents

Table of Contents
(continued)

Foreword

Detective Rick Castro
Child Abuse Unit
San Diego County Sheriff's Department

I believe that the definition of sexual assault only defines a small portion of what it truly entails. If the public had a better understanding of how sexual assault and abuse damages a victim's being, there would be a larger outcry for the victims. Suicide, isolation, depression, drug addiction, loneliness, lack of self-worth, and the inability to develop strong lasting relationships, are only a few examples of the effects of sexual assault and abuse on a victim. I feel that sexual assault and abuse is a hidden pandemic. The lack of resources, education, and parental involvement are contributors to the growing problem.

> Sexual assault and abuse is like electricity:
> It hides behind walls,
> Insulated from the public,
> Sometimes deep underground,
> Reaches around the world,
> Will shock you when you find it, and
> Must be handled with care and respect...

The quote above came to me while I was fishing in the Eastern Sierra's. I was fishing near an electricity producing plant and I could hear the humming sound of electricity coming from the high power lines directly above me. All around me were warning signs of underground power lines and the universal symbol of a person being shocked. All of a sudden, the words of the above mentioned quote came to me.

I have interviewed thousands of victims in my career, but only a few have ever touched my soul and reinforced that the job I am doing is God's work. I had the honor and privilege to interview Lorina Pyle, a true survivor and, a warrior. Although Lorina's story is horrific and incomprehensible, I believe that through her passion, strength, survival skills, and commitment to God, she will be a voice to the countless victims searching for someone they can cling to and empower them to come forward with their story.

In this book, Lorina will take you on a journey that people only talk about in private. She will inspire and empower readers and victims to act now by sharing their story as she has done here or by getting involved with organizations that work with and for victims of sexual assault.

I love the work I do, but even in moments of peace and relaxation, I still think of all the victims of sexual assault and abuse that are waiting for us to identify, rescue, and empower them.

God bless all the victims...

A Blessing to the Author

Thank you and many blessings to you Lorina, for being who you are, a truly remarkable woman who has come through life experiences that no one should ever have to endure. Sadly to say, this is more common than not. You are a beacon to our "Innocents," the countless thousands of young people all over this planet who are abused on a regular basis because they have no protection and are too afraid to tell.

It is a great privilege to have been even a part of the healing that you so badly needed in 2006, when you showed up at a healing circle I was leading. One look at you told me that you were in total desperation! Thankfully, my training in transpersonal inner-child work and other studies, allowed me to help you bring forward your dreadfully cocooned, in great pain, inner child. You had the strength of both heart and soul to go back, embrace and re-empower her. The wounded child could no longer stay shut off in the traumas of her early painful experience. Bringing together that traumatized child with the adult you I was working with acted like a domino effect to help you in your determined search for healing.

Since that time, you have so diligently done all you could to heal yourself and now your path will lead others to their re-empowerment and healing, in turn, creating a unified wholeness within you. It has been so wonderful to watch you learn, heal, and grow into the wonderful minister you have so earned. Your selfless and extremely difficult choice to bear your innermost rifting, painful experiences so that others can be brought into wholeness to heal from their injuries is a gift of great love.

Many others would have quit. So many others have along their journey. I greatly honor your intentions to help others find their voices and the internal power that they themselves, along with these predators, have believed were taken away. But, because of you and your remarkable being, so many young ones who are internally dragging down their adult, and sometimes not yet adult selves, shall have the opportunity to find a way out of that prison of secrecy and pain.

I wish you all good in your continual trek to teach and heal these people and lead them into their beautiful wholeness.

Standing in admiration of your warrior lady spirit,

Rev. Jean Holmes, U.C.M.
A.C.H.E. Certified Transpersonal Hypnotherapist

Rev. Jean is an internationally respected medium, teacher, lecturer, and ordained spiritualist minister with the Universal Church of the Master, who holds the Golden Light of Christ Church charter. The Universal Church of the Master is Rev. Jean's headquarter church,

She is active in the International Federation of Spiritualists in Europe.

www.higherwisdom.com

Introduction

This journey would never have been possible without help from my spiritual friends, meditation, and the support of my loving family. I never could have imagined how difficult writing this book would be, but somewhere deep inside me, I knew I had to tell my story. To be able to share my life's experiences as a child, I have had to change the names of the people involved, but I assure you, this story is my unbelievable truth.

The name for my series of three books, The Unbelievable Story About My Truth, comes from my belief that no one would believe my story because it was so unbelievable. Who would believe that a near eleven-year-old child would torture and sexually abuse a four-year-old baby? Who would believe that a father would kidnap his own child from a loving mother just to put that child in the hands of a physical, mental and emotional abuser or in the care of near strangers? Who would believe any of the horrific things that were done to me, often in the name of love or for my own good? But, it is my truth.

I know now that I must have had to go through this and survive for a very significant reason or purpose. If sharing my story, my strengths and weaknesses, can somehow help others to find a way through their own personal hell to help themselves, then my life and experiences will not have been in vain. My original purpose for writing this book was to use it as a very important part of my healing process. As I went through the process, it became clear to me that it was for more than just my healing. If someone who reads my story knows a child in the same circumstances, my words can help them to understand what the child has been lead to believe about their existence and be better able to help the child to speak out. And, upon hearing my story, I can only hope that it will give adults, no matter their age, the courage to face their own dark fears and pain to find a way to forgive themselves any poor choices they made along the way. For all, young and old, the message is that they matter. It is never too late to tell! They no longer have to be ashamed or carry the secrets of what someone else did that created what became their damaged reality.

I was brainwashed into not telling, like most people who have been molested and or abused. I was belittled and made to feel worthless so that I didn't feel like anyone would care if I did tell. I was taken over emotionally, mentally, and physically at the tender age of four and from then on, for most of my life, I continued the abuse by holding on to and believing the negative and hateful things that my abusers had implanted.

Like all of us, I spent my young life asking God "Why me? Why are you allowing this to happen to me? Why did you put me here? Why can't I just die?" I truly hated being alive. I truly hated me! I had no reason to be alive and even more so, it seemed as though no one else wanted me here either. I was a waste of time, a burden, and an extra mouth to feed. I was just a mistake, an ugly little girl that no one could possibly love. I was constantly being reminded that I was stupid and worthless and that I would never amount to anything. But none of that could compare to the violence and fear imposed upon me from the sexual abuse.

One question I've heard from so many, including psychiatrists, is why didn't I tell? Tell somebody, anybody? Surely someone would have been able to help. This is not true in the eyes of the abused. I was ashamed, embarrassed, too terrified to tell. Who would I tell? How would I tell? What should I tell? My thoughts were, if I did tell, sooner or later I would be returned, back to my step-mother and step-brother. That would mean going back and being punished, but this time, not just for being stupid and worthless to them, but for "telling." In my mind, I was better off sticking it out and just hoping for a miracle. But, that miracle never came.

When little girls should be playing with dolls and friends, going to school to learn how to read and write, draw and paint pictures of their favorite things, I was experiencing physical abuse, mental abuse, sexual abuse, rape, sodomy, depression, anxiety, and had constant thoughts of suicide. My step-brother was the worst of all evils. He was the tormenter, Satan himself in sheep's clothing. The very sound of his voice made my heart pound as I would scramble for a place to become invisible. The second worse evil was his mother, my *true* evil step-mother.

It has taken years of fighting through the fear and intense soul searching to get to where I am now, both mentally and emotionally. It has been very difficult to put my feelings and words to paper. I have experienced memories that were stashed away so deep that as they were triggered and exposed, I had to concentrate on healing them. I had to learn to be gentle, loving and kind to myself, something I was never taught to do. Remembering the details and re-experiencing a lifetime of feelings made me finally understand why I always felt so dirty, stupid, cowardly and worthless for so much of my life. As I mentally traveled back into the past, I was able to honestly see and understand how I obtained my fears and sense of worthlessness. That repetitive brainwashing from such an early and formative age kept me in the chains of being a victim for most of my life.

I am now free from those chains. I have broken free from the chains of fear, from the chains of judgment, from the chains of self-loathing that weighted me down and held me back from the life God has shown me I deserve; a life of love and happiness. That is what God has intended for all of us to know.

My name is Lorina and this is the beginning of the journey of my unbelievable story, my truth; this is how I became DAMAGED.

I was born in Price, Utah on June 21, 1966. My father, Del, was thirty-eight and my mother, Daisy, was only twenty. My mother was my father's fifth wife, but she would be far from his last. She married young to get away from her life at home with her own mother, Alice. At the age of five, my mother had contracted scarlet fever, which developed into polio. Six other neighborhood children also got sick with the disease, and died. My grandmother resented that she had to take care of her daughter, and would tell her that the only reason she survived was that even God didn't want her.

To be honest, I don't really remember my mother being in my life. It wouldn't be until many years later, as a young adult, that I would find out the truth about why she was absent from my life. I would learn that when I was just three years old, my dad and my mom's brother, Denny, kidnapped me by stealing me out of our front yard when I was playing. My grandmother, Alice, was in on the plan too. Whenever I asked about my mother, I was told so many different stories that it was too confusing for my young mind to follow. Eventually I learned not to mention her or ask any questions about her.

One of my earliest memories was at the age of three when I got my first best friend in the whole world, a new puppy. I named her Tassey. Looking back, I realize it was probably a way to distract me from asking about where my mommy was, but at the time, it was the most precious gift ever.

I could clearly communicate at this age but I knew that I was better off to speak little, listen well, and keep myself occupied. I enjoyed being around the adults and listening to them. I was like a little sponge; soaking in everything. I would play as quietly as I could around them, so they wouldn't notice me. I had no problem carrying on a conversation with myself and was in deep thought most of the time. Maybe that solitude is why my memories have remained so vivid over time.

I can picture my room at my Grandma's house as if I were sitting in it right now. My crib was white. The floors were wooden with round, woven throw rugs. Above my baby crib, there was a small shelf that held a snow globe that I always played with when I woke up. There was a mirror behind the shelf where the snow globe sat. Sometimes when I would get up to grab the snow globe my reflection would catch my attention. I remember quietly staring into the mirror, looking deep into my eyes wondering "Who are you?" I tried to look beyond my physical self. I didn't understand it but somehow I felt that there was more to me than what I could see. In a curious way, this was very interesting to me. I understand it is hard to believe a young child could think and feel with such depth. To this day I can't explain it, but my memories come from that viewpoint, that crib, that shelf, that snow globe and mirror. And, as I grew older, I knew this awareness was something I was to keep to myself.

There were two doors, none leading outside, just two separate entrances to my room. I was kept in that room many hours a day but I learned to enjoy my time alone. I would lie still playing with the magical snow globe. I would sing and my voice echoed in the room. To me it sounded great. I had to be very careful not to let Grandma Alice hear me. She didn't care too much for singing.

My grandma was a tall, scary woman to a little girl like me. She scolded me quite often. We had a large white bath tub with the large feet. I was scared to death of what I perceived to be a monster. I was alright when I was inside it playing, but when it was time for the plug to come out, that's when all hell would break loose. I remember cramming my body up against the back of the tub screaming for dear life. I just knew I was going to be sucked down the drain. I would cry and scream, while Grandma yelled at me to shut up or she'd really give me something to cry about. This would become a daily ritual.

I vaguely remember my grandfather; but I'll never forget how large he was and most of all, how he spoke through a hole in his throat. He was the nicest person that I can remember being in my life by this age, and the first person to introduce me to religion, or at least a sense of it. We would walk together on a dirt road to get to church. I can remember that my first time in the church I was surprised to see a bird bath. I asked why they had a bird bath inside and my grandfather explained to me that it wasn't a bird bath but filled with holy water for the people to cleanse themselves before entering God's house. There was a beautiful picture on the wall of Jesus, walking in a garden. When I asked about the man in the picture, I was told he was the Son of God and if I ever felt lonely or afraid he would be there for me. All I had to do was call on him and he would protect me. There was something about Him that made me feel good and safe inside.

I also recall people lining up to speak to God behind a wall in a small room. I didn't understand any of it. I asked why I couldn't speak to or see God myself and I was told it was because I wasn't old enough. I was very curious about how the world was made and how God came to be. It was so confusing to be told I would have to ask Him after I die, and then and only then would I be allowed to know. Until that time, I was just to know He exists -- always has and always will – I was not to question Him or the Bible.

When my grandfather came home from work he would take me for walks and talk with me. Sometimes he would take me for rides in his truck. He worked for the electric company. I remember this because he would take me to his work sometimes where there were very large spools that held electrical wire. I really enjoyed the time I spent with my grandfather because he made me feel special. He would also rescue me from the cruelty of children who made fun of me and called me names Whenever he noticed me outside crying or arguing with other children, he would bring me inside, dry my tears and tell me to just ignore cruel people, that their words just weren't true. I am grateful for his love and patience with me. Surely it was his loving kindness that took away the fear of his very visible disability (speaking through his throat) which normally would frighten any child.

I had two uncles who lived at my grandma's house, David and Denny. I don't remember them as much as I remember the room they shared in the basement. They weren't very nice to me. They didn't hit me or call me names; they just didn't have any time for me because I was annoying to them. They would try to scare me, to keep me away from their room, by telling me that monsters and magical bears slept with them and guarded their room when they were gone. They were sure to let me know these creatures did not like little girls. Sometimes my grandma would ask me to take something, like clean laundry, to their room for her during the day when they were at school. Just the thought of going down to the basement was very frightening to me, but I knew better than to not do as I was told. My first time going downstairs, with both hands full, I remember stepping slowly and carefully down the steep creaky stairs. When I reached the bottom, I looked into the darkness searching for the string to turn on the light.

The cold, damp basement smelled funny, kind of musty. The floors were wooden and in some places, there was dirt. There were wooden shelves lined with jars filled with a variety of vegetables and jams. David and Denny's beds were on each side of the room. Blankets and clothes were on the beds and floor. Spider webs filled the corners. I felt like I was in a whole other world. Frozen with fear, I looked around the room carefully to see if I could see the creatures that I was warned about. I couldn't see them but I felt as though something was watching me. Remembering what my grandpa told me about Jesus, I prayed for him to protect me. I took in a deep breath, felt a calm warmth come over me, and knew that Jesus was there with me. This gave me the courage to turn the light back off and get back up the stairs without running.

I was about to embark on what were to be the best memories of my childhood where I experienced happiness and felt nurtured, but unfortunately it was the shortest period of my life.

"Meet your new mommy." This was a phrase I would hear many times throughout my childhood. This time, however, I was being introduced to the only woman who tried to fit the bill, to the best of her ability, showering me with lots of love, caring, and understanding. Her name was Mary Jane but she preferred the name "Tommie" over Mary.

Tommie couldn't have any children of her own and the pregnancies she did have all ended up in death and heartbreak, a sadness she would always carry with her. She married my father in 1969 when I was three. The marriage would only last just under a year and eventually became another sad loss in her life and in mine as well. But in that short time, I came to know and love her. She gave me many things, most especially, a sense of security. She gave to me a wealth of love, knowledge, understanding, self-love and wisdom. She became my mommy. I stopped sucking my thumb and I didn't wet the bed. I clearly remember her teaching me how to sing "The Itsy Bitsy Spider" while swinging with me on her lap on my purple and yellow swing set, my favorite colors to this day. *(Although she has passed away, in my prayers I still say to her, "Thank you. I love you.")*

Every day, Tommie took the time to teach me songs and safely swing me. Sometimes she would fill up a kiddy pool and sit and splash with me. She would set me up in a chair with my favorite doll and a cup full of yogurt while I watched her exercise, passing on to me a life-long interest of working out. She always kept me close to her, teaching and nurturing me. Dressing me in the prettiest dresses, adorning my hair in ringlets, she loved showing me off. I felt very special because Tommie always made me feel so important to her.

Our last holiday together was Easter. I remember that I was very ill. It was the day before Easter and I just knew the Easter Bunny wasn't going to bring me anything. She lovingly assured me everything would be just fine. Easter morning, I woke up before everyone else and crept into the kitchen. I rubbed butter all over my chest and throat thinking this would make me better. My dollies were sick too, so I rubbed butter all over them. When Tommie woke up, she was so very understanding of my reasoning and cleaned me up, and even helped me bathe my dollies.

Suddenly there was a knock on the door and she asked me to answer it. To my wonderful surprise, there was a large beautiful purple Easter basket full of candy! I excitedly scooped it up and flew into my bedroom so I could dump all the goodies out onto my bed. Then I noticed the bedroom window above my bed was open and sitting on my bed was a great big, awesome stuffed red, white and blue teddy bear with big brown button eyes and a big black nose smiling at me. What a treat! This has remained one of my favorite holiday memories. Sadly it was to be my last love-filled holiday. My world was about to be changed forever.

My dad took me away from Tommie just as he did my real mom. No warning, no explanation, no reason. It wasn't until a decade later, when I was fourteen and reunited with Tommie, that I learned the real story. With arms open wide to draw me desperately and lovingly close to her, fighting through tears cascading down her cheeks, choking from the strain of the pain in her throat she told me of her heart breaking separation from my father and me. Everyone who ever knew Tommie also knew the story of her never ending search for her long lost little girl. To her, I was an answered prayer, a blessing since she could never bear any children of her own. I was her pride and joy! She told me that at only three years old, I had an impeccable vocabulary, beautiful full length golden blonde hair and the face of an angel. She said that I was the one sure thing that sealed the deal between her and my father. It wasn't until much later that I learned he presented me as bait to the women he wanted. His famous line "Not only do you get me, but you will get to raise this needy little girl." For Tommie, it was a temptation too great to pass up.

Within a year's time, my father had moved his focus of desire to yet another woman. When Tommie confronted him with this, it was the beginning of the end. She later admitted to me she was very much in love with my dad, a love that somehow never did end, even with all his emotional and heartless cruelty. She described that last day spent with me. As she did, she spoke with great sadness mixed with anger toward my dad. I could feel the unbearable ache in her heart as tears streamed down her face. She recalled my father telling her, no matter what happened between them, she would be allowed to raise me, assuring her he realized she was the best mother I could have. He always had a knack for being able to say just what he knew someone needed and what they desperately wanted to hear. His lies would be protected for far too long.

She explained that, on our last day, he told her he was going to take me to the babysitter to have her wash my dirty clothes, and then he would bring me back. Her angry response to him was, "I have been washing her clothes the whole time I have known you. I certainly don't require anyone else to wash them now." Dad calmly responded back that he understood how she felt and he agreed. He convinced her they needed to spend some romantic quiet time together and it would be a great idea if she would make a nice dinner just for the two of them. He let me pick out my favorite things to take with me for the day. As we prepared to leave, she happily picked me up hugging and kissing me, telling me how much she loved me. She put me down and said goodbye, blowing me kisses until my father's van was out of site. We had no way of knowing we wouldn't see each other for eleven years.

Tommie shared that she had spent that day preparing for what she thought was going to be their reconciliation dinner and a romantic evening. She told me how she went happily to the grocery store, picked out all the right things for a great dinner, got home, cut fresh flowers, and made the perfect meal. Her hair was styled, her make-up perfect and she was dressed to impress. She sat in the glowing candle light, beautiful, smiling and radiant. She sat patiently, watching the candles burn down as the hours passed. Finally she blew out the candles, while hoping that he just didn't realize how late it had become.

Filled with worry, Tommie got in her car to drive to his shop. To her relief, there he was, working away painting a sign. He confirmed that he hadn't realized how late it was, telling her he was on a very important deadline. He told her he was very sorry and since she took the time to look so beautiful, the least he could do was take her out for dinner. He worked for about another hour with her lovingly and patiently waiting for him. Finally, they went home and he got cleaned up. After they went out for dinner and drinks, they came home and made love all night. According to Tommie, it seemed as though they slept for maybe an hour or two when he woke up and made love to her again, one last time. He then kissed her goodbye, saying he would be back with me before noon. As he told her he loved her and drove away, she had no way of knowing that was to be the last time she would see him.

Tommie spoke of how she waited all day, and well into the night, before she went searching for him. As she pulled up to the shop, she was flooded with a feeling of dread because the shop was empty, and all of his belongings were gone. Panic overtook her, and she drove everywhere she could think he might be, with friends, relatives and all the popular bar hangouts. No one had seen him and no one knew where he was. It was as if he had disappeared into thin air. There was no sign of him or his things anywhere. Her heart was shattered that day. Not only did she lose the man she loved, she lost the only child she had ever known as her own. All the promises, all the devotion, all the love, vanished without a trace. Dad's family and friends never offered any comfort or information; they were quite accustomed to keeping secrets for him. They knew that anyone who wanted him in their life was required to make him their number one priority. Loving me too devotedly was her big mistake.

"Meet your new brother."
Innocence, trust, security... Gone forever! 1970- 1971

My dad took me to my maternal grandmother Alice's house in Teasdale, Utah. I remember being with her when he introduced me to Dolores, telling me she was to be my new mommy. This was the day of my entry into a life of hell. It was 1970. The number one song on the radio was "When You're Hot, You're Hot." When Dad and Dolores married, I was four years old. I went with them to the court house. I remember how beautiful my new dress was, pink, yellow and purple chiffon with a silk belt. It looked like rainbow sherbet. When we left the court house, I twirled down the sidewalk feeling like a princess as we walked to a café to celebrate. Dad gave me a whole dollar to play songs on the juke box. I had so much fun that I fell asleep in the car when Dad and Dolores took me back to my grandma's house so they could enjoy their honeymoon night. Ironically, this life-changing day was one of the last happy days of my childhood.

I distinctly remember Grandma Alice's house, her large round wooden table, the hard wood floors, the strong odor of coffee and cigarettes. There was a large kitchen with the sink that sat beneath the large picture window, where my grandma always washed my hair. Even when I stood on the chair it was hard to bend over far enough, so my head could reach the faucet. The counter hurt my ribs and her fingernails would dig into my head as she scrubbed vigorously. When all of the shampoo was rinsed out, she would wring my hair out so tight it would pull and hurt the skin on my head and face. It seemed as though it took forever, because my hair was so long, reaching all the way down to the back of my legs. She told me that Dad and my new mom would be back for me later on, to take me away to a new home.

The adults sat around the large round table, while I chased Tassey in and out and underneath their legs. I remember being told to settle down somewhere because tomorrow was going to be a busy day. We were going for a long ride and I would be meeting my new brother, Danny. How could I settle down when I was going to get a brother?

We drove many miles before picking up Danny. There he stood my new brother. This was so exciting! I would now have someone to talk to and play with, someone who could protect me. The first thing that I noticed about him when we met was he had a great smile and he looked fun. He was almost eleven years old and much bigger than me. He looked like he would make the perfect big brother. After we were introduced, we got into the car and we drove a really long time before stopping.

We were on our way to Delta, Colorado, to meet more of my new family members, Dolores' family. I was told that Tassey wouldn't be able to join us until we moved into our new home because it would be too long of a trip for her. I'm not exactly sure whose home we visited, but I remember it being the home of one of Dolores' family members. It would be a trip that haunted and affected me for the rest of my life. This was the first time I was molested by Danny. I still remember parts so vividly that I can actually smell the rotted musty smell of old cars. I clearly remember his voice, the look on his face, and the way I felt. This was the end of my childhood innocence, and became a descent into a darkness no child should ever experience.

The place we were visiting looked like a junk yard, although it was just a very cluttered yard with a lot of old broken down and rusting abandoned cars, washing machines, refrigerators, and even a couple of old school busses filled with more junk. With the eyes of a small child, I remember thinking, "Wow! What a great place to play!" We parked the car and went into a crowded, bad smelling, junk-filled mobile home where I was quickly directed to go outside and play, that it would be good for me to get acquainted with Danny. At that moment, it seemed as though I couldn't be happier. Now I was going to have someone to play with, to stick up for me, and look out for me.

We both ran out of the trailer happy to stretch our legs after the long drive, ready to run, play, have fun and go exploring. I was so excited. We ran to the junk cars and pretended we were driving.

We made driving noises, pretended to shift the gears, turn on the blinkers, honk the horn, and all kinds of fun things. We were racecar drivers, bank robbers, and mobsters. Then, Danny got this really good idea that we should share the same car. He would be the driver and I could be the passenger. There was no way I could have known what would happen to me next. He told me to look out of my window to see if anyone was coming. Playing along, I checked and told him no one was in sight. I gave him an "it's all clear" yell.

Danny called my name and when I turned toward him I noticed his pants were open and he had his penis out, making it big and hard. Over and over he kept telling me to touch it, saying "This is what you do to be in a family. Mom and your dad do this to show they love each other. It makes your daddy very happy. Don't you want to make me happy? Don't you like me? You want to make me happy don't you? If you don't do what I tell you to do, then I can't be your brother and our parents will be very unhappy. We won't be able to be a family and it will be all your fault. No one will like you anymore. Everyone will be mad and never speak to you anymore. Your dad will take away your puppy. You will be all alone and my mom will leave your dad. Then he will never be happy again and it will be all your fault. Just try it you'll like it."

I was confused, scared to death, and truly believed I had no choice in the matter. Danny's manipulation worked and I was now completely under his control. He proceeded to coach me on how to touch and hold his penis. He told me to pretend it was a melting ice cream cone and I had to lick it all around, everywhere. Impatiently, he told me to suck it like it was a lollipop. My mouth was sore and my jaw was cramping; tears were running down my face, and my nose began to run. I wanted to run away. I didn't like this at all. Trying to pull away, he grabbed my head and pushed me down with all his strength.

He wouldn't let me have any air. He smelled sweaty and gross. I was sweating profusely too. I had very little air left in my lungs, and was in a complete panic. Tears mixed with sweat, and soaked my neck and my hair. I was whimpering and trying with all my might to pull away but I was no match for his strength. He pressed both of his hands down firmly on the top of my head thrusting his penis deep into my throat. I was gagging and gasping for air. My will was gone. With blackness falling over me, a hot disgusting goo filled my throat. As soon as he allowed me to pull my head away, I was throwing up over and over, spitting and gasping to catch my breath. I was in complete shock, unable to understand what had just happened. It is beyond my ability to even put a word to how I felt. Stunned and confused, I cried helplessly.

He quickly gained his composure and acted like he was concerned as he helped me wipe the puke out of my hair and off my dress. Immediately he informed me that I could never tell anyone. He said my dad wouldn't marry his mom and everyone would hate me. We wouldn't be able to be a family. If I told, my dog would run away. If I didn't keep quiet, I would destroy everyone's life, especially my own. I was so confused and terrified. No matter what I did, I would destroy everyone's life? This was the worst day of my young life. But, it was only to be the beginning of an absolute hell for me.

As we rode back to my grandmother's house, nothing was said. My smile was gone. My heart was empty. I felt completely trapped in my own darkness. We were there only long enough to collect my belongings and Tassey, and then it was off to Palisades where I was to begin living in my new home. We left from my grandmother's in Utah in the evening and drove for what seemed to be hundreds of miles. I fell asleep.

Before morning, the car broke down. I remember being awakened by Danny. We were still in the car and it was very frightening because we were in a dimly lit garage. The inside of the car was still pretty dark. I didn't know why, but the car felt wobbly and unstable. I sat up to get a better look around. I was terrified by what I discovered. We were high off the ground.

We were in a gas station garage, the car was lifted and the garage lights were off. A dim light and voices were off in the distance in the gas station office. I guess our parents decided there was no need to wake us up to work on the car. This turned out to be another perfect situation for Danny, the predator. He reminded me of the terrible thing we did earlier and told me I was to repeat it all over again. I started to cry and begged him not to make me go through that again but there was nothing I could do to stop him. He moved his body back and forth enough so I could feel the car sway. He told me if I didn't do what he wanted, the way he wanted, he would make the car fall and he would blame it on me. He said I would get spanked with a belt, no one would like me, and that they would take away my Tassey.

Once again I was alone and at his mercy. It was just as horrible as the first time. He smelled sweaty and gross. As I gagged and cried, he thrust himself down my throat holding onto my head. Once again, I was gasping for even the slightest bit of air. My hair was soaked from tears, sweat and snot. I could taste vomit coming from my throat. Choking and struggling, finally the hot disgusting goo spilled from my throat and mouth. He commanded that I swallow every bit and lick it all up or he would make me do it all over again. I did exactly as he said. There was no way I could go through that again. I felt so disgusting and dirty. All I could think of over and over again, was what I had been going through since meeting Danny. In my helplessness, I cried and cried.

He made it very clear to me that if I said anything to anyone, something terrible would happen to Tassey. Maybe he would do the same thing to her as he did to me, or maybe he would just make her disappear. Either way he would tell everyone what a bad girl I was and that I would be in very big trouble. No one would like me and no one would ever want me. I would be a total outcast. He then told me that I was the real reason Tommie left my dad and that no one really liked me because I was too much trouble to take care of so I'd better keep quiet or his mom would leave too!

Even at four years old, I remember this incident as if it happened only yesterday. At that moment, I no longer thought I was the beautiful, happy little girl everyone had commented that I was. It was all a lie that adults used to cover up the truth. In my mind it all made sense now. I was truly worthless, ugly, unwanted, a burden, a waste of time, and that's why my dad couldn't find me a home or a mommy. I believed it must have been the reason my real mommy didn't want me. These thoughts and feelings were engraved so deeply that they remained my truth until the age of forty. I suffered countless battles with myself over these "truths" for years. Senseless manipulation implanted by one human being upon another.

This was only the beginning of my new hell on earth. Holding Tassey close in my arms, Danny told me if I cleaned myself up and quit crying he would get our parents attention so they would let us down. Quickly, I took some deep breaths, calmed myself, wiped away my tears, and tried as hard as I could to act normal. When my appearance was satisfactory to Danny, he rolled down the window and yelled until he got his mom's attention. He asked her if they could let us down, saying we both had to use the restroom. She went and told Dad, and soon we were let out of the car.

After using the restroom, Danny was told to keep me entertained and out of the way of the adults. He got candy and soda from the machines, which he tried to bribe me with, trying to convince me what a good person he really could be. He told me that he really did love me and that he was going to be my best friend and the only true person I could count on. He would always tell me the truth, always protect me and stick up for me. Instead of feeling comforted, I was more confused than ever. I remember that after these episodes, I never really trusted anyone again, especially him. Even the trust in my dad was gone forever. Although I loved my dad, I became afraid of being alone with him, wondering if he was going to do what Danny did. Now, I believed deep down, that all boys and men were the same, and that the ones who weren't molesting just didn't have the time or the desire, at that moment. The age of innocence for me was now over at the ripe old age of four, still a whole year away from kindergarten.

Along with Danny, I had a stepsister, Kelly, and two other stepbrothers, Justin and Karl. I never had any problems with my other stepsiblings. The oldest stepbrother, Karl, was old enough that he never lived with us. The second oldest stepbrother, Justin, and my stepsister, Kelly, lived with us off and on. Danny's living arrangements with us were more on than off. In a very short time, he introduced me to many new bad habits, trying to make me believe he was sharing secrets with me that would make us close. In actuality, he was creating addictions and tools for him to use against me so that he would be able to have even more control over me. By the time I was five, I remember getting up in the morning and scrambling around looking through ashtrays in the house and in the car ashtray hoping to find a cigarette. It wasn't to look cool or to feel older; it was because I craved them.

Many, many bad things were now set in motion in my life, bad habits and uncontrollable impulses as well as inexcusable behaviors. I was now having terrible nightmares, every night, any time I fell asleep. I bit my fingernails. I was very withdrawn. I had no friends. The worse of all the evils was I wet the bed. I tried to stay awake all night, so I wouldn't fall asleep, but I just couldn't stay awake. I wasn't lazy and not once do I ever remember wetting on purpose or being too lazy or scared to get up. I never wet the bed out of anger or spite. I simply slept too deeply. Sometimes I would dream that I was using the toilet in the bathroom and it seemed so real that by the time I woke up, it was already too late. I tried many times to hide my mistake, in various ways, knowing the shame, punishment and belittling that lay ahead. When Dolores took me to a doctor for my bed wetting, he confirmed that it was not a medical problem, which made everything ten times worse for me. Now Dolores felt totally justified in how she had been treating me. I was ridiculed and had many abusive punishments. In Kindergarten, my punishment was to stay smelling of urine. Dolores said it would help me to "straighten my sorry ass up if everyone knew what a piss pot Patty I was."

From the beginning, the kids in school wanted nothing to do with me. On my first day, I didn't know what to expect at all. It was fun, at first, to be around other children, but no one would sit near me. I didn't know at the time that it was because of my ugly clothes and the odor of urine. No one ever took the time to explain to me about how school worked and what to expect. So at recess, I had no idea what was going on. Was it time to go home? I thought "Well, I'll just pretend I don't know what to do and I'll stay here because I don't want to go home anyway." The kids that I asked told me that I should go home but I decided to stay. Finally, the bell rang and it was time to go back into class. It was a good thing I had stayed; I had been saved from another possible severe punishment. The next recess was not so nice. It was slightly raining and it seemed my whole class was outside teasing me, telling me maybe now I wouldn't smell so bad. Then they started singing rhyming songs with my name attached while laughing, pointing and teasing. This was just a taste of what was to come for many years. After that first day, I was to remain an outcast, always fighting, getting lousy grades, and having zero self-esteem. At this point, I didn't know which was worse, my home life or the time at school.

The overwhelming emptiness was being deeply engraved day after day. At this point, most of the adults in my life just ignored me or made me feel like a burden. It seemed as though everyone I knew thought I was strange, stupid and dirty. I was referred to as "Del's daughter" and "just like him." I would always be unpredictable, not trustworthy, with a bad behavior problem. I was treated as a difficult child, but the only time anyone ever paid attention to me was when I did something wrong. If I was ever a good girl, it went unnoticed; I was never praised. I was only thought of as a burden and, deep down in my heart, I truly believed it.

The most confusing adult I knew at this point in my life was my stepmom, Dolores. She acted very differently to me around other people than she did when we were by ourselves or with her children. When we were alone, she would tell me that I was worthless, hopeless, stupid and ugly, and a cancer to the human race. She loved to remind me that I should be forever grateful that she would even take the demanding, demeaning, thankless job of being my mother, because no one else would be willing to take the time to deal with such an ugly stupid little girl. Adding to this, she emphasized that I wasn't as special or pretty as I was previously told or thought I was, so the sooner I got that ridiculous notion out of my head, the better off I would be. The only real reason anyone would ever say anything nice to me would be because they wanted me to do chores. Every day, I was reminded that I wasn't anything special and never would be. Every day was a complete hell and, little by little, they got increasingly worse.

My nightmares were escalating. I often had to throw up when I got up in the morning. If I threw up anywhere other than the bathroom, that would call for another beating. My only friend in the world was Tassey. At least she was being treated better than I was. My beatings were getting worse and it seemed everything I did was wrong; the worst was wetting the bed. While still only five, I remember Dolores being extremely angry at me for wetting the bed. She threw her coffee cup across the room, jumped up and threw me down onto the floor, yelling and flailing her arms at me. She repeatedly asked me "Who the hell do you think you are?" Telling me I didn't deserve to be alive. She ripped off my nightgown and grabbed me by my hair. Furiously, she dragged me down the hallway, calling me names, telling me how worthless I was and telling me she would teach me a lesson I would never forget. She picked me up by my throat, violently shaking and choking me. She threw me down on the bed with a large circle of urine. She then put my face down into the wet spot with what felt like all her force. She held onto the hair on the back of my head and ground my face back and forth into the urine. She was yelling at me, at the top of her lungs telling me that if I wanted to act like an animal, that I would be treated like one. She pulled me up by my hair, threw me into a corner, and told me to stand up with my nose touching the wall and my hands behind my back. I was informed that, if I moved one muscle or hair on my head, she would rub my face into the bed again, spank me and put me back into the corner. She told me if my dad found out about this that he would take the belt after me so I better just keep my mouth shut.

With tears streaming down my face, I was made to stay like that all day instead of going to school.   My legs ached endlessly. I tried to shift my weight from side to side without being noticed as I stood naked in the corner. As part of my punishment, I was to have no food or water all day. Delores was good to her word when it came to threats of punishment. When Danny came home from school, Dolores sent him to the store to buy diapers. When he came home, she told me for my own good she was going to teach me a lesson so that I would think twice before wetting the bed again. It was Colorado in the winter and very cold outside. It fit well into her plan. Knowing that everyone else would be dressed warmly, it would bring even more attention to me being outside with only a diaper on. She ordered Danny to put a diaper on me and instructed me to walk around the block with only the diaper on. No shirt, no pants, not even shoes. Now everyone could see what a piss pot I really was. I cried, begged and pleaded but nothing did any good. She had her mind set and there was no changing it. It had to be done. I was a very bad girl and I deserved exactly what was coming to me. With my head down, outside I went. I had never felt such shame and humiliation.

It was freezing and the cold sidewalks burned my feet. I never looked up to see how many people saw me but I could hear many of the comments. I did hear laughter but I never looked up to see who it was coming from. My main goal was to get back home as soon as possible. Making it back to the front door, I was quickly escorted back into the corner. I could hear Dolores and Danny laughing as she commented how that should teach me a lesson. They were exchanging comments on how funny I looked in the diaper and how it was the first time they had actually seen my worthless little ass move pass the speed of a crawl.

I don't deserve to be loved. I don't deserve to be alive.

My heart and my spirit were crushed. I hated myself more than anyone else possibly could. I wanted to die. From that moment on, I truly couldn't understand why I was even born. I felt I truly did deserve everything bad that happened to me. I felt as though I was frozen to the bone. My legs ached and the pit of my stomach burned from no food or water. I stood still until darkness fell. At Dolores' direction, Danny put me into the shower and turned on the extremely cold water. I washed as fast as I could. The water was so cold it felt as though it was burning my skin. I had a very painful throbbing pain in my head while quickly trying to rinse out the shampoo. Finally I was allowed to get out. The dry towel felt so nice. I quickly put on my nightgown and was placed back in the corner until my dad got home from work and dinner was on the table.

Food never tasted as good as it did that night. I was the first one finished. I still wasn't allowed to have any liquids to drink but I was too terrified to complain. When Dad asked me how my day was, I didn't dare say anything other than fine. I couldn't even bring myself to make eye contact with him I was so ashamed of what a bad girl I had been. I was afraid he would beat me with the belt like Dolores told me he would. Nothing else was said by anyone about the day's earlier events. Dolores then instructed me to kiss Dad goodnight and get into bed. When I got to my room, she quickly followed me in. She told me I was lucky she didn't tell on me. She firmly stated that I better not have any accidents in my bed or she would send me to school in a diaper. I was so thirsty it felt like my throat would stick together when I swallowed. I tried hard not to sleep. It seemed as though every time I drifted off I would dream of a big glass of water or milk, or a clear running creek.

I was so dehydrated that even tears couldn't form. I was exhausted, but afraid of falling into a deep sleep. Fortunately, the lights were out and the sound of the TV was silent, so quietly I snuck out of bed, got some dirty clothes out of the hamper, and put them into a pile on my bed. I wanted to be sure if I had an accident overnight, no one would know. Sure enough, as usual, by morning my panties were wet as were the dirty clothes. Panicked, I quickly took off my panties, put on my night gown and stashed the wet things back into the dirty clothes hamper. I snuck quietly back into my room and into bed. I heard Dolores leave her room. I could feel her presence as she walked down the hall and into my room. So many thoughts raced through my head. Telling her the truth was certainly not one of them. As she stood there glaring at me, I could feel the hate I had for her flow through my veins. She looked evil with her jet black hair, her never empty hands, always grasping a cigarette in one and coffee or alcohol in the other. She was a large, tall, strong woman and had an ugly sounding voice with a fake laugh. This beast, as I saw her, was my mother. "Get your ass out of bed now!" she commanded loudly. I jumped up not knowing what to expect. I could feel my body tremble. She ordered me to pull back the sheets. I did and they were dry. She told me to turn around and raise my arms up. As I did, she checked my night gown for wet spots. Thank God I passed her test. Now I was to get ready for school and hurry up. After dressing as fast as I could, it was time for the daily ritual of my hair being violently pulled by being combed and braided. Dolores didn't believe in hair brushes. Only fine tooth or rat tail combs were used on my hair. This was torture considering my hair was very fine, thick and almost knee length. Many tears streamed down my face during this process but I didn't dare to ever make a noise or complain. If I didn't hold my head firmly still, she would repeatedly slap my head or thump me with her firm long thick red fingernails.

There was never time for breakfast; there was never breakfast food in the house anyway. Liquids were now completely out of the question. It was understood that I was to walk to and from school. If I was too slow getting there or home I would be spanked. The walks home at this point were the worst part of the day, because waiting for me at home was Danny. He was my babysitter and the molestations were daily now. He had progressed in ways of getting me to perform for him. His favorite was to suffocate me. If I refused to do anything he told me to do, he would cover my nose and mouth until I had no air and would show some form of submission. I would nod my head yes or try to grunt the sound of okay. Sometimes he would barter with me, telling me he would let me have food or water, or a cigarette which now, even at my young age, I felt as though I needed. It was so terrible; the trades were never worth it. The smell, the act, the taste, the pain, the sickness, I could never erase, but I had no choice. I was trapped. The only way out was death. Why couldn't I let him just kill me? I hated him and I prayed for death, but I wanted a painless death. I just couldn't handle the suffocation, it was simply too extreme. To be without air was just too unbearable.

As far as Dolores was concerned, she would have preferred that I never be allowed to have a drink of anything. I had to always be one step ahead in everything I did, every day. I found resources for drinking water. I would drink out of the dog's dish because I couldn't turn on the hose outside. Dolores had keen hearing. I learned quickly that she could hear when the outside water was on and instantly knew I was sneaking water. Another beating! But she never caught on to me drinking out of the dog dish. The same went for the bathroom. I wasn't allowed to turn on the sink water at all. I discovered I could very quietly sneak the back lid off the toilet and with my hands, scoop out fresh cold water from the back of the toilet. It sounds disgusting, but when you are so very thirsty, it's a life saver. Thank God for my dog Tassey. I had become quite accustomed to her dry dog food as well.

I rarely saw Dad anymore. He was either at work or on his way home to pick up Dolores to go straight to the bar. Dad was very into the VFW. He spent most of his free time there. He also played saxophone in many of the local bars on the weekends. Sometimes I got to go to the bars where he would label me as the "Kitty Girl." Again Dad found a way to use me for his benefit. The "Kitty" was an empty white bed pan with the words "Don't forget the Kitty" painted on it. I would walk around to all the tables and patrons and hold it out while people put money in it and then bring it back to the stage. It was actually donations for the band members. I felt very embarrassed doing this but I was glad to be away from home and it felt good to think my dad needed me. On one special occasion at the VFW, they were having a Halloween costume contest. I was so happy that my parents were going to let me participate. They dressed me up as a hobo. My costume was homemade and it was kind of embarrassing. I wore Dolores' messed up black wig, Dad's work boots, some old paint rags as clothes and my dad marked up my face with black charcoal. I had a long stick with a bandana filled with newspaper tied to it that I carried over my shoulder. I don't remember who won the contest but I do remember I had a lot of fun that night. It was very late when we got home and I forgot to sleep on the floor next to my bed, my latest solution to my bed wetting problem. I happily lay down in my bed and went to sleep.

When I woke up in the morning I could feel the cold wet sheets. Fear engulfed my entire body. Now what am I going to do? So many solutions raced through my mind, but any way I looked at it, I was in trouble. Big trouble! I knew Dad and Dolores were both very drunk when we got home, maybe it would dry in time. Danny also knew they would be sleeping late so he came in early to molest me. Now I was double horrified. He noticed right away that my night gown was wet. When he ordered me to suck him as he stood in front of me, I told him "No, I can't, I don't feel well." and I told him I would probably throw up. I started crying as he forced my face into his groin. In a low threatening growl, he told me if I knew what was good for me I would do what he said. I tried to, but sweat began to run down my neck and face. I tried to hold back but vomit spewed from the sides of my mouth and ran down his stomach and legs. Now he was really pissed. "You did that on purpose you little bitch, didn't you?" He jumped back wiping himself off as he was telling me, "I could have helped you but now you're in really big trouble." I was still throwing up, crying and begging for him to please not tell. "I'll do what you want," I cried, over and over repeating, "I didn't mean to and it won't happen again." But it was too late. He hated it when I threw up; to him it was inexcusable. I heard him run to my parents' room and bang on the door. I could hear Dolores' voice and Danny telling her "the piss pot is at it again." I heard Dolores say that she would take care of the situation as soon as Dad left for work. Danny came back into my room and taunted me as he told me to strip my pissy sheets and sit with them in the hallway, where the dirty things belonged.

I had to sit across from my parent's room where I could easily hear the bed squeaking and their disgusting sex noises. Finally the noises stopped and my father emerged dressed for work. Quickly behind him, Dolores assured him she would take care of me and that I wouldn't be a problem anymore. Her hair was a mess, her make up from the night before was smudged; she looked horrifying to me in her nasty robe. As she walked around, scratching her crotch, she ordered me to get my worthless ass in the kitchen and make her damn coffee. There would be no dawdling because I knew she meant business. In the distance I could hear Danny and her talking but I couldn't make out exactly what they were saying. I did know, however, that I was in very deep trouble. What was it going to be for my punishment this time? It was never as easy as a simple spanking. Would I stand in the corner all day? I could handle that. Would it be the diaper routine? I prayed that it wouldn't be that. Even having my face rubbed in urine wasn't that degrading.

How could I begin to even imagine how the two of them could have conjured up a whole new level of emotional pain? As soon as the coffee finished perking, I poured her a cup and carefully brought it to her, being careful to stand at arm's length just in case she decided to thump me on the head, something she loved to do. Her nail would hit my forehead so hard I could feel my skin scrape under her nail. She sat her coffee down and lit her cigarette instructing me to go to the bathroom and take off all my clothes and wait for her, quietly. Danny would walk past the bathroom door often, just to antagonize me. He would point his finger at me, shake it and laugh saying "Your ass is grass. I told you, you were going to get it!" Then in a childish way, he would sing his made up piss pot Patty song. I didn't dare to talk back, or cry or make faces. I knew he was right and there was no feeling sorry for myself, only fear and shame.

Looking up through the water I wondered...
am I going to die like this?

How could I be so bad? What was wrong with me? Why couldn't I be what everyone wanted? I knew what was expected of me. Why was I such a difficult person? In my mind, I was rightfully awaiting punishment, but I was still scared. I wondered why they didn't just kill me if I was so much trouble to them. I wished I was brave enough to run away. So many thoughts ran through my mind until suddenly, I heard her miserable smoker's cough coming toward me. My heart began to race as she entered the bathroom with Danny right behind her. I felt cornered. I tried not to cry but could feel my eyes fill up with tears. Dolores was quick to tell me; "You better not cry you ball baby. You know you deserve what's coming to you. I told you I was sick and tired of this bullshit. You're lucky I'm not taking the belt after you." She grabbed my arms tightly as she picked me up off the floor, shaking me and yelling in my face, "What in hell is wrong with you? What is it going to take for me to get it through that stupid stubborn little head of yours? You're nothing but a worthless god damn piss pot."

Now the tears were pouring down my face. I shook uncontrollably as she told me she was going to really give me something to cry about. She turned me around slapping my butt. As my hands automatically went behind me to help protect my butt, she slapped my legs, and yelled for Danny to fill up the tub. I was in for the worse experience of my life. The tub was half full when she told me to step inside. As I put the first foot in, I realized the water was cold as ice. I jumped pulling my leg out. "It's too cold!" I blurted out. She replied "Good! Maybe this will teach you." She picked me up and put me back in the tub with both feet standing in the water. The tub was now almost all the way full. I have never felt anything so cold in my life. It was so painful.

They both were standing there, blocking me, trapping me like an animal. Dolores told me to sit down in the water. As hard as I tried, I just couldn't make myself do it. Danny was more than happy to participate as he pulled my stiff legs out from under me. I went splashing down into the freezing water. Danny held me down by my shoulders and Dolores was yelling at me cursing for splashing her. Without meaning to or realizing it, I was fighting back. I was like a wild cat in water. I was in so much pain, all I knew was that I had to get out. Their strength overpowered me and I was becoming weak from the cold. I could feel my body being pushed further down into the water. My shoulders went under and I was pinned. Danny pulled at my feet and Dolores pushed down hard on my shoulders. It was a nightmare, only worse, because I was awake! For a moment it was as though time stood still.

I don't remember when I stopped struggling. I don't even remember breathing or even needing to breathe. My head was now completely submerged under the water. I opened my eyes and looked up. I could see Dolores staring down at me. She was completely emotionless. I wondered to myself if this was it. Am I going to die like this? All I could hear was mumbling that sounded like loud humming. For a moment everything seemed to fade and my will was completely gone. As I started to fall into darkness suddenly my legs were released with a jolt and my upper body came to the surface. Air! Beautiful air! I could breathe. For a time, I didn't even notice that I wasn't breathing because of the coldness. As I looked around, Danny and Dolores were nowhere in sight. Terrified I didn't dare move. Dolores yelled from a distance that I was to keep my dirty ass in the tub until she told me to get out. I stayed put, until she and Danny entered the bathroom. She sat on the edge of the tub with a cigarette in one hand and coffee in the other. I had to stay in there until all the water drained out. I shook uncontrollably. My teeth chattered loudly. I was literally cold to the bone. When it came time to stand up, the numbness was just starting to wear off and the pain was now setting in. I could feel pins and needles stabbing through the bottoms of my feet. My knees shook in waves. My head ached as it never had before. This was the worst pain I had ever experienced. I was told to put on a fresh night gown and get into my room, back into the corner where I would be spending the rest of the day with no food or water.

Hearing the anger still in her voice, I knew I had to obey, and quickly. My hands, feet and head were still in pain and felt heavy. My coordination was gone, but off to the corner of my room I went, where I stayed through the day and into the night. Finally thawed out and the tingles gone, I was devastated as I heard the family at the dinner table.

The smell of food made my tummy hurt but worse than that, I heard Dad ask about me. All that was said is that I was still in the corner in my room where I belonged. He never asked any more questions, or commented, nor did he stick up for me at all! So empty, so worthless, even my daddy didn't love me anymore. I really didn't deserve to live or eat or be in the same room as the family. I wished with all my heart that I could disappear. At that moment, I decided to never ask for food again or smile or care about myself. I was truly crushed inside. I never told Dad about any of the events that happened when he wasn't around. At this point in my life, I realized I was alone and it was the world against me. I had no safe haven. No one really loved me. I was a mistake, in the way of everyone, a waste of space and time, certainly not worth the effort of understanding or loving.

Danny was right once again. He had always told me if I didn't do what he said for me to do and do it to his satisfaction, he would make my most prized possession disappear. The next day, my Tassey was gone. For days I looked, called and cried for her but the love of my young life was gone forever. I thought of her often, but if there was one thing I learned at this tender age, it was that nothing lasts forever, especially when it concerned things, people or places.

Violence was Just a Way of Life Chapter 7
I lay still as my parents violently argue and
destroyed everything around them. 1973-1974

Time seemed to become a blur to me. We moved so many times to different cities and states. When we did, it was usually in the middle of the night. Dad seemed to have a habit of running up the bills until we would have to sneak out of town. That left me never knowing from day to day where I was going to live. I changed schools so many times that I had grown used to being the outcast. It was always the same thing, the first day or two, people seemed to like me, but before the week was through, they would begin to know the real me, stupid, smelly, ugly, worthless me, and word spread like wildfire.

When we lived in Denver, Colorado, the weather was painfully cold. I walked the path to school alone every day. I don't remember how many blocks away from home the school was, but I'll never forget how long they were, and how miserably cold I was. I didn't have warm clothes; I didn't even have socks, just shoes. In the winter it seemed like it snowed every day and when it didn't, it was still freezing, wet and slushy. I tried so hard to be brave. I certainly didn't want the extra attention, which I knew would always boil down to trouble for me. The tears would uncontrollably roll down my face. I couldn't feel my thumbs or the tips of my fingers at all. My hair, fortunately, kept my ears warm but my nose was frozen and would get so red that I resembled Rudolph, Santa's reindeer.

Without fail though, no matter how much I prayed for my dear God or Jesus to help me, by the time I walked halfway to school, I could barely walk. I couldn't feel my feet. The only thing I felt was extreme pain. It was as though I had two large ice blocks for feet. Every step I took felt like knives piercing through the bottom of my feet and into my legs. I would lose my balance. It must have been pretty noticeable because people would pull over in their cars to ask if I was alright. I would never look or respond because of fear and embarrassment. I just kept praying, forcing myself along.

Many times I would chant to myself, "I think I can. I think I can." I was still young enough to believe in the story of the Little Engine that could. I'd say to myself, "If he can make it, then I'm sure I can." And make it I did, but I was a mess. Every day I waddled into class and every day they took me to the nurse's room where they began to thaw me out. I'll never forget the pain. It was unbearable. Being frozen is one thing, but thawing out is a whole new dimension of pain. First, there was a feeling of knives and needles, then intense itching. Dolores always accused me of being a wimp and convinced my dad that I was doing it for attention. As for the school, I got used to the routine and eventually learned to bypass class in the morning and just go to the nurse's office. I could hear the staff talk about my parents, how they could rarely get hold of anyone and when they did, there was no cooperation. They seemed to be on my side, but still nothing was ever done to help me. This continued until we moved again.

As time went on, the only thing that changed for me was that my degree of being molested intensified and my parents began to fight daily with nightly bouts of physical abuse. Many times I woke up to the sound of screaming and crying, and things being thrown and broken. I never got out of bed. I pretended I was sleeping and would stay motionless. When it was finally light outside and all had been quiet for a while, I would quietly creep out of bed and each time, to my amazement, I would find the house demolished beyond belief. Broken silverware drawers would be strewn across the kitchen with the silverware everywhere. There would be broken glass, the dining table tipped over; chairs and lamps would be broken, and new holes would be in the wall. Entering the living room, I had to be careful of where I stepped, because of broken lamps, shattered ashtrays, and fragments of ceramic that used to be knick-knacks blanketing the floor. End tables were thrown about and the couch tipped over with newspapers everywhere. I always felt so guilty when I came into these scenes, as if somehow I was to blame. Immediately, I would start to clean up, doing it as quickly and as quietly as I could, anxious that I wouldn't finish in time. Each time, Dolores would be the first to emerge from the bedroom. Her presence and looks alone mortified me. She always acted as if nothing had happened. She would snarl, "Well! Where's my coffee? Haven't you made it yet? You know your dad is going to want his newspaper. Get your ass in gear and stop screwing around." Then she would go back to the bedroom where I could hear my parents have loud sex while the whole trailer shook. It was repulsive and confusing. This routine happened at least two to three weekends a month.

Danny continued to live with us more on than off. There was not one day that went by that he didn't suffocate and threaten me to provide his sexual favors. I would have given everything up, warmth, food, shelter, love, even life itself, in exchange for never being molested again. This was by far the worst thing I suffered. When he was in charge of babysitting me, it would happen all day or all weekend long. My life was shit. I was shit. I hated my life, my world, but most of all, the fear of being suffocated. I'll never forget it, no matter how hard I try. The feeling of the sheer panic of it is still fresh in my mind. Even now, I occasionally get panic attacks. And when I do, I put myself into a meditative state and focus on my breathing. This is the only way I can reassure myself that I'm okay, that this is "now" and I'm safe. Still, there is always this other side of me that doesn't believe he won't show up at my door someday to finish what he started thousands of times before. He started when he was a child and continues his evil to this day. I now know of so many lives he destroyed. I feel so guilty knowing he continued creating lasting memories of torture and hell for other helpless children.

In my elementary school years, I may have been getting older on the outside but the scared child hiding within me never seemed to age or become any wiser. Ashamed and terrified, that little child hid behind the walls of anger, guilt, confusion, and frustration, knowing deep down I was ruined, worthless and not worthy of being loved by anyone. Believing this is what makes the abused child stay hidden.

I remember another one of our moves, another new state, another new house, another new school, but not a new life. When we moved to Amarillo Texas, it was exciting at first. But as usual, the brief excitement was trampled by fear. The house there was actually very nice. The yard was covered with some kind of clear green marbles for decoration. It was in a really nice neighborhood with other nice houses. The school was only a couple of blocks away. I could see the playground from my yard.

Danny had become very interested in wrestling. For him, I seemed to be the perfect guinea pig for his wrestling practice as well as perfecting his goat roping skills. Many times, when I would least expect it, I was told to run and I knew just what that meant; I was just about to experience pain. If I was caught, which was almost always the case, he would tackle me to the ground, tie my legs together, my arms together, and then tie all of them together like the cowboys would tie goats or calves. But he didn't let me go as quickly. He must have enjoyed doing this because, like the molestations and suffocations, this also became a daily ritual for him. Any time I walked down the hallway or across the living room I was a target for one of his wrestling moves.

His wrestling was more like a beating. He took full advantage of my limberness, bending and twisting me. But he would also smash me and jump on me. He would do all the moves he saw from TV wrestling, as well as the designated wrestling holds from school competitions. Constantly looking over my shoulder, I was always jumpy and had the shakes. I had become a very skittish, bruised and carpet-burned child. My parents never took my protests seriously, saying, "Oh you're just fine, don't exaggerate. Your brother was just playing with you." or "Quit being a baby. I don't want to hear it, Lorina. I have better things to do with my time than sit here and listen to your bullshit."

It was hopeless! I was hopeless. I was all on my own and there was nothing I could do and nowhere I could go. This was my life; no matter how much I prayed, it didn't change. It couldn't change. No one believed me when I tried to say anything. No one listened. No one cared. I still wet the bed and was still being punished for it. I was always grounded and not allowed to have anything to drink except for small amounts at meals, when we had meals. Meals, even food in the house, were always dependent upon how much alcohol was being consumed at the time.

It seemed that everything in and around my life worked in a roller coaster fashion. Sometimes we had a normal family type of life and sometimes everything was chaotic. The only thing that was somewhat consistent was my having to go to school. But school was still horrible for me because I was such an outcast. Daily, from the time I woke up, I was terrified of Danny. I hated being alive. Dad still worked long hours, and anytime he left with Dolores, Danny began his torture routine. In the middle of the day, I would hear the neighbors, washing their cars, mowing the lawn or playing with their children, but no matter how loud I screamed, no one seemed to hear me, or maybe they had just become accustomed to screams that came from my house, because no one ever came.

Suffocation!

Chapter 8

In a panic I would search for air through the
cracks of his fingers until falling into blackness.

Suffocation was the worst. Danny would pin me on my bed, and I would fight for every breath I could take. Would this time be it? Will I get away? How can I trick him? Why won't anyone help me? In between struggles, I tried to scream, "Help me! Help me!" From behind his hands, between the cracks of his fingers, I could see the light outside the window. I could hear life going on outside, but still I was there, trapped! Sometimes this would go on so long that I would see the day turn into night through the cracked fingers, through the blankets, beyond the edge of pillows or whatever he was using to smother me. He always took me to the edge of death by suffocating me. Sometimes I could see the sick satisfaction in his dark evil eyes, as he would stare into my mine until I blacked out. When I would come back into consciousness he would do it again until he broke me down or until I was so weak that he would force himself on me, hitting me and threatening me. He had perfected breaking me down. I would have run away from home, but I was too scared to even do that. I wasn't afraid of being homeless; I was afraid of being returned. What if I got caught? What level of tortuous punishment would that bring when I was returned?

One weekend, I was so overcome with fear that I was willing to try something very risky. Dad and Dolores were leaving early to paint a big sign and weren't expected to be home until late. I didn't want to spend one minute, let alone a whole day, with Danny, so I came up with a plan. I watched out my bedroom window waiting for them to leave. My heart pounded so fast. I was trembling all over and my mind was crazy with anxiety. As soon as I saw the van backing down the driveway, I ran as fast as I could, straight out the back door and around the house. I hid under a bush in the front yard so quickly that I was there before the van was out of sight. I waited there for a while to see if the van might return because they had forgotten something. As soon as I heard the sliding glass door open in the backyard and Danny yelling my name, I bolted. I ran as fast as I could to the schoolyard and never looked back. I scurried behind tree after tree, just like in the movies. I wanted to play on the swings, the jungle gym, the slide, but I knew he would be coming to look for me as soon as he found out I wasn't hiding in the house. I was scared, but I was safe and free, for now. That was worth any amount of trouble I was going to be in later. I knew that if I could sneak back in, when Dad got home, Danny wouldn't tell. How could he? He knew why I left and I don't think he would risk my telling on him. At least I hoped that's the way he would think.

Thinking like a child, I decided to go play at a girl's house that I didn't know very well, but maybe she would let me come in. It worked! I was in a home and safe. Within a couple of hours, Danny was knocking at their door. I instantly started to cry and begged for them not to tell him I was there. I convinced them he would hurt me, that it wasn't my parents looking for me, only him. I never shared any details of how he would abuse me; I just said he was very mean and wouldn't stop picking on me or wrestling me. Thankfully, they agreed to cover for me. I was so frightened that he would see me, that I curled up into a ball and hid under an end table. I could hear his voice at the door. I heard him telling them if I came over that "She had better get her butt home, and quick, if she knows what's good for her!" In hearing this, the parents waited until he left and then told me I had to leave because they didn't want any trouble. I understood and agreed to leave. I was shaking so bad that my teeth were chattering.

As I left the house, I was ready to run. My eyes searched frantically everywhere. I prayed he wouldn't see me. I didn't know where to go or what to do. I snuck over to some bushes in the neighbor's yard and crawled under them and waited. Many times I could hear him yelling out my name, but I just stayed put. Finally I drifted off to sleep. When I woke up it was dark and I panicked, not knowing what time it was. I was afraid that Dad had come home before I could sneak in. Without giving it a second thought, I climbed out from under the bushes and ran into the house. The van was gone; the house was dark and still. The front door was unlocked, so I rushed in and there was Danny, lying on the couch, watching TV with all the lights off. He actually seemed relieved that I was home. He jumped up and pointed out a bowl of candy that was sitting on the coffee table.

My parents hadn't come home yet and he was ready to cut a deal. He never asked where I was. He just told me about a problem he had with the dishwasher. He put liquid soap in it and left the house to buy the candy. When he returned, there were soap bubbles everywhere in the kitchen, living room and garage, and the living room rug was still wet. Wanting to stay out of trouble, he decided if I took the blame for it, he would let me pick out what I wanted from his candy and forget about running away for the day. That was a great trade, I thought, and agreed. Five minutes later, my parents pulled into the driveway. I don't know why this whole incident scared Danny, but he was actually nice that night and the next day. It didn't last though; things went back to normal before I knew it. I never got away with that trick again. He was onto me and kept an even closer eye on me from that time on, especially if my parents were leaving. I have a lot of terrible memories in this house in Amarillo. Every day that my parents weren't home, when I got home from school, Danny continued his torment and sexual abuse. He would search for me, trap me, suffocate me and throw me on his or my parent's bed forcing me to stay on the bed while he took off his shoes and pants. To this day, I cannot stand the feeling of sitting on the bed when someone else puts on or takes off their shoes, or even bumps the bed for that matter. It doesn't matter who it is; it makes me feel sick, scared, and sends me straight back in time. Now as an adult, I make special requests of my friends and family so that I don't have to suffer these flashbacks. They are all so wonderful and cooperate without asking questions, even if they don't understand.

Danny had terrible demands and rules. I was controlled like an animal, scared and shackled, knowing what was expected of me. The sickness grew in my stomach; sweat would start to roll off the sides of my face with each of his movements. When he was finished disrobing, I could smell him. He smelled so bad, sweaty and unclean. This alone would make me gag. When I gagged, that really pissed him off. God forbid if I threw up! When I couldn't hold it back, he would punch me in the back of the head and make me lick up every speck of puke off his stomach, penis, scrotum, and legs. God knows how much I truly hated this. Why couldn't I just do what he wanted and do it right so I wouldn't be punished? The pain in my jaws was terrible, the smell, the taste everything about it was disgusting. I experienced so many ugly days like this in that house.

One Good Memory Chapter 9
A little taste of love, or was it just an illusion of love?

I remember one Christmas vividly while we still lived in Amarillo. I was indescribably miserable with a very sore throat. Dad and Dolores were home early from the VFW. They were almost always completely loaded when they came home from there; and usually, when they were drunk, there was physical violence. But this night, it wasn't so bad. I timidly knocked on my parents' door and Dolores appeared. It was late and I was supposed to already be asleep, but it hurt so much when I swallowed that I had to do something. Surprisingly, this ended up being one of the few times Dolores was nice, almost pleasant. She ordered me back to my room and told me she would be there shortly. When she came into my room, she had some Vicks rub and a smile! She rubbed the medicine on my chest, back and throat, then she wrapped a towel around my neck and carefully pinned it. She smelled strongly of alcohol but it didn't matter to me this time because it almost felt as if she really cared. I was so starved for love and affection! It was a wonderful feeling as she sat on the edge of my bed. She actually asked me if there was anything else that I wanted. I answered her admitting that I was hungry and she told me she would get me some food. This was unbelievable! I was never allowed food, especially a drink, at night. Even more shocking, she was bringing it into my room. Wow! She came back with a turkey leg.

That was the first time I had ever seen a turkey leg. It wasn't on a plate or napkin; it was just handed to me as if it was a chicken leg. Oh boy, was I shocked. I thanked her as I took it from her. Then she did something she had never, ever done before. She kissed me on the forehead! When she left my room, I eagerly ate the leg even though it hurt my throat really bad. The pain didn't seem to matter so much because of my overwhelming feeling of love. That one moment in time even made the abuse seem bearable. This was to be one of the only good memories of Dolores. This expression of real caring only happened the one time, but I'll never forget the feeling it gave me.

The next day, when I woke up, it was obvious that I had the mumps. My neck on one side was huge and it hurt twice as bad as it did the night before. My mind drifted back to what happened before I went to sleep. Remembering the love and kindness that Dolores had shown me, I wondered if it was a dream. I sat up and looked around. There it was the turkey leg bone. It really did happen. Wow, maybe she really does love me, I thought, as I got out of bed. When I entered the living room, I soon realized that the niceness was over and I was greeted with, "Well piss pot, did you wet your bed last night? You better clean your damn room and then go lay down. You're sick and you're not going to play today so don't even ask." Suffering from a hangover, her beauty was gone. Her care and affection was gone. I commented on how bad my throat hurt and she told me to go to my room and she'd be there with the Vicks. I should have known it was too good to be true. I was lucky to even get a taste of her being nice. I expected a replay of the night before but I was about to experience just the opposite.

In she came, her voice rough, her hair a mess, and there was black makeup under her eyes. It was obvious her hangover was once again getting the best of her, and as usual, I was her emotional punching bag. She informed me I'd be staying home from school today, and if I knew what was good for me, I would stay in bed and not be a nuisance. She quickly rubbed the Vicks medicine on my neck and chest, nothing at all like the night before. Then the worst happened. She told me to stick out my tongue and instructed me not to swallow the Vicks as she put a teaspoon on the center of my tongue. She said it had to sit there until it melted. If I had swallowed it, I would have to start all over. It was so awful. I kept gagging and tears were rolling down my face. Every time I started to gag, she would thump me in the forehead with those long red fingernails. It always hurt, and she knew it. She did it every day because, according to her, I always deserved a thump or a slap upside the head, because I was worthless and stupid. So, she sat in front of me and waited for the Vicks to melt, saying that she had to sit and watch me because I couldn't be trusted.

I was so happy when I could finally swallow. I laid back and listened to her tell me "Don't you even ask for water or anything to drink. I'm not washing any sheets for little Miss Pisspot Patty today." I didn't answer back. I never did. She was so evil. I knew she wouldn't hesitate to slap my face or choke me while shaking me violently. I just held in my tears and acted appreciative for her efforts. Inside I cried. My heart crumbled, as I thought to myself, "How could I be so stupid the night before? She couldn't have loved me. Not even for a second. She was right. No one could or ever would." The only good thing about today was there was no Danny. He had to go to school. All I had to do was be quiet and unseen and my day would be pleasant. I didn't get any food but I could sneak to the bathroom to sneak a little water from the toilet tank without Dolores seeing me when she was taking little naps. I would sneak into the bathroom being careful not to touch the door so it wouldn't squeak. I wouldn't turn on the light and I carefully removed the back lid of the toilet. Using a cup from my play teacups, I would quickly scoop up the water out of the toilet and drink as much as I could, as fast as I could. I had perfected this routine over the years. The water was so cold and felt good on my dry, sore throat. God, how I hated my life! Every day was an obstacle. All I could look forward to was turning eighteen to get away, or hopefully, that Danny would die. Both seemed so far away and absolutely impossible.

My life was being uprooted again but I was ready for a change. I hated the school I was in and I still didn't have any friends, at least, no one liked me. Dad came into my room early and told me to get in the van because we were going for a drive. It made me glad to know that Danny wasn't joining us. I knew it would be a long drive because Dolores had packed a cooler full of food. We drove for hours until we finally stopped in a small town with a large hill with a big "W" in white rocks on it. It stood for Walsenburg, Colorado. It was 1974. The year stands out clearly in my mind because it was one of the worst years of my life.

We pulled into the driveway late in the afternoon. There was a great big wrought iron fence with a large gate that was chained and locked. Behind the gate were a house and three run-down buildings. The house was where the graveyard caretaker used to live. One building was the embalming room and the other two were for storing the tools used for the grounds and digging the graves. There were no more head stones or bodies because, from what I was told, a long, long time ago there was a very big storm and the river had overflowed. The cemetery flooded so much that the coffins came out of the ground and were floating around, and even down the river. I don't know how much of it was true but there we were in what was quite obviously a cemetery. That was why the yard was so large. It was covered in weeds and very creepy. Dad unlocked the padlock and opened the gate. He drove the van in and said, "We're here. Let's have a picnic." I didn't know what to say or even think. Everything was so old. There were spider webs everywhere. It felt abandoned. Dad and Dolores walked into one of the buildings and I followed. It was dark inside except for the light that seeped in through the cracks in the ceiling and the walls. The wooden floor was covered in thick dust and it creaked when we walked.

Something just didn't feel right about the place. It felt like that we were being watched. The whole property had a haunted feeling. Dolores laid down a blanket and started preparing sandwiches. We all sat on the blanket as Dad asked Dolores what she thought. He said: "This will be one of my workshops. We can live in the house until I find a mobile home to buy. We'll fix up the yard and prepare a nice spot to park the trailer." She didn't hesitate in answering "Yes! This will be perfect." I was so disappointed and very scared, but I didn't say a word. We finished our food and Dad gave us a tour of the other buildings, the house, and the grounds. I know I saw shadows that moved quickly and lurked around the corners. I felt the presence of darkness but I knew better then to share my feelings with my dad or Dolores. By this time in my life I became very good at calling in Jesus and commanding the evil and darkness to go away. Over and over, there were loud, clanking sounds of freight trains passing. The highway was right outside the gate with fast moving traffic and diesel trucks going by. I had lived in strange places before but this was certainly one of the strangest!

Dad hurried us into the car saying we better leave before it got any darker because there was no electricity and no lamp posts; it would soon be pitch black outside. The next morning it was barely light when we were home again, pulling into the driveway. I was so relieved that I didn't wet my pants in the car because I had accidentally fallen asleep. Dad changed his clothes and left to go to work. I could hear Dolores talking to Danny about the place to where we were moving. She almost made it sound inviting, but I knew differently. For two days, we packed and cleaned. On the last day, when Dad came home, we were finally ready to load and leave. Dad drove his van while pulling a rickety old white trailer full of his paints and tools, and we were in the black Thunderbird pulling another old rickety trailer full of our dishes, clothes, and other household items. We moved so often that we never had time to really accumulate a lot of things. I wasn't happy to move where we were going, but I was happy to leave this hell house. As I looked back out the car window at the house, for some reason I told myself, one day I will realize I was happier here than I ever knew. But, I was also hoping I would be wrong.

Another chapter in my life closed as another opened. We arrived back in Walsenburg while it was still dark outside. Just as Dad said, it was pitch black. He had to pull the car up just right to use the headlights to unlock the gate. Once we were in, he relocked the gate. We just slept in the car that night. I tried to stay awake for fear of wetting my pants, but even more afraid of having to go to the bathroom outside in the dark.

Shortly after the sun came up, it was hot and beating down on our black T-bird. For some reason, everything looked more welcoming. It's funny how sunshine can change your outlook sometimes. Dad, Dolores and Danny were all still asleep. I quietly snuck out of the car and went exploring. The weeds were very tall in between the buildings. Everything smelled old. There were so many places to hide. I found a long skinny stick and buried it into the ground. Then I found a plastic lid and stabbed the stick through the middle. This was my pretend steering wheel. I found three large sticks and three rocks large enough to sit under the sticks that would create gas and brake pedals so I could pretend I was driving.

I decided I needed to go look for a gearshift stick so my pretend car would be perfect. I was in a world all of my own until I heard my name being called, angrily. I looked up and there was Dolores screaming at me from the car window. I could feel my throat clench as I jumped up. God! She always made me nervous and scared. Just the sight of her frightened me. I walked toward the car and she opened the door letting her dog, Cindy, out as she yelled, "Damn it Lorina! Didn't you have enough brains to let the dog out of the car when you got up? Didn't you think she had to pee? Why must I tell you everything? I swear you are so stupid!" Then she turned to Danny and nicely asked him if he could please go find a place to feed Cindy, saying she had to count on him because I don't have a brain in my stupid little head. "Well, it looks like it's going to be a great day," I sarcastically thought to myself.

This may have been a new beginning, but at the same time, it was the same old hell. The house was cold and small. My bed was in a small room between the living room and the kitchen. There was a door that separated my room and the living room but it was to never be closed. This was a great thing though because I could quietly watch TV through the open door. My little space had no privacy, no window, just peeling, yellow wallpaper and a creaky cold floor. My life in this house consisted of trying to remain invisible and being a dirty little sex slave to Danny. Even though there were lots of places to hide, they didn't do any good. If I didn't come running when Dolores called, I would be in for a.day of being yelled at, slapped, dirty looks, and endless lectures. But, if it was just Danny, I would take advantage of the hiding places as soon as my parents were gone. Other than rare trips to Horseshoe Lake with Dad, I had no out, no friends, and no family. It seemed as though there was nothing to ever look forward to. I talked to myself and to my imaginary friends, and made friends with the grasshoppers.

Chapter 11

A New Level of Terror

I'll chop you up like a deer and throw you away.
No one will miss you anyway!

One day, Danny surprised me with an opportunity to have fun and took me to the river to go swimming with him and some of the friends he had made. We both knew this was against the rules but he made it sound so fun that the consequences didn't seem to matter. It was the only time he made me feel like I was included in anything good. We waited until my parents left, and then we snuck down a narrow dirt path covered in tall grass. It was like a small jungle. We zigzagged over rocks, under a fence and over a wall. I was totally lost. Finally, we came to an opening. There was a big tree, water, and other teenagers! They were smoking and drinking, having a great time. I watched them as I sat away from the water. Suddenly, Danny said we had to hurry back before our parents got home, so off we ran. Somewhere along the path, I stepped on some broken glass and cut my toe deeply in a tender place. Danny dragged me along and told me to quit sniveling about my foot, saying if we got caught, my ass would hurt a lot more than my toe. I kept quiet the rest of the way moving as fast as I could. Blood was everywhere and I was leaving a trail. At home, we tried to stop the bleeding but nothing seemed to work. By the time our parents got home, I was scared half to death. They would want answers and I didn't know what to say. I knew I was in trouble any way you sliced it. Everyone was going to be mad.

I decided to lie to my parents because, in my mind, Danny was the worse one to piss off. When they got home, I said I cut it playing outside in the back yard. Dolores asked me where the glass came from and I could only say I didn't know. I don't know how she knew I was lying because our yard was huge, but I knew I was busted. I could feel fear shoot through my whole body when she insisted that I show her where in the yard that I got cut. Reluctantly, I went out to the corner of the yard and told her that it was the place it happened. She looked right at me and said, "Where's the glass? Where's the blood?" It was over. I knew her look of hate. She yelled: "You lying little bitch, what in the hell is wrong with you? Why can't you tell the truth? You're about as worthless as your father!" I knew what was coming. I ducked but she grabbed me by my hair, pulling me up, slapping me. She screamed, "I'll teach you not to duck from me you little asshole." I cried as she slapped and kicked me all the way back to the house. "You wait 'til your dad gets home. You're really going to get it then!" I was ordered to lie on my bed and informed not to move, eat, drink, or talk. She was right. I was a worthless liar. I deserved everything I got.

Dad got home later that night and the trouble started all over again. He made me tell him where I was when I cut my foot as he snapped the belt in his hand. I had to tell. I told him Danny and I went to the river. I told him I stayed away from the water but it didn't seem to matter. He told me he had to spank me for going there and for lying. I complied with his instruction to bend over the bed. I cried as the leather snapped at my flesh over and over. The snapping was loud and scared me even more. When it was over, I could feel the welts rising and my butt felt red hot. I know I did wrong and I deserved all of this. I wished I could have just disappeared. I was told I didn't need to eat, by Dolores, as she walked over to my bed. "When are you going to grow up? You can't be trusted and no one wants to be around you." She had a large pot of soapy water that she sat in front of me on the floor and told me to put my foot with the cut toe in it.

The water felt so hot and my toe hurt so much. I kept pulling my foot back out because it was so painful and each time it earned me a thump on the forehead with her long fingernails. She told me to quit being such a damn baby and pushed my foot into the water. I cried, silently, as the tears poured down my face. She looked at me with an evil smile of satisfaction and said, "That's what you get for being a goddamn stupid brat. Maybe next time you'll use your brains, but I doubt it because you don't have any." She ordered me to leave my foot in the water until it became cold. She dried my foot with a towel and announced that I was grounded for the entire summer break. I would have to stay in my bed for several weeks. For some kids, that might have been unbearable, but for me, it didn't seem so bad. I wasn't allowed to leave our yard anyway, and I didn't have any friends, so it was no big loss for me. Besides, I thought, if I had to stay in my bed, then maybe I wouldn't have to do so many chores. Being grounded didn't sound like such a bad thing to me until I found out what grounded meant.

Grounded didn't mean no chores. Grounded meant I didn't exist. My bed was in the dining room area so I could see and hear everything, but everyone just acted like I wasn't there. I usually felt ignored, but this was far worse. I wasn't allowed at the table and wasn't allowed to watch television. But worse than that, being grounded to my bed meant I couldn't avoid Danny. My only escape from Danny had been to stay clear of him whenever I could. But now I was like a caged animal, caught in my little space where he knew I was all the time. Believe me, as soon as my parents left for anywhere, he took total advantage of my confinement. Pinned in my spot, he could come at me, forcing his penis in my mouth, making me suck it until my jaws ached. I choked and gagged from the smell of him. It was so revolting. I hated him so much! His face, his smell, his voice! If I cried or tried to turn away, he would punch me in the back of my head and threaten to make me do it all day. So I would try to do it just like he told me hoping that he would finish so it would be over. The worse part of it was he always expected me to swallow his disgusting fluid and, if I didn't, he would yell at me, call me names, hit me more, and make me do it all over again. When I couldn't swallow what he shot off, he would become enraged. I couldn't understand then, or even now, how he could be offended when I was the one being violated. My God, I was an eight year old child, not a prostitute! There was no reasoning with this monster at all, ever.

That summer, it felt like he was at me all the time, daily, sometimes two, three, four times a day. The more Dad and Dolores were gone, the more it happened. I tried everything I could think of to get out of it, but nothing worked. I couldn't run, I couldn't hide, and crying only seemed to give him more power through his anger. He had no compassion, no feelings, and no soul! Once, I felt I just couldn't, wouldn't do it anymore. I didn't care what he did or said to me, I wasn't going to touch him anymore! Of course, he wasn't going to take no for an answer. He left the room for a minute and came back with something in his hand. He jumped on my bed, pinning me down by sitting on me. He put one hand on my forehead and showed me a knife he had in his other hand. It was so scary looking, sharp, pointed and curved. I now know that it was a carpet cutter's knife. He made sure I got a good look at it as he moved it closely across my face, down to my throat where he pressed it firmly against my skin. He whispered in a low, menacing voice how worthless I was and always had been. He told me how no one would even miss me if I was gone. He made it sound so simple, so easy, the perfect crime. He could cut my throat and watch the blood drain from my lifeless body. Then, he could skin me, just like a deer and chop up my body into pieces and put them into a garbage bag. I would be hauled away to the dump where I would never be found. He reminded me again that I would not be missed and that finally my family's problems would be solved. They wouldn't have to find a place to dump me off anymore. All he had to do was tell our parents that I didn't listen, and he went back down to the river to play. Then by the time he realized it and found me, I had fallen in. He would tell them how he tried to save me but he couldn't. Since they would be looking for my body in the river, they would never think to look at the dump. Knowing they would never think Danny was guilty of anything, I became terrified. The thought of dying that way. Being cut up was more than I could handle in my mind, so I gave in. Again, he won; my strength of will was broken by the horror of the pictures he painted in my mind.

Why Didn't I Tell?   Chapter 12
There was no one I could trust, no one cared.

Why didn't I tell? Why? No one would believe me. No one cared about me. No one even liked me. No friend, no teacher who noticed me, no one but a father who rarely spent a moment with me, a stepmother who wished I was dead, and a monster who only used me to torture and satisfy himself. There was no one I could trust and I never met anyone that made me feel safe or secure. How could I tell anyone how disgusting and dirty I was? I was embarrassed of the things I had done. But mostly I was terrified of what would happen when they told my parents what I was saying. I knew that all hell would break loose for telling our family business, something Dolores warned me never to do. Even if my parents thought there was a chance Danny could be hurting me, they would only ground him and then I would be in more trouble than ever. I didn't know I was a victim, I only knew confusion and terror. All I could think about was surviving from day to day, moment to moment, breath to breath.

It's hard to find the right words to explain the feeling. Unless you have felt the absolute panic of not knowing if you would take another breath, like almost drowning or getting something caught in your throat, you won't understand. I can tell you that you will do anything just to have a breath! As your mind races, your arms and legs flail around, your head jerks from side to side as your body moves any way it can, like a fish squirming and jerking when pulled out of water. You use every bit of strength you have until the darkness starts to close in around you, sound fades away, and everything goes black as your limbs go limp and you believe it is over. When you awake, you are helpless, broken, and your soul seems lost to you. You are resigned to do whatever is commanded of you. That's how it was with me. Stripped of my strength, my will, and willing to do whatever was demanded of me to not go through the suffocation again. It was a game to Danny and I knew the rules. Break them, and I was a punching bag and still had to take his penis shoved down my throat. But follow his rules, do whatever he wanted just the way he wanted, swallow without choking or puking, then I could have water and food. And, if I did it well enough, maybe I could watch television or get to smoke a cigarette.

When other kids were praying for and dreaming about fun things, birthday parties, or what they would get for Christmas, I was dreaming and praying just to have a normal loving family, enough food to eat, and to not have to do the things I was being forced to do or having to choose to do them to stay alive. I would look at the kids around me and think about how lucky they were to not have to do sexual things or be afraid every day. I would think and wonder about how life would be if I could have been with my mom, my real mom. I wasn't allowed to speak of her. Dad would just tell me she was a helpless alcoholic who didn't care about anything or anyone. He said she had a lot of medical problems and probably wasn't even alive anymore. Dolores would always tell me that my real mom didn't want anything to do with my dad or me because we were both worthless. All I knew was that she was gone, was probably dead and like everyone else, she probably didn't care about me or love me. Even thinking that, I longed for her, I just wanted to meet her, at least just see her. I held on to the hope that maybe she would want to find me, to rescue me, but that hope would fade. Deep down, I knew it was only a dream I had, that she surely didn't want me and never thought about me.

Now I found myself fantasizing about how I could painlessly end my life. I would look at the trees and envision myself hanging. But what if I just hung there choking and not being able to breathe and not die. If only I had enough guts to run in front of a big truck on the freeway and end this torture. I didn't want to die from suffocation and it terrified me to think of being cut up. I didn't want Danny to have the satisfaction of killing me either. If only I could die in my sleep or get hit by a car. Something sudden, so my suffering would be over, everyone's suffering would be over! Why couldn't God let me die? Jesus could make the scary dark shadows disappear, how come Jesus couldn't make Danny and Dolores disappear? I was stuck in hell. Not knowing what to do, I felt so helpless. I couldn't help but feel that I must deserve all this pain and heartache, after all the terrible things I had done. I was always in trouble, I never listened, and I was a bed wetter, a nail biter, and an ugly, rotten, worthless waste of time that would never amount to anything! It seemed all I was good for was doing chores, even though whatever I did was never good enough for Dolores. She was very particular about how she wanted things done, and it always had to be done perfectly and quickly. If it was less than she expected, I got spanked, grounded, and had to do the chore over again until it met her standard. And God forbid, I broke a glass or an ashtray.

To her, nothing was an accident. Every mistake I made was because I was clumsy and stupid. Every time I vacuumed, I heard, "You can do better than that." Every time! Even now, whenever I peel a potato, I think I need to peel it thinner. The smell of coffee, a newspaper lying on the floor, simple little things take me back to my years with her and I still cringe! Sometimes, I would try to do extra chores that weren't asked of me, hoping to be recognized for my effort. It always backfired on me. Instead of a compliment or thank you, I was just reminded that it was my home too and I should be doing everything without having to be asked! I couldn't win. I couldn't wait to grow up and get away from her. I hated the sound of my name. I hated me. The sound of her voice would echo in my mind many years after she was gone from my life.

I never understood her, even now as I look back. Was it the alcohol or was she just a cruel, mean person? The one memory I have of her being halfway nice to me, the night I was so sick, she was drunk. No one else was ordered to do anything, except for Danny being told to babysit me when they wanted to leave the house. She would constantly tell me that what she did and said was for my own good, and that I should grateful she was there.

Dolores had strange rules. For example, I wasn't allowed to use a hairbrush. I can remember once, after she had washed my hair with dish soap without using conditioner, she sat and watched me use a fine tooth comb because hairbrushes weren't to be used on wet hair. It was so painful and took forever because my long, thick hair tangled easily. I couldn't understand why, if I was so ugly and worthless, that it mattered if I used a hairbrush or a comb?

Another really strange memory is my getting in trouble every day for coming home from school dirty. I don't know how I got so dirty, I really don't. I didn't have any friends that I played with; I never played ball or games with other kids. Every day I told myself I was going to stay clean. I know it wasn't my lunch because I was always so hungry I never played with my food. It went straight from the tray into my mouth. But, lo and behold, whenever I got home and Dolores was there, she would tell me to look down at my clothes and say, "Look at you. You're a pig. You should be ashamed of yourself. Go change your clothes and get in the corner until dinner." It was a scene played out day after day after day.

Something was up. Something was different today. When I came home from school this particular day, cousins were visiting. They were older with a daughter about four years old. Dad and Dolores were leaving for a while to go buy a mobile home and the cousins were staying over. It was nice to have a break from Dolores. Danny went with them. It was so wonderful not to be afraid, even for a little while.

A new home! Like everything else in my life, it wasn't the chance for a change I had hoped for. The mobile home was being put on the same property but at least we were getting out of that creepy house, even if we were in the same yard. I was finally getting my own bedroom and, my own bathroom. Well, sort of. I had to share the bathroom with Danny but I was very happy about it because now I would be able to sneak drinks of water more easily.

The big day was here. They moved the mobile home into the big yard and stabilized it. It was so much bigger than our house and it smelled so new. It had orange-brown shag carpet with a big ugly picture of orange flowers right in the middle of the living room wall. Brown paneling covered the walls.   There were two big orange-colored glass lamps on each side of the couch and a recliner with a bright reading lamp for Dad. There was a bedroom on one end of the trailer with a small room in the middle, my room. I soon understood the meaning of "the same shit different day." What I thought was to be a blessing quickly became a nightmare. My parents alcohol consumption became worse and there was more fighting, more often, and more violently. Instead of an extra room to hide from Danny, it turned out to be just an extra place for him to molest and torture me. The trailer was stifling hot in the day and freezing at night. The heat enhanced the smell of the house, and the smell of new carpet is, unfortunately, a trigger for bad and fearful memories for me even now.

My sixteen year old stepsister, Kelly, came to stay with us briefly. When she arrived, she announced that she was going to marry her military boyfriend. Dolores was furious and said no way! Kelly needed Dolores' permission since she was a minor. Everything seemed even stranger at this time as I watched from the shadows, so to speak. With Dolores freaked out, Kelly locked herself in a small camper that was parked in the yard and refused to eat or drink, or even come out, until Dolores agreed to let her get married. Kelly had won, but I didn't. With all the attention focused on Kelly and her problem, Danny was molesting me that much more.

Now that Kelly had gotten what she wanted, everyone seemed much happier, for the time being anyway. Her husband, Jim, was much older than she and was a Vietnam vet. He had a lot of mental baggage from the war. Even though they moved away, they still came to visit often. Not often enough as far as I was concerned, because I just loved Kelly. She seemed to be the only normal person in my life. Although I loved having Kelly there, I soon learned that Jim too was a predator, although much different than Danny.

Once, Jim and Kelly came to visit over a weekend and stayed in Danny's room. I was very excited because we were going to have a big Spanish omelet breakfast. Jim had been bragging about how his omelets were the best you would ever taste. But, in the morning, instead of getting together to cut and prepare all the ingredients as planned, he lay in bed suffering from a hangover. I became the messenger that went back and forth from him to the kitchen, between peeling potatoes. Every time they sent me to him to ask what they needed next, he would signal me to come closer to him and he would put his hand in my panties and move his fingers around touching me while whispering to me, asking me if it felt good. This was completely unusual to me. I didn't know what to say or how to act. This wasn't any way that Danny had programmed me. I was always the toucher, not the touchee. What was I supposed to say? What was I supposed to do? If Kelly found out she would hate me. I just couldn't face that, so I did nothing, I said nothing. I just stood there like a deer in the headlights. I always wondered if Dolores sensed something though, because after my third time of being sent to his room, she announced that I now needed to stay out of there because I had no business being back there alone with a grown man. Okay, I thought, whatever that meant. A little late! But I wasn't going to ask, and I had nothing to say. She was so unpredictable and never made sense. She's the one who sent me back and forth in the first place. This was nothing new for her though; Dolores always contradicted herself by telling me to do something, then asking why I did it. It was always so confusing to me. I lived the saying, "You're damned if you do and damned if you don't." With Dolores, you never knew from one day to the next how she was going to react. Most of the time she was mean, calloused, and in no mood for any nonsense. Whenever she looked at me, I swear my face always reminded her of chores that needed to be done. I tried my best to avoid her and Danny, but I couldn't because Dad was always at work or at the VFW bar.

I don't quite remember how it came about but I met a boy that came to visit his grandparents across the highway, which was the street in front of the gate to our property. We actually became friends! His name was Gregory. I had to sneak to visit him but it was so worth the chance of getting caught. They were the greatest people I had ever met, so friendly and always asking if I was hungry. I felt so comfortable there. Their house sat in the middle of their property. Although it was a junkyard, it wasn't a scary junkyard like the one I had experienced in the earlier part of my life. It was pleasant and organized. Further out from the abandoned cars and junk there was a field that was completely filled with sunflowers. This was my secret field of protection that I would reflect back on many times throughout my life. Whenever I would get the opportunity I would sneak across the highway to their house then through the yard to the sunflowers. Their scent made my heart happy, and they were so tall that when I laid down in them I felt that I became invisible. I didn't even mind the ants. Sometimes I could hear Dolores or Danny yelling for me. I would just stay there until I couldn't hear them anymore. The feeling of security and protection was worth the trouble I would get into later for disappearing. I never shared this beautiful place with anyone.

The house had two stories but the kids were only allowed to play downstairs. Gregory had a sister that was there too, but I mostly just played with Gregory. They had a piano in the house and the grandparents actually encouraged us to play it. And, I had my first taste of Fruit Loops there. They were amazing! I ate so many I got blisters on the roof of my mouth. Their home was just like I had always dreamed a normal home would be like. Even after Gregory and his sister went back home to their parents, I would escape to go over there and just hang out. I felt so safe and secure in their home, but I couldn't tell them about my life across the road. I thought they wouldn't like me anymore. Brainwashed and living in total fear, Danny had convinced me not to tell anyone.

Eventually, Dolores found out where I was going and put a stop to it immediately! She was always against me speaking to anyone outside our immediate family. She would scold me saying, "Our business is our own damn business so shut your damn mouth and stay in your yard or you won't be allowed out of your bedroom." I remember thinking to myself, what happens to adults when they get older? How can they be so mean? Don't they remember when they were kids, how easily their tender feelings could be hurt? Why can't adults talk to kids like they talk to other adults or friends? My parents spoke nicer to a dog than they did to me. When I would think these things, I would make a promise to myself to remember how I felt in my heart and to never forget how it feels to be a kid. Even now, as an adult, I remember it like it was yesterday and I try to speak with consideration to my own children. I'm not perfect by any means, and sometimes my mouth gets the best of me, but I always correct my wrong actions with them and let them know when I am aware that I have hurt them and that they never deserve to be hurt. Dolores was so overly protective about our personal business and there were so many secrets to protect. I know that now, but I didn't understand any of it then. And, I was caught up in so many secrets of my own.

With the exception of Kelly's visits and my short time across the street, everything seemed to get worse when we got the mobile home. My parents were drinking and fighting all the time, we went without food more, and our heat and electricity were turned off often. Dad and Dolores started going off on separate drinking binges. Once, for a short time, Danny left to go visit his dad. It must have been some kind of school break because Dolores was stuck with me in the daytime. She didn't trust leaving me alone during the day because she knew how much I loved going to the neighbors. That wasn't going to stop her from going to the bar though. She talked the owner into letting me come with her. This was great for me. The bar always made me feel at home, the smell was so familiar. And the other drunken adults were great! They gave me food, played pool with me, and gave me money to play the jukebox. Whether I was just with Dolores at the bar or with her and my dad at the VFW, the times in my life in bars were always happy.

Once, when Dad had been away for about three days, he learned what had been going on. He was furious! I could hear the yelling from my room saying, "My daughter will not be raised in a bar!" I remember Dolores yelling back, "Then raise the stupid brat yourself because no one else will raise her sorry ass." He just stormed out of the house. I heard his truck door slam and he sped off. Great, I thought, I get to deal with Dolores on my own now. I stayed in my room, and as I feared, she eventually yelled for me. I went into the kitchen. She told me to sit at the table. As I did, she sat a can of spaghetti in front of me and snarled, "There. If you get hungry, eat this." Canned Spaghetti? What's this stuff? Then she stormed out the door. I could tell by the makeup and perfume she was wearing that she was off to the bar.

Big Changes Chapter 14

Could it really be? No more Dolores, no more Danny!

I was alone. No Danny, no Dolores, no one to yell at me, no one making me do anything. I turned on the record player and listened to some old 45s, and drank all the glorious water I wanted. Wanting to prove that I wasn't so worthless, I decided to clean the whole house. When I finished, I tried to eat the can of spaghetti but it tasted bad to me and I barely ate any of it. I went and got some of the cigarette butts I had stashed to smoke so I wouldn't be hungry anymore. As time ticked on, it soon became very late. I thought the house looked perfect and I decided to go to bed.

I don't know how long I was asleep before I heard a loud bang in the corner of my bedroom. My eyes popped open but I didn't move a muscle. It was so dark I could barely see. I could hear crying and saw a dark shadow crouched down between my dresser and closet doors. All of a sudden, yelling and heavy footsteps echoed through the hallway. I was frozen in fear! What in the hell is going on? Suddenly, in the doorway of my bedroom, Dad appeared naked except for a cowboy hat and a pair of cowboy boots. He was searching for Dolores and he was furious! He was calling her a fucking whore and announcing, "If you want a cowboy, then here I am! I'm the only cowboy you need, bitch! Where are you?" Although he stepped into my room and looked around, he couldn't see the silent dark shadow in the corner. Now I knew who it was, Dolores, and at that moment, I felt sorry and scared for her. I didn't move or make a sound. He turned around and stomped out, his yelling fading off down the hallway. Although I could hear Dolores whimpering and crying in the corner, I drifted off to sleep.

In the morning, I woke up wet and cold. I had wet the bed again! Then, I remembered about the night before. Dolores was gone and everything was quiet. With no one in sight, I felt relieved that no one would know. I snuck my bedding into the dryer to quietly cover up my unforgivable mistake. I went down the hall and crept into the living room. I saw that my parents' bedroom door was shut so I turned on the TV real low, and sat close, careful not to wake anyone. Then, the door cracked open and there she was! She was wearing dad's bathrobe. Her hair was messy and she had black eye makeup all around her eyes. God, how she frightened me! She immediately started barking orders "Get your dad's newspaper! Have you made coffee yet or are you just going to sit there on your ass and do nothing, as usual." Well, so much for feeling sorry for her. Obviously, she didn't notice all the cleaning I had done the night before. Oh well, nothing new. She coughed, scratched her crotch, and then turned around and went back into the bedroom.

Very little time went by before you could hear them having sex. They were so loud and they made the trailer shake. I don't know why, but this just made me sick. When the door cracked open again, I knew this was my queue to bring in the coffee and newspaper. Their room smelled horrible! The smell of sex, alcohol and cigarettes lingered like a suffocating cloud. They acted like it was just another normal day, like nothing happened the night before. Was this normal? Did other families act like this behind closed doors? I wasn't sure, but something inside of me said -- no, this isn't normal." But, this was my life.

Days and weeks went by. Life wasn't great but it was tolerable without Danny. Much too soon though, he returned and my life of a living hell was in full swing. Another night when I was sleeping, I was awakened by loud yells and the sound of glass breaking. I recognized the sounds instantly. It was Dad and Dolores at it again but she wasn't hiding this time. It was horrible! They were cussing and calling each other names, followed by loud crashing. Again, I just pretended that I was asleep, and didn't move. I didn't even take a full breath fearing they would hear me. If there was one thing in life that I had learned so far, it was out of sight, out of mind. I drifted off to sleep even with all the lights in the house on and the loud noise of fighting. When I woke up in the morning, all was quiet again. I crept out of my room and peeked into Danny's room. He was there. He must not have heard anything last night. I don't know how, but I know I didn't hear his voice in the yelling. I went down the hallway toward the kitchen. Oh, my God! What in the hell happened here? My parents are crazy!

It was a disaster. I wondered if they were okay. The dining room table was tipped over; three of the four chairs were broken. Glass and ceramic were in pieces everywhere. All of the drawers were pulled out and thrown on the floor. Pans and bowls were strewn about. Plates were shattered. Everywhere I stepped there was something on the floor. The living room too looked like a battleground. One of the two orange lamps was broken and the end tables were tipped over, nowhere near where they normally sat. Books were ripped and thrown around the room. The recliner was on its side and the couch was tipped over too. Silverware from the kitchen was thrown all over.

Dad's bedroom door was closed. I carefully put my ear against the door to see if I could hear anyone moving or breathing. I could hear Dad snoring. I hurried into the kitchen and quickly, but quietly, started to clean the mess. My heart raced and I breathed shallowly. I felt panicked and, for some reason, I thought if my parents woke up to this mess, I would be in big trouble. I put the drawers back, except for the broken ones. I picked up the pots and pans, and the dishes that weren't broken and put them away. On my hands and knees, I picked up the broken glass. Quietly, I gathered up the silverware off the floor from around the house. When I started picking up the tables and tried to right the couch, my parents' door opened and there she was! She was pissed off and glared at me. Closing the door behind her, she walked toward me shaking her finger at me. "What in the hell have you done here, you stupid ass? Can't you mind your own business? No one told you to touch anything! Can't you keep your fucking hands to yourself? Why are you always doing things to piss me off?" I couldn't speak. Did I miss something? What did I do wrong? "Why did you clean this up?" she went on, "I wanted it to be left the way it was, so that your father could see what he did last night! But no, you had to go and ruin everything just like you always do! You're just a worthless brat!" As I look back now, it seems like the angrier she was with dad, the more she took her anger out on me. She never spoke to Danny with that tone. As far as she was concerned, he could do no wrong and she acted as though it was them against me most of the time.

I remember taking a class trip to the library one time. I found a book that I really wanted but I didn't want to return it, so I snuck it out and took it home. This was the first time I ever stole anything. I remember it so well because the book was called, Are You My Mother?, by Dr. Seuss. I felt I would be able to relate to the character in the book because deep down, I longed for my real mother. I read the book over and over, especially when Dolores threatened to disown me. With Danny back home, Dad spent less time there. He and Dolores would start arguing and Dad would leave. Then Dolores would leave. It was like they tried to make each other mad by seeing who would stay away from the house the longest. This was the worst thing for Danny and me because they wouldn't pay the bills or buy food, leaving us with no heat or electricity and nothing to eat. Somehow, Danny always had cigarettes and he was never too hungry to molest me. Life was dreadful! Dad let some people from the bar stay in the old house on our property, and when Dolores was gone, I tried to escape from Danny over there as much as I could. Danny knew this and would tell on me for going over there so that I would get in trouble. It was his way of getting back at me for running away from him.

One evening, before I went to sleep, Dad, Dolores and Danny were home and everything seemed normal. But, when I woke up later, no one was there. I took advantage of the situation and ran over to the new neighbors' house. When I knocked on the door, I knew I was busted when I saw Dolores and Danny sitting at the table. Everything seemed so serious. Dolores was holding a towel with ice on her nose. The neighbor invited me in. Dolores acted nice asking me if I was hungry. She always put on an act in front of people. We both knew she couldn't care less if I was hungry or not. The neighbor asked if I wanted to watch TV. I looked at Dolores. She nodded her head yes and said to go ahead. Wow, this was strange! I turned on the TV but tried to listen to the conversation in the other room. I really couldn't hear what was being said, but from what Dolores told me later, Dad left to go to the bar to play saxophone in the band and while she was sleeping, someone broke into our home, snuck into her room and punched her in the face breaking her nose. She said it was dark and she couldn't see anything but swore that she knew it was my dad. She woke up Danny who took her over to the neighbors' house.

According to Danny, when my dad came home around 3 a.m., he confronted Dad saying that Dolores was next door with the neighbor claiming he had attacked her. Danny said Dad seemed confused and angry. Then he marched next door to the neighbors' house. He stepped into the doorway and asked her what was going on. Danny said Dolores stood up and yelled, "You damn well know what happened, you son of a bitch!" He said she turned to walk out of the room and that Dad then reached over and picked up a large cast iron skillet from off of the stove, throwing it at her head, barely missing her, bouncing it off the doorframe. Then he stormed away mumbling and cursing. Danny said if the pan had hit Dolores, it would have killed her. When no one was in the kitchen, Danny showed me where the pan impacted the wall and sure enough, in the wood there was about a one-inch gash. That next day, things were really weird and everyone left me alone. Putting all the attention on Dolores was fine with me.

The next morning, Danny and Dolores were gathering some of their things to leave. Dolores told me that if she and dad got a divorce, I would have to go to court and that she wanted me to ask the judge to stay with her. I don't know why she would want me, probably just to piss off my dad. I just said okay and hugged her. I said, "I love you," which really meant nothing, and then said goodbye. I acted sad for her sake but inside I was relieved and happy to see her go. Yeah!! Could it really be? No more Dolores, no more Danny! It was so hard to believe, but it was a wonderful thought.

The day passed and the house remained quiet. Dad came home later that night and seemed surprisingly happy. He told me to get some things together because I was going to stay with my Aunt Agnes for a while. He made everything sound fun and exciting, like an adventure. He told me I would be staying at the neighbors' house for the next two days and then we would drive to the airport so I could fly on an airplane by myself to Salt Lake City. He told me to be brave, that I didn't need to be afraid. What he didn't know was what I feared the most had already left.

My last days at the neighbors were great! Not only was she nice to me, but she also treated me like a person. She let me help her make dinner and fed me until I was full. She taught me how to make the most delicious thing I had ever tasted, fried potatoes with onions and eggs mixed into one dish. She helped me pack and gave me a beautiful silver-sequined clutch bag to take with me. She wished me luck with my new life and told me to always think of her when I looked at the purse. That was the last time I ever saw her.

Dad picked me up and we drove for hours through the night. By morning, we arrived at the airport. It was cold and snowy. I was so excited, not nervous at all. Dad walked me to the plane and talked the pilot into showing me the cockpit. It was fascinating. There were lights and buttons everywhere. The stewardess was beautiful and very nice. I remember thinking that I wanted to be a stewardess when I grew up. In that space and time, I felt very special and lucky! Maybe things were going to be better from now on. Or, maybe not, only time would tell.

I arrived in Salt Lake City and there to meet me was my Aunt Agnes. She was nice enough at first but soon, she didn't want me around either. The only reason why she took me in was because she couldn't say no to her favorite brother, her only brother. Little did I know, Danny or no Danny, the molesting would continue.

Keeping quiet, thinking things wouldn't get worse,
was a big mistake.

I was really used to moving by now. New places and new faces didn't frighten me. What I hated was changing schools. It was always hard! I was terrible at making new friends and to make matters worse, my clothes were always raggedy and outdated. This made me an immediate target for ridicule. School was no better there, than anywhere else I had gone. The class work was different from my old school's so it made it very hard to understand what was going on. I had this problem at all the schools I attended. Dad transferred me so much that often the records from the previous school I attended hadn't even arrived before I was being transferred again. Aunt Agnes didn't understand my problem with wetting the bed at all and, in some strange way, she seemed to take it personally. Furious, she would yell at me telling me to strip my bed and get dressed, that I could just "go to school smelling of piss. If I could lay in it, then I could surely go to class smelling of it." That in and of itself didn't help to make school any better. At this new school my new nickname was Skunk. There I spent my time either fist fighting or being alone.

Soon, Aunt Agnes gave me the no drinks allowed policy but at least, when I stayed with her, there was food and I got to eat. It seemed the meaner and more hateful Aunt Agnes got, the nicer and friendlier my Uncle Steve got. At first, he was the greatest. Sometimes, if Aunt Agnes left in the morning to go to work before Uncle Steve, and I wet the bed, he would let me shower before school. He never yelled at me, he always smiled and made funny noises trying to make me laugh. He loved to hide behind doors and around corners to jump out and scare me. As the days went by, my uncle got more and more friendly. I was his little buddy and, sadly, he was probably my best friend except for their daughter, Abbey. I just adored Abbey, but she never stayed home because she was studying to go on her Mormon mission and, Aunt Agnes always yelled at her too. Although I loved and trusted her more than anyone, during the little time we spent together, I never confided in her or anyone.

It was a ritual for my aunt, uncle and me to watch TV after dinner before bed. Uncle Steve always invited me to sit on his lap and when Aunt Agnes wasn't looking, he would share his beer with me. I loved it because I was usually thirsty. When Aunt Agnes would flip out and start yelling at me, he would try to interrupt and distract her. He always went out of his way to be my friend, and God knows I needed one! He'd slip me a couple of dollars here and there, give me a later bedtime and sometimes he'd even let me skip school. Why was he so nice? It wasn't until later that I learned it was because he had other things in mind. He was earning my trust and adding up good points on his side so that I would keep his secrets. When I sat on his lap, sometimes he would tickle me so that I would squirm around on his lumpy lap. I knew it was more than a game or an accident because I could feel his body lift up when he would push down on my body. As I look back now, I ask myself "Why did I put myself in that situation?" It's not a good excuse, but the only reason I can think of that makes any sense is that he was the only nice person in my life at the time. If I made him mad or deprived him of what he wanted, I would have no one. Who would protect me from my aunt? Except for him, I had no friends at all. In my mind, I believed that if I rebelled or told, they would send me back to Dolores and, back to Danny. That thought terrified me more than my new form of torture. At least he wasn't physically hurting me. He was definitely the least of those two evils.

Keeping quiet, thinking things wouldn't get worse, was a big mistake. He started insisting on tucking me into bed on his way to bed. This is when his tolerable games began to get horrible! He would pull my covers up to my chin, then fold blankets up at the bottom exposing me from the waist down. He would turn out the lights and quietly come over to me, kneeling down over the bottom of my bed. Cautiously, he moved my panties over to the side exposing me. He would start licking me. This was so confusing. I was confused and petrified. My body would stiffen without my even thinking. As before with Jim, this sexual abuse was new to me and, like before, I didn't know what to say or how to act. My mind was racing. What if Aunt Agnes was to walk in? The most confusing part was that it kind of felt good and was repulsive at the same time. Every time he heard my aunt cough or move around, he would jump up. He became good at being sneaky. When he would hear my aunt coming, he would creep into his room before she reached the end of the hallway, pretending he was there the whole time. One night, during his tucking me in, I started to pee a little in his mouth. He stopped and asked me straight out, "Are you peeing? I told him no that I wasn't. He still kept doing it though. It didn't make him stop and, in a strange way, it gave me a little self-respect. It was my way of getting back at him.

I hated facing him in the mornings because I always felt embarrassed about what had taken place the night before. It was harder to face him when my aunt had already left for work. When I was alone with him, I was jumpy and afraid. I knew he wouldn't hurt me physically like Danny did, but I knew that what he was doing wasn't right and it felt very creepy. He loved to put his arms around me, hugging and squeezing me. His body hugs were disgusting! They consisted of lifting me off the ground and rubbing my body up and down and side to side on his groin area. One morning, during one of his overbearing hugs, he had to change his pants because he had a large wet spot all over the front of his pants. He acted as if it was no big deal and simply went to his room and changed. I felt so dirty and so ashamed.

This relationship continued in the same way the whole time I lived with them. I couldn't tell anyone. Who would I tell? Who would believe me? I didn't feel like anyone cared about me anyway. Maybe that's why I was also afraid of getting my uncle in trouble. He wasn't a good person but he was one of the very few "friends" I had. Reflecting on it, I can see how mixed up my logic was. But back then I didn't understand the manipulation. With Danny, it was life or death. But with Uncle Steve, it was guilt, alcohol and loneliness that kept me silent. How can I tell on him and get him in trouble? All he ever tried to do was be my friend, get me out of trouble, and make me laugh. Once again, I remained silent. I kept his dirty secret. By now, I was a good actress; always masking my feelings, pretending everything was okay.

Christmas was coming and I got some exciting news. Dad was coming to pick me up and we were going to start a new life together again. All I could think was how nice it would be to be away from Danny and my uncle! And, if I was lucky enough, maybe Dad will have found a new mommy for me, one that will love me and not hate me for wetting the bed.

The Worst Words I Could Ever Hear   Chapter 16
All my hopes for a new life, a normal life, were gone!

All my thoughts and questions were answered soon enough. Christmas morning, Dad woke me up. He told me to come into the kitchen because he had a surprise for me. I was so excited! Was it a gift? Maybe it was a puppy? Or maybe a new mommy! As I stepped in the doorway, my heart dropped. I couldn't believe what was there! I could see matted black hair, a coffee cup, and a smoldering cigarette. Oh my God, could it be her? Was this my surprise? Then I heard her voice, and that fake laugh. My worst fears swelled within me. They were back together again. She called me over to give her a kiss and a hug. She was everything I remembered, that foul-smelling cigarette, coffee, and night-before alcohol binge stench. My mind raced with a million questions but I just stood there frozen in silence, praying that they were just passing through town. All hope was shattered when Dolores uttered the worst words I could hear, that everything was going to be alright and we were going to be a family again. That we were going to start going to church and be happy. Reaching out to me, she said, "Now come and tell me how much you love me, show me how much you missed me." Like a robot, I moved toward her on command. I was stunned. In a moment, an instant, all my hopes for a new life, a normal life, were gone! I felt my spirit break. All I could pray for now was death.

My life was changing again, a new town, a new school, but with the same old problems. Yes, some things never changed. We left Salt Lake City the next day to move to Salida, Colorado, but first we had to stop and pick up Danny.

New Year's 1976 was right around the corner. For some, this was exciting, but for me, it meant nothing. We didn't move into a home or apartment like most people. We had a very small camper trailer that Dolores pulled behind her Thunderbird while Dad drove his van pulling his scaffolding. This is how we always traveled. We pulled into a KOA campground. I hoped that we wouldn't live there long. It had a heated pool and a playground, but living there was still dismal. It took very little time to set up the trailer and with that, Dad and Dolores were off to the bar. I was mortified! Danny wasted no time in molesting me. It was worse this time because there was no place to go, nowhere to hide. If I wanted out of the camper, I had to perform his sex acts. If I wanted to eat, or play anything, I was at his mercy.

Dolores signed me up for school and as usual, school life sucked. Not only was I wearing ugly clothes that were too small, my shoes were holey and I had a faint smell of urine. At least the school bus picked me up in front of the campground. My parents were gone a lot and Danny was in charge of me all the time. Sometimes, he would throw something together for us to eat, his special goulash. The strange thing was, whenever he let me go outside while he was fixing me something to eat, when I got my food, it tasted funny. It tasted like a nasty kind of medicine that Dolores would sometimes give me. It wasn't just this time, it happened many other times before. Once, when I asked him why it had the strange taste, he would just reply, "It tastes just fine to me so eat it or go without." As I look back, I wonder if he was trying to poison or drug me. There were many times I experienced this "taste" and whenever away from Danny, I never tasted it. It couldn't have been an accident with his cooking like he once suggested. He usually made something with macaroni and he told me the weird taste came from boiling the pasta. I've cooked a lot of pasta as a mother over the years and, not once, have I ever tasted that strange taste.

Living in the KOA did have its advantages. When I was allowed to go outside, there were many places to hide, like the bathrooms or the showers and there were lots of tall weeds by the playground. Sometimes I would just lie down in the middle of the weeds and stare at the sky until I drifted off to sleep. This often landed me in big trouble. Danny would get really mad when he couldn't find me. He'd tell my parents he was calling and looking for me and I wouldn't answer which earned me a sound spanking. But it was always worth the trouble I got into just to have the time alone, safely hidden for a while.

Sometimes, we got to go visit Dolores' brother, David. He lived in Salida too. I loved going there because they had delicious apples and everyone was always so distracted that they didn't notice how much I ate. It was an old home with a very old smell. Uncle David was old and was losing his eyesight. His wife, Susan, was a snappy old woman, and Dolores didn't like her much. When she was face to face with her, she acted like she liked her, the way she did with me. But once she was away from her, she would do nothing but call her names and complain about her.

Dad and Dolores came home from work early, and sober, one day and were excited to announce that we were moving out of the KOA campground into our own place. We would be right next to Dad's work. Once again, the promise of a new and better life was just another letdown. We pulled up to an abandoned gas station off one of Salida's main streets. Dad parked the camper on the side of the building. We walked into what used to be the office and Dad said, "This is it! If you have to use the bathroom, then use the one in here." The whole place smelled. It was old, and the sink was barely clinging to the wall. There was no shower, no tub, and no privacy. In my young life I learned to never believe that things couldn't get any worse! Dolores showed me how to boil water and combine it with cold water in a bucket so that I could take what she called, a spit bath. When she washed my hair, it was with the water from the hose outside. I remember the pain of my head freezing it was so cold. This place was another disastrous experience! The only good things about this new beginning was that Dolores cooked and it made the camper smell good and Danny couldn't touch me with Dad and Dolores around because there was nowhere he could be alone with me to molest me.

For the first week or two, my parents got along. We were going to church on Sunday's and sometimes on Wednesdays. I loved church. Dad worked hard in the gas station garage he converted into his workshop. As usual, even this came to an end. Dolores and Dad were back to their binge drinking and I was being left alone with Danny. I was spared his attacks for a week and a half when Justin came to stay with us in the camper. He was really nice to me and I liked him. I felt safe around him. Even with him there, Danny was able to hurt me the minute Justin left to go anywhere. To keep from being discovered, he would drag or coax me out into the overgrown weed field behind the gas station and molest me there. Even when I tried to fight him off or screamed, no one heard me, no one would help me, and once again, there was no one I could tell. I couldn't say anything to Justin; Danny was his brother. Who would he believe? As far as I knew, and truly believed, no one cared.

Luckily, we weren't there for long, before my parents came home with great news. We were moving again, only this time, we were moving into a house. I would still be going to the same school as I did when living at the campground, and the garage. It didn't really matter to me though because school still sucked. I was still an outcast feeling out of place and embarrassed, with no one to speak to or play with. At school, I wished I could just disappear or not exist, just like at home. The only thing good about school was that I got to eat lunch and drink water. Moving day came and I was excited by the thought of moving into a real house. It was much bigger than I expected and I finally got my own room. It was small, but it had a door and some privacy. There was a living room, dining room, and three bedrooms. It had a very large window above the sink that overlooked a giant field. There were a couple of barn-like buildings next to a path that led to a large fast running creek.

It was my job to keep the furniture dusted, the bathrooms cleaned, the floor vacuumed, and the kitchen clean. While living in this house, cleaning the kitchen was more of a release than a chore because of the large picture window that over looked the field and creek. Big beautiful deer and other wildlife would graze peacefully. In the morning, the sunrise was amazing and in the evening the sunsets would paint the clouds in pastel shades of pink and blue. There weren't many opportunities to feel happiness in my heart, but these sights were what I would hold onto. Danny was still abusing and molesting me but he started working with Dad, so he had less opportunity. Dolores started staying home more, sewing blankets and even cooking dinner and occasionally, making breakfast. Dolores wasn't drinking as much, and she and Dad were fighting less. Church and music were part of our lives again. It almost felt as if life might be starting to get better. Once, as I was looking out the kitchen window while doing dishes, I saw two big, four point bucks, walking and grazing in the field. They were so beautiful and graceful. They just stood there, perfect and picturesque. As I was watching, it made me think of how much we had in common. When it wasn't hunting season, their lives were peaceful and they seemed content. When Danny wasn't home and my parents weren't fighting, I was also content. I've always remembered that moment. Sometimes I bring it back to mind and go back to that peaceful moment, as I remember it. It was humbling.

This house was probably the best we lived in but, as usual, it would only last for a little while. Since the house was large, it was too expensive to heat properly so it was always cold. It had a furnace that burned coal and Danny was able to use this to his advantage. We would be sent down to a room under the house to get buckets of coal. I hated going down there because this was where Danny would regularly make me do sexual favors for him. I felt as if I was already choking, and being in a room full of coal would make it nearly impossible to breathe. It was dark, dirty and eerie. Filled with spider webs, it was a small area that didn't look or feel safe. Sometimes, Danny would molest me in the barn-like buildings in the backyard. Any time he could get me alone and out of sight, he would suffocate and molest me. It didn't take long before I started hating this house as well. Every nook and cranny represented the sex acts that Danny would force upon me.

Everything else started to fall apart, like it always did. Dolores started going out and Dad began working later and later. I tried to stay in my room and listen to Christian music or read books, as much as I was allowed. One night, when I was sleeping, Dolores woke me up telling me that Dad and Danny were in a bad car accident. I didn't know what to do or say. I am sorry to say now, that deep down inside, I was hoping that Danny had died. Fortunately or unfortunately, only the car was totaled. We had to drive a couple of hours away to go pick them up. We pulled up to a gas station where they were outside waiting for us. They were shaking and complaining about being frozen cold. On the way home, they explained about how the accident happened and said the car was too demolished to get anything out of it, Dad's paint supplies, tools, even some fabric Dolores had in the trunk.

Although they were faced with driving in a blizzard, with icy foggy conditions no normal person would drive in, Dad decided he wanted to get back home that night. He regularly ignored others' advice, and never cared whether or not he was putting other people in danger. That night, it was no different. When they were crossing a two-lane bridge in weather they could barely see through, at the last minute, they saw a full-grown cow, and realized it wasn't moving. Faced with slamming on the brakes that would surely put them in a spin, sending them down the side of the bridge into the icy river below, Dad decided he had only one choice, hit the cow dead on in the middle of the bridge and just hold on for dear life. Plowing directly into the cow, it demolished the Mustang. The front was completely smashed in and cow guts were all over the engine. The top of the car had smashed down on top of them and all the windows were shattered. The trunk was caved in and the taillights were broken out. They walked away leaving the car on the bridge. As they climbed out and cleared from the wreckage they could see the cow lift its head just as a diesel truck driving by hit it, decapitating it. The truck driver pulled over and got help for them. That was how they were able to contact us.

That wasn't the only bad news our family received this week. In one phone call everything would change, once again. It was Justin. He was asking Dolores to come to Alaska. He had gone into the hospital because of stomach pain and found out he had cancer. He had been living in Alaska and according to his letters; he really loved it there. He was going to have surgery and chemotherapy and wanted her there. Within two days, she left to be with him. Everything from that point went downhill quickly. I was left in Danny's care and Dad worked or played saxophone at the bar most every night. When Dolores finally came home, she said the operation went well and they removed all the cancer. But, she couldn't handle the stress and started to drink heavily again. It seemed as though every day now she had a Bible in one hand and a cigarette and beer in the other. Instead of cooking, she was crying or spending her time at the bar. Dad began to drink more too, and like always, they began fighting again. I became more and more addicted to cigarettes because they were easier to obtain than food. School seemed much harder and I was falling way behind. It felt like everything was falling apart again. By the things that Dolores was saying to me, I felt as if the hard times and everyone's sadness were my fault. She repeatedly told me that if it weren't for me, she would've left my dad a long time ago! She would say to me, "You're the reason I'm here letting your dad knock the shit out of me and treating me like crap. If I didn't stay here with you, then you wouldn't have anyone or anything. I'm the only one who cares or truly loves you. Even your own mother couldn't have cared less about you. So you should thank your lucky stars. No matter what happens, you stick with me because I love you. Your dad's full of shit and all he does is lie. He doesn't really care about you and never did. He just used you as a tool to attract women saying 'Look at this helpless child. She needs a mommy."

She told me when I was younger and my feet would freeze walking to school that she would tell him I needed warm boots and he would tell her that he was broke and couldn't buy anything. But that same evening, he would come home with a new suit. That just broke my heart. Maybe my daddy really didn't care. I couldn't really talk to him because I was afraid of him. He didn't abuse me but he always seemed annoyed by me, like I was to be seen and not heard. He always said nice things about me to other people when we were together and would introduce me. But as far as him saying anything when we were alone, it just didn't happen. Sometimes, I would try to talk to him. I would take a deep breath to speak but nothing would come out. I could feel my heart racing, would clinch my hands to try and stop them from shaking but still nothing would come out. I kept repeating this process until I just gave up. I had no outlet, no one to trust, and no one to talk to. Dolores continued to warn me daily not tell anyone about our problems or our family. No one at school or anywhere needed to know our damn business!

I prayed a lot and spoke to God and, believe it or not, I never lost my faith. No matter what, I always believed in the Bible and loved God. But, I still hated my life; I still looked forward to death. I wanted to go to Heaven and, regardless of what Dolores told me, I always believed that I was going to go to heaven when I died. No such luck for me; God had different plans for my life. It wasn't until much later that I was able to see why I had to go through this hell.

Somehow, Dolores got a side job as a motel maid. On Saturdays, she let me come with her and help her clean. I really enjoyed this because it let me get away from Danny. I cleaned the bathrooms and always did a good job at it, so she let me keep coming with her. That quickly ended though, when her drinking became more out of control. One Saturday when I woke up to go, Dolores met me in the kitchen. She told me Dad was in the living room on the couch and to stay away from him. She said he was hurt and he'd deserved everything he got. "Don't talk to him, don't feel sorry for him, just ignore him," she instructed. I remember being very confused and didn't know what to do. Even though Dad wasn't very friendly to me, he was still my daddy and I loved him unconditionally. He never paid a whole lot of attention to me and we didn't speak a lot, but I admired him and thought he was the smartest person on the planet. In hindsight, I realize my fear of him was more from intimidation.

Danny was in his room when Dolores left the house. I ignored Dolores' orders and crept into the dining room to peek around the corner at Dad. He heard the floor creak and called out my name. Slowly, I walked towards him to see what he wanted. He asked me to bring him a glass of water. I didn't really get a good look at him until I handed him the glass. He looked terrible. I could feel the tears well up in my eyes. I couldn't say a word. I thought to myself "Oh my God, what happened to you?" There was dried blood in his hair, cuts and scrapes all over his face, and his eye was swollen and black. I couldn't help but cry for him.

Still, I didn't make a sound. Dad motioned for me to come close and he hugged me. This made me cry out loud. He asked me to bring him some aspirin and as I went into the kitchen to get them, Danny appeared. He stopped me and told me to get ready to go because we had to walk to Uncle David's house to meet Dolores. I took the pills to Dad and said goodbye. When he rolled over, I could see large gashes in the back of his head. I went and got a bag of ice for him. I just set it where he could see it when he rolled back over because I was afraid to wake him up. He looked like he was in so much pain. I felt so bad for him. It didn't matter what Dolores said, I couldn't understand how anyone could deserve that.

I dressed warmly for the walk to Uncle David's house. It was freezing outside. It had been snowing off and on and the roads were covered with ice. It was so slippery that even walking was dangerous. On our walk, Danny asked me "Don't you want to know what happened to your dad?" "Yes," I answered. He told me that Dolores was in the bar drinking. She was sitting on the barstool when Dad walked in through the back door. He was so mad to see her sitting there, drinking between two men that he walked by her and slapped her in the head, knocking her to the floor. Then he walked right out the front door. The men that were sitting next to her jumped up and ran after him. They chased him down outside and beat him unconscious. That explained Dolores' attitude, but I still felt bad for him. We waited for hours at Uncle David's for Dolores, but she never showed up. This was nothing new. Sometimes Dolores would stop at the bar for a quick drink but ended up staying there until closing. She didn't always make it home either. When this happened, she and Dad would fight for days.

Dad healed and went back to work. but now he rarely came home. Once again, we had no groceries, there was no coal for the heat, and he didn't pay the electric bill. Danny left to go visit his dad for two weeks and Dolores would sit with me at night at the dining room table wrapped in blankets. I would have to listen to her stories while she drank beer and smoked cigarettes. I didn't ask for food; I knew better. I just listened and learned. We read the Bible by candlelight and she told me about how rough her life had been and how lucky I was to have my life and her in it. The days went by and Dolores climbed back out of her pity pit and, unfortunately, Danny came back. Dad got the electricity turned back on and as quickly as everything fell apart, somehow it came back together again.

My parents tried to get along around Thanksgiving because my stepsister Kelly and her husband were coming to visit and Justin was moving back from Alaska. His cancer was in remission. It ended up being the best Thanksgiving we ever had because we had food and everyone was there and sober. After dinner, Kelly took a walk with me down the trail in the backyard to the creek. At that moment, I felt so close to her. We stood next to the water. The edges were frozen. The air was cold and crisp. It was beautiful there. It's funny how being with the right person can change your whole perspective. I had been down by the creek many times before with Danny, but it never seemed beautiful before. I loved to talk with Kelly and spend time with her because she always treated me as a person instead of a nuisance. In that moment, I wanted to tell her about Danny. I wanted to ask her to take me away. Every time I went to say something, I would inhale thinking, "Okay, I'll just blurt it out." It didn't happen. I just couldn't do it. Something meaningless would just come out of my mouth. Deep down, I was terrified that maybe she really wouldn't care either. I was trapped in my own skin. I guess I deserved everything that happened to me. Danny was right. I was a worthless coward. At the very least, I got to spend some time with Kelly and everyone else was nice to each other for a day. As soon as the guests left, everything returned to normal. Dolores and Dad were fighting again and back to binge drinking. Our cabinets were pretty empty but somehow, Dolores was good at creating something out of nothing, when she felt like it.

Christmas was approaching fast. Dolores kept re-enforcing that we wouldn't get anything because my dad didn't care. I believed her, because Dad didn't come around much anymore. When he did, they would just fight and he would storm out of the house. Dolores got a side job at a store. She said she would get two paychecks before Christmas and bragged that she was the only reason that we would even celebrate. In a sense, it was true. As the weeks passed, it seemed like everyone but us was decorating.

There was only one week left until the holiday and Dolores brought in a skinny, scrawny little tree that only had about six branches. It didn't matter to me though. I was so happy just to have a tree and I loved it.

This year, Dolores showed a side she had never shown before. She actually seemed to care and I'll never forget how she took the time and effort to create a joyful memory. We didn't have any decorations so she just got some household items together to make our own decorations. Empty egg cartons, yarn, empty spools of thread, it wasn't fancy to look at, but it worked. That is one of the fondest memories of Dolores that I ever had. Something must have come over Dad too, because two days before Christmas, he came rolling in with a tree and decorations. This must have made Dolores happy because right away, they disappeared into the bedroom where they stayed all day. To my surprise, I got to put our Charlie Brown tree in my bedroom, making me very happy. Danny and I decorated the tree Dad brought home. Every time Dolores came out of the room, she made me redo the icicles. She would say, "If you're going to decorate, then it better be done right." She wanted them to be put on one at a time and only one per branch. Yep it seemed as everything was back to normal again.

The day before Christmas, I did something very wrong. Danny went to his friend's house and Dad and Dolores were still in the bedroom. One present at a time, I snuck into the bathroom and carefully unwrapped, rewrapped and snuck each one back under the tree. I didn't get caught and to this day, I don't know why I did it. It left me disappointed. My advice to anyone who would think of peeking at your gifts would be, don't do it; it's not worth what you may or may not find. Just wait, because it's hard to pretend you're surprised. I know I should have been happy that I got anything at all and don't mean to sound like a whiner, but I never got what I asked for. This time though, I was surprised that Christmas morning with a gift that hadn't been under the tree. I got a watch and I cherished it.

Time went by fast there in Salida, even though we lived there longer than anywhere else I remember. Every day was still unpredictable. Danny was still tormenting me any time he was home. Dad and Dolores drank and fought off and on. Sometimes there was a family atmosphere and sometimes it was cold and lonely. Occasionally, my parents would have me stay at friends or acquaintances during rocky times. There was a particular Mother's Day that I can clearly recall. We were going out with Dad to a big VFW picnic. They were also celebrating the bicentennial. One of the activities was letting the kids catch fish barehanded out of a blocked up creek. They called it the Huckleberry Finn Picnic. It was great! When we got home, Dad gave me a Mother's Day gift. This puzzled me and still does to this day. Here's a man that forgets most holidays including my birthdays, but he got me a Mother's Day gift. I was only ten years old. I didn't argue or ask any questions. I just gratefully accepted it with a kiss and a hug. What was even more puzzling was that it was a Zebco reel. I didn't even own a fishing pole. It never did make sense to me but I loved and treasured it just the same.

It was supposed to be getting warmer since it was spring, but no such luck. Another storm came in and it was freezing. Dad and Dolores were fighting as usual, and for the last week, the electricity had been turned off. Wrapped in blankets, sitting in candle light once again, Dolores explained to me that sometimes it was good to sit in the dark. She would get me so frightened that I always felt there were bad guys watching me, waiting to get me. She warned me that bad people lurked around at night and liked to look into windows. She told me that it's better to be afraid of the light then it is the dark. If you're in the dark, people can't see you but if you're in the light then you're a target. She even had me afraid of my dad sometimes, saying on the nights he didn't come home that he was really outside lurking around watching us through the windows. I didn't really understand this but I didn't want to ask her any questions either.

The power wasn't turned on for days, and it was freezing. Danny left for a couple of days. It was just Dolores and me at home. Getting off the school bus, I couldn't wait to get home and wrapped up in a warm blanket. The house was still. I was so happy that no one else was home. I was very hungry but there was nothing to eat. I found some cigarette butts in the ashtray and that was just as good as food, if not better. Not only did the smoking curb my appetite but it also calmed my nerves. I sucked down all the smokes I could find, picked up the house and cleaned the ashtrays. This way no one would know I smoked them; it would just look like I cleaned the house. I went to my room and bundled up into my blankets. It was completely dark when I opened my eyes. Someone was yelling for me. It was Dad. He's home again and maybe, I hoped, he has food. I rushed into the dining room where he stood holding a bright lantern. In the doorway of the kitchen, I saw a dark shadow. It was Dolores. She had come home too.

They were moving around quickly acting frantic. Dad pointed to some boxes and told me to take them into my room and fill them up. He lit another lantern and sat it in my room. "Hurry up," he said, "and pack what you want. Then go help your mother. We have to be out of here before daylight." Carrying things out to the van and car, my feet and hands were so frozen that I could barely feel them. My fingers couldn't grip very well and I couldn't feel my toes at all. I had been through this before and I knew better than to complain. I learned to make a game out of it by trying to carry as much as I could outside before they could ask me to do something else. As dawn started to break, the pain from being cold was unbearable. Whatever was left in the house by the time of sunrise would be left behind.

After leaving the house, we drove to a motel about 25 to 30 miles out of town. It was much colder there and even though it was May, snow blanketed everything, and was still coming down. We lived in a small room with one bed. Dolores used a hot plate to cook on and we used a cooler for perishable items. They made me a bed on the floor at the foot of their bed. Obviously, they had made up again because I had to fall asleep to the sounds of them having sex that night. Even though we were so far out of town, I didn't have to switch schools. I was in the same school in Salida longer than any other school in my life; I just had different bus stops. It still didn't make much of a difference because I didn't have any friends. I didn't get along with any of the teachers either.

The next day, I was instructed on where to catch the school bus. I stepped outside and it was freezing. You could see ice patches on the ground and everything was white and glistening. I heard the school bus coming and something came over me. I couldn't breathe well and my heart was pounding! All of a sudden, I was terrified! Knowing that Dolores wasn't watching me, I hid behind the car. It was still packed completely full of our stuff. I watched the bus stop, open the doors, then close them and drive away. There were no other kids at the stop, so no one else saw me hiding. I waited until the bus was clear out of sight before I went back to the motel room. I walked in and Dolores said, "Well, what in the hell did you forget now?" Before I could think, a great lie just popped out of my mouth. I quickly said, "Whoever told you about the bus stop must have been wrong about what time the bus stops. I stood out there the whole time and the bus never came." Dolores grunted "Well, you'll just have to stay here with me today then, because it is too far for me to drive you today. Just keep to yourself and don't bug me." That was fine with me. The next day, I wasn't able to pull the same stunt because this time, Dolores sent me outside a half hour earlier. By the time the bus arrived, I was a lot happier about getting on. I was so cold that I couldn't feel my feet or hands.

At school, like at home, I seemed to have a knack for saying or doing the wrong thing. I remember sitting in the hallway almost every other day writing "I will not talk in class." or "I will not disrupt the class." There were a lot of "I will not in class" days. Looking back, I don't understand why I did the things that I did. One day, during recess, I decided I was going to see how far I could get away from the school and then make it back before recess ended. Of course I had to show other kids that I could be cool by letting them notice me cross the street off of school grounds. Well, they noticed me all right. Someone told and I was busted. A teacher came and got me and took me straight to the principal's office.

The principal, Mr. Thompson, was the only person in the school I actually liked. Sure, he reprimanded me, but I could handle that. It was calling my parents that petrified me. Surprisingly, as strict as my parents were, I didn't get in that much trouble for bad things I did in school. I now realize that my parents didn't look at school as a benefit for my future but more as a place to put me during the day, like a mandatory babysitter. But, during the time I spent at Longfellow Elementary, Mr. Thompson and I would be on a first name basis. Somehow, I think he knew my life was a mess, so in little ways, he tried to be comforting by saying nice things or giving me a snack or just by letting me sit in his office and read when I was supposed to be "in trouble."

We only stayed at the motel for a couple of weeks before we relocated again. This time, we moved to a trailer park. We moved into a small trailer that had only two bedrooms. That meant, now I would have to share with Danny. Dad said that this was only going to be temporary because they were having the mobile home we lived in before moved to this trailer park. I hated sharing a room with Danny! I felt so trapped. I was a 10-year-old sex toy. Dolores always told me how stupid I was, well maybe, if I was so stupid, it was probably from the lack of oxygen to my brain from Danny suffocating me all the time. I didn't have as much fight in me as I used to have. He still enjoyed provoking me into battles though.

Is this the way a family really is?

No sooner did we get settled in, than my parents were back into the bar scene. Now, it was the Elks Lodge and the VFW. No matter what it was called, it was still a bar, and they still drank and they still got into fights. One evening when Danny was babysitting me, he was watching TV in the living room and I was supposed to be going to sleep in the bedroom. I heard a knock on the door. Then I heard the voice of Michael, one of the few friends Danny had. They hadn't been friends for very long but I knew which one he was because I thought he was really cute. I couldn't make out their conversation but for some reason, they came into the bedroom. Danny was showing him where I was but never turned on the light. I lay as still as I could, pretending to be asleep. I heard the boy tell Danny that he thought I was really pretty. Inside I smiled. Danny replied that they better leave the room before I woke up. Barely peeking, I cracked my eyes open just slightly, and watched Danny leave the room. Michael walked toward me and knelt down. He gently kissed me on the lips and then quietly left the room. I drifted off to sleep that night feeling so special and happy. I never told anyone about that experience. I just felt good thinking that there was someone out there that liked me.

Soon, living there was no different from any other of the other places we lived. Bills weren't getting paid and the heat and electricity were regularly getting shut off. My parents were rarely home at the same time. Dolores and Danny started drinking bottles of whiskey together now. I was always hungry and thirsty and it seemed as though my head never stopped hurting. I remember walking down the long dirt road to the bus stop thinking, "I must be the only 10-year-old in the world that knows everything about sex." Of course, that unfortunately was not true, and I certainly didn't know everything about sex, but I definitely knew more than I ever should have! One day, Dad came home from work early when I was by myself. He told me to grab a few things because I had to go stay with some friends because he and Dolores were going out of town for a while. This was nothing new to me. Dad did this off and on the whole time I was with him. Sometimes I knew the people he left me with and sometimes I didn't. Sometimes he picked me up in a couple of days and sometimes he picked me up in a couple of weeks or months. Eventually, it stopped mattering to me. I was very subservient and learned to just go with the flow because I knew that I didn't have any control over my life. I gathered up a couple of shirts, pants and panties, and jumped into Dad's van. I was too scared to ask him where we were going or how long he would be gone.

We pulled up to a large beautiful home. We walked up to the front door, and to my complete surprise, Mr. Thompson opened the door. Immediately and silently, I panicked. It wasn't because of Mr. Thompson, because he was always a pleasant and kind person to me; it was because I didn't belong in a home like that. Everything was so nice. What if I wet the bed? He wouldn't like me anymore either. He had a couple of sons and a very pretty, well-dressed wife. Everything in the home seemed perfect. It was clean and decorated so elegantly. I could only dream of having a home like this someday. Everyone was so polite and courteous to each other. We all sat at the table for dinner. Their family was so perfect; everything there was so perfect. I knew I didn't belong there but I sure wished that I could. They made a bed downstairs in the family room for me. When Mr. Thompson came in to check on me, I started crying. He tried to comfort me by telling me my dad would be back soon. Reluctantly, I told him that wasn't the reason I was upset. I admitted to him that I had a problem with wetting the bed and I was scared to go to sleep. I was so embarrassed but I didn't know what else to do. I asked him to please not tell anyone because I was so ashamed. He was so kind and understanding. I had never experienced this kind of reaction. I thought he was going to be mad and not like me anymore like the other people in my life. He assured me that this would be our secret and he remade my bed to be prepared for an accident. He told me not to worry, that he would help me with my wet or dry bedding in the morning. He laid out a towel and told me if I needed to shower when I woke up, that it would be okay. We said prayers together and then he left a night light on for me in case I needed it.

In the morning, he helped me just as he said he would. This was so unlike anyone else I have ever known. He didn't make a big deal out of me wetting the bed. He took care of it all, assuring me everything was all right. He had to leave early because he had a meeting to attend. He kissed me on the forehead and started to leave. Before walking out the door, he turned to me and said, "After you shower, the boys will be upstairs waiting for you to eat breakfast. Have a good day." As I showered, I looked forward to spending a day in a normal home. This was truly a dream come true, to live without fear. I knew this wasn't where I was going to stay for long, but I sure wished that it could be. I dressed and hurried upstairs. The boys were waiting at the table for me. It was a beautiful dining room table with six chairs. They pointed to an empty place setting and said they were waiting for me before they would eat. It was a great warm feeling. I felt important, and I felt so happy! We were only having cereal, juice, and toast but it was the best breakfast I ever remembered having. I learned one important lesson about what not to do after eating cereal though. After I finished the last bite, there was still milk in the bowl. I lifted the bowl up to my mouth to drink the milk and I heard the boys gasp. Quickly I set my bowl down and asked what was wrong. The boys looked completely shocked and the oldest one said, "It's a good thing our mom isn't here. We are not allowed to finish our milk like that. We're not supposed to ever put our mouth to any plates or bowls, only glasses or silverware." They told me their house rules were you drink your milk out of the bowl using your spoon and whatever is left you wash it down the sink. To me, I thought that was wasteful, but I apologized and thanked them for the tip.

When Mr. Thompson returned, he gathered us up to go play basketball. This was the first time I had ever played. It was great fun! After dinner, everyone was downstairs in the family room. The oldest son mentioned that he was a wrestler. I boasted that I bet I could pin him and everyone laughed. He asked his dad if it would be okay to let me try. Mr. Thompson said yes but warned him to take it easy on me. I quickly responded that he didn't need to take it easy on me because I could take it. No matter what he did, he couldn't pin me. I pinned him about four times before his dad said that was enough. I know he didn't just let me win either because I really was tough. After all, I had been fighting for my life with Danny for years. I felt so strong and proud of myself.

I only got to stay with the Thompsons for about two weeks before Dad came back to get me. I hated leaving, but as usual, I didn't complain. Once again, my safety, warmth and love were gone again.

If only I could find a way to kill myself that wouldn't hurt.

Returning back to the trailer, everything was the same. Absolutely nothing had changed. At school, I had bragged about the days spent staying with the principal's family and beating his son at wrestling. I didn't realize it at the time, but that ended up being a bad thing. The principal had to pull me aside and asked me not to say anything about the wrestling again because the rumor had gotten around and his sons' buddies were teasing him about getting beaten by a girl. I agreed and never brought it up again.

The holiday season was approaching and I knew there was no way it would be a repeat of the previous wonderful year. It would just be like all the others. One of the worst things about the holidays was the time off from school. Sure, I hated school but I hated being home even more. There was a small playground in the trailer park that just had a swing and a merry-go-round. I didn't mind how rundown it was, or how cold it was, I was just happy to be able to go outside and be alone. Many times I remember sitting on the swing winding myself up to just spin around and around.

After having a taste of how normal families lived, I felt even more sad and helpless. The thought of suicide seemed to consume me daily. I wished I could find a way to kill myself that wouldn't hurt. What a chicken I was! I was too afraid to live and too afraid to die. I never questioned if there was a God; I believed in him for as long as I could remember. In my heart, I always knew there was a heaven, a place where there was no fear, no pain, and no loneliness. This is the place that I wanted to be and this is how I looked at death. At one point, I really wondered if I was living in a world of robots. I know it sounds crazy but the cruelty of most of the people in my life thus far seemed just as crazy. From my earliest years, I looked at every day as being a good day to die. Not so that people would miss me or feel bad, because I thought just the opposite. I thought everyone would be happy and relieved if I was gone. I guess I was selfish in this way because I just wanted my pain to end. I just felt tired... tired of just existing. I wasn't just feeling sorry for myself; this was truly how I felt. I had no way of knowing that this feeling would over shadow me throughout my life.

It was almost Thanksgiving and Danny and I were on school break. He and Dolores seemed closer than ever. They stayed home smoking and drinking all day, every day. Coffee in the morning, and by noon, they were opening a fifth of whiskey. By the evening, they were loud and belligerent. In one of their drunken stupors, they decided to give our poodle, Tuffy, a haircut. This turned out very bad. They used an electric razor on him and he had bald patches all over his body. It didn't make any sense to me because it was cold and snowing outside. It was my job to take Tuffy outside to go to the bathroom and he already would shake for being so cold. I didn't know dogs felt embarrassment but it became obvious that they do. After they cut his hair so badly, he hid behind the toilet for three days. I could totally relate and I felt sorry for him.

Dolores came home from the store with a turkey and announced that this year, it was my turn to clean and prepare it for baking. I was worried. This usually meant I was going to be yelled at for screwing something up. Although I wasn't stupid, I had a hard time understanding what adults were telling me. I didn't dare ever say no to anything she told me to do. She told me to take the turkey into the tub and give it a bath. I didn't know if she was joking or serious so I asked her what she meant. As usual, I got the same answer, "Are you stupid? Don't you know what a bath is? Take the damn turkey into the tub and wash it inside and out! And bring me the bag that's inside the turkey. And don't use soap on it." As weird as it sounded, I filled up the tub and bathed the turkey. After I dried it and took it into the kitchen, Dolores had another surprise for me.

Sitting on the kitchen counter was an opened fifth of Black Velvet. She told me I was going to help her and Danny drink it because she felt it was her job to teach me never to drink again. She said that she was going to teach me a lesson I would never forget, that after this experience, I would never want to drink. This was very confusing to me, but I had learned early on, never to argue with or disobey Dolores.

Danny was the drink mixer, Black Velvet and Coke. It was terrible! With the first glass, I almost puked with each swallow. When I started on the second glass, it wasn't so bad. By the third glass, I wasn't doing so well. The room was spinning and I felt hot. I couldn't stand up very well. All I wanted to do was lie down. I felt sick and stumbled to the bathroom and threw up. I lay on the floor next to the toilet. It felt cool and comfortable. In the background, I could hear Danny and Dolores laughing and making fun of me. I didn't move. They were telling me to get up… that I wasn't finished drinking yet. but I didn't move. I couldn't move. Everything went black.

Someone must have moved me during the night, because I woke up on the bedroom floor. Everything hurt and I was thirsty, very thirsty. Dolores was in the kitchen cooking the turkey. When I heard her go into the bathroom, I snuck into the kitchen and guzzled down two tall glasses of water. I don't know why but for some reason, the water made me feel drunk all over again. The Black Velvet bottle was still sitting there and it still had a little bit in it. Just the looks of it made me gag. Normally, when I got up, I would find an excuse to go outside. I would take out the garbage or offer to clean out the car, anything to sneak a cigarette. Not today! I asked Dolores if I could go to the playground for a while since the turkey was still cooking and, to my relief, she said yes. I didn't want a cigarette; I just wanted to be outside in the fresh cool air. I lay on the merry-go-round and stared at the sky because every time I closed my eyes, everything started spinning. Dolores was absolutely right. I never wanted to drink Black Velvet again. To this day, just looking at the bottle makes me shudder. I can distinctly remember the smell and the memory.

Within a couple of days, I was back to normal, whatever normal was. Dad was rarely home over the last couple of months and now it was almost Christmas again. Dolores hung up some of the decorations from last year, but it didn't look like we were going to get a tree this year and there wasn't a present in sight. I knew better than to pout or act disappointed around Dolores or Danny because they always had something mean to say. They were always quick to remind me how I didn't deserve anything anyway and that I should just be happy I had a roof over my head. I believed they were right, I didn't really deserve anything. My own dad didn't want to be around me or he would have come home. Kelly was supposed to come visit and I knew she would give me something. At least that made me happy inside. About three days before Christmas, Dad showed up and he had a tree. What a wonderful surprise it was! Even though there were no presents, I was happy just to have a tree. Although Dad was home, he didn't talk much or even acknowledge me but I loved having him there. I would take off his boots for him and rub his feet. Sometimes, I would bring him a pot of hot water for him to soak his feet. I would rub his head. That was my dad's favorite thing in the world, to have his head massaged or his hair combed. I enjoyed doing these things for him because even though he obviously didn't show love to me, I loved him and wanted to show him.

It was the night before Christmas and I fell asleep waiting for Kelly to show up. When I went to sleep, there wasn't one present under the tree but, when I woke up, there were presents. I was shocked and excited. Kelly had come through and saved Christmas for everyone. Unfortunately, she didn't stay long. She had to leave the very next morning. The holidays passed and everything was back to normal in our house, the drinking, the fighting, and Danny suffocating and molesting me several times a day. In January, our mobile home that we lived in in Walsenburg was finally moved to Salida, and was put in the same mobile home trailer park that we were living in now. We didn't move into it right away because there was too much snow and it was too cold to block it properly and do what they had to do for it to be safe for us to move in. Danny had the keys to it and used it to his advantage. With it being empty and with no one around, this was the perfect place for Danny to molest me. I hated this trailer with a passion. It reminded me of all the bad times in Walsenburg. The smells and the memories intensified the horribleness of being molested in it again.

It was so cold and dark, even in the daylight. Danny would command me to go over to the trailer every day so he could have his way with me. Why would I go? Why didn't I just say no and not go? I learned to obey because I knew the consequences. Unless you have ever been strangled, suffocated or held under water against your will, you can't possibly understand how your body feels when it panics struggling for oxygen. My task was always the same and always horrible. It never got any easier. I always cried and gagged. The tears and snot still ran down my face. My jaw still ached and felt as though it would lock. None of this mattered to Danny. All he was interested in was that he would be satisfied to the fullest. "How could people actually enjoy this?" I wondered. To me, it was pure torture and it didn't matter how fast or how slow I performed it, it seemed to take forever for him to ejaculate.

The longer it took the meaner and more forceful he would get. Didn't he understand that I wanted this over more than he did? My jaw hurt so bad that I would have to stop and rub it with my hands. This infuriated him. He would tell me, "Now that you stopped, you have to start all over again." I remember it like it was yesterday. Whenever I recall these experiences, my body tenses up, and my forehead and top lip become covered in sweat. I remember wondering how many other kids at school go through this. Or, was I the only one? How can one human being put another human being through this? No matter what Danny said, I truly believed deep down, that I didn't deserve this. Sure, maybe I didn't deserve water because I wet the bed. I certainly didn't deserve new clothes or even food because I was stupid and unwanted. I could live with that. It was the molestation and the suffocation that truly made me pray for death. But, because I couldn't find a way to kill myself that wouldn't hurt, I would dream of the day when I would be able to leave home, swearing that I would get the hell away from Dolores and Danny forever. I was only ten, and still had a long sentence to serve.

We finally moved into the trailer, but things didn't get any better. Before, whenever we first moved into a place, it seemed like my parents would at least try to get along for a little while. Not this time. This mobile home just seemed to have so much negative energy that it affected everybody. Dad didn't come home much and Dolores got a waitressing job, so I got to sneak out of the house a little more. I made friends with a strange boy that lived with his mom and sister. He had two rats for pets. I didn't know that people kept rats as pets until then. Because Dolores didn't approve of me having any friends, I tried not to mention them. I knew she wouldn't have approved of them because she hated dirt and anyone that looked dirty. This never made sense to me because I had met family members of hers who were nice people but they literally lived in filth. These new friends of mine were nice but their house didn't smell very good. It kind of smelled like burnt toast and rats. The strangest thing to me was that they didn't wash their dishes until every single last dish was dirty. I just didn't understand that at all. I didn't judge them for it, it simply made no sense to me. All I could see and all that really mattered was that they were nice. They treated me as an equal and the boy didn't act strangely toward me at all. Not like Danny. I was grateful to have someone to walk with, to and from the bus stop.

Danny finally found out about them and told Dolores. She put an end to that friendship immediately. When she found out that I was doing something she didn't approve of, she would do strange things to get back at me and then act as if it was totally normal. One day, when I came home, I saw my toys outside hanging out of the trash dumpster. These were things that I had had since I was a toddler, basically all of my life. My favorite giant purple stuffed turtle, my baby dolls, were all thrown in the trash. My heart was shattered. She wouldn't let me take anything back. She yelled at me, telling me I was too old for that crap and I didn't need any of it anymore. I still have issues with anyone throwing something of mine away or telling me to throw something away. Because I was rarely allowed to go out and wasn't allowed to have any friends, those toys, those worthless stuffed animals she threw out, were my friends, my family. I could take care of my babies without being criticized for doing it incorrectly. Even at my age, I still talked to them and cuddled them, but not anymore. They weren't replaced with anything either because as she put it, I didn't deserve anything. I was truly, truly alone now.

Out of the blue, my teeth started hurting. I had never had this kind of pain before. Dolores' solution was to gargle with warm salt water and let an aspirin dissolve on the tooth that hurt. It worked temporarily but in the morning, by the time I got to school, it was unbearable. I tried to ignore the pain but it was just too much. I had to go to Mr. Thompson's office daily. The teacher and office staff were very frustrated with me. I could hear them talking on the other side of the door where I was sitting. Their comments were rude and callous. They would say things like, "Don't her parents make her brush her teeth? She's probably faking it to get out of class. It's always something with this girl. She's nothing but trouble." Day after day, for about two weeks, I was in and out of the office. They would put a red numbing liquid in my mouth and just send me back to class. Several times, they tried to call my house and they sent notes home with me, but all that did was infuriate Dolores. She got mad at me for going to the office and said the school needed to mind their own business. I was in trouble for being in pain! I was in pain because I couldn't brush my teeth. I couldn't brush my teeth because I didn't have a toothbrush. If I could brush my teeth, then I would have access to water. I still couldn't have water because I was still wetting the bed.

Mr. Thompson was getting aggravated but he told me his anger wasn't directed at me. He said he was upset that my parents hadn't taken me to the dentist. One day he said enough is enough, that the situation needed to be addressed now. He made me leave the school with him. We got in his car and started to drive to my house. I told him I was afraid that this would get me in trouble, but he replied that it just wasn't right to let me suffer like this anymore. As I look back on it now, I realize someone did care, but at the time I didn't see it that way. I just thought that he was sick of me coming into the office every day. We pulled up outside my house and walked up to the front door. He told me I should knock first and I said "Why, I live here, it's okay." Boy, were we shocked when I opened the door! My parents' bedroom was directly off to the right-hand side of the front door. Right there, in plain sight, was Dad and Dolores naked and in the middle of having sex. Mr. Thompson said "Oh excuse me!" and we quickly backed up and shut the door. We both just stood there, silent, embarrassed beyond words. We stood outside until Dolores opened the door in her bathrobe and invited us in.

Dad came out of the room and neither he nor Dolores seemed bothered at all by what had just happened. Mr. Thompson apologized and still had a red face as he explained that something needed to be done about my teeth. Dolores immediately commented on how this was my own fault for not taking care of my teeth. Mr. Thompson stood up for me saying, "These things happen." and went on to say that now the help of a dentist was needed because it was disrupting my schoolwork and that I was in a lot of unnecessary pain. At first, they admitted that we didn't have any insurance and they really couldn't afford it. Reluctantly, they finally agreed that they would take me. They did take me that day and, Dolores scolded me all the way there. She was so angry, telling me I would have been better off if I would have just stopped being a baby and wiggled the teeth with the cavities and pulled them out myself. I actually tried to do it, but it was just too painful. She was almost right. After examining me, the dentist decided to pull two of my back teeth because they were so bad. I remember screaming from the pain as he pulled them out. My parents said they could hear me all the way out in the waiting room. The pain of having the teeth pulled was worth it because when it was over, it was so much better. There were no more daily trips to the school office. No more humiliation from the staff.

He Shared the Secret

Chapter 20

*He had the perfect sharp knife at home to butcher
me with so I better keep my mouth shut! 1977*

Danny was going to visit his dad for a week. Dad and
Dolores were working. For once, I could actually look forward to
going home after school. I could go home, do my chores and drink
water without getting yelled at. I could sit in peace and quiet and
feel safe. The front door was unlocked because I didn't have a key.
When I got home, I went into my bedroom. I was shocked to find
Danny's friend, Michael, sitting on my bed. His back was against
the wall and I could see he was in his underwear. I froze. I didn't
say anything. I just stood there in the doorway. He told me to
come in and sit on the bed. He pointed to an open magazine and
told me to read the story on the open pages. I recognize the
magazine. It was one of Dolores' called "True Detective." I hated
those magazines. I would hear Dolores talk about them. They had
horrible unsolved crime stories in them that were supposed to be
true stories. I was too afraid to read them because when my parents
went out drinking leaving me alone at night, I was afraid something
would happen.

I will never forget the story that he told me to read. On the
front page, there was a cat and the title read, "If Only Misty Could
Talk." The story was about a young woman who was missing.
After no one had heard from her, the police decided to search her
apartment. There they found her in a trunk in her closet. When I
turned the page, there was a picture of the trunk open with her body
inside. It was cut up in pieces the way a deer is cut up to put in a
freezer. It went on to say that the cat was the last to see her alive
and was the only witness they had to the crime. I looked at
Michael, afraid to think why he would want me to read this story.
Michael confessed to me that Danny had told him everything about
what he did with me and he wanted to know if I was as good as
Danny said I was. My heart sank. I could feel sweat rolling down
the sides of my face. My whole body felt hot. I couldn't breathe. I
was frozen with fear. Pointing to the magazine, he told me that
would be me if I didn't do what he told me to do. He went on to
say if I dared to tell anyone, he would carve me up just like that

poor girl I just read about. All I could think was, "How could this be happening? I thought he liked me. He seemed so nice!" I prayed that a car would pull up. It was so quiet I could hear my own heartbeat.

He told me to come over to him and do the same thing that I did to Danny. He said he didn't want to hurt me but he would. He raised his voice saying the quicker I got started, the faster I would be finished and it would be over. Like a robot, I did as he said. I went over to the bed and he removed his underwear. I did as he asked but I had to stop many times because my jaw ached. He was much larger than Danny. The horrible smell and taste was the same. My tears and sweat didn't affect him either. All he was concerned with was ejaculating. When he finally did, I threw up all over. I expected him to be mad and start yelling at me or even hit me like Danny would but it didn't bother him at all. He just used my blanket to wipe off the puke and then got dressed. Michael started to leave and turned back to remind me about the magazine saying he had the perfect sharp knife at home to butcher me with, so I better keep my mouth shut. Then he walked out as I lay on the floor at the bottom of the bed. I had no idea that it was possible to feel any worse, but I did. I only moved once after he left and that was to take Tuffy out to go to the bathroom.

It was dark when my parents got home. I heard them open my bedroom door, but I didn't move. They didn't even notice me as I lay there on the floor in the dark. I didn't get up the rest of the night. I cried all night and didn't care about water, food or cigarettes. I truly must be worthless. Now it wasn't just a family secret. I wondered how many others Danny had told. In my child's mind, I wondered if the whole world were robots and if they were out to get me. What in the hell was I here for? Is this how my life would always be? Is this all I'm good for? I totally withdrew after that, but no one seemed to notice or care.

The following weekend, I was alone watching TV when Dad and Dolores came home in the evening. They both stunk of alcohol and cigarettes and Dolores still had a beer in her hand. Dad sat down with his newspaper and Dolores sat across from me announcing that she had something important to talk to me about. I sat up trying to show her she had all of my attention, but instead, she just asked me a strange question. "Do you know what a period is?" "Yes," I answered, "it's the dot at the end of a sentence." "Quit being a smartass," she responded. I really had no clue what she was talking about. As she started getting into her explanation, I was so embarrassed! She began to explain to me about menstruation right in front of my dad. She covered the basics about what to do if I started bleeding but she never explained about hormones or boys or what was wrong or what was right. She didn't ask me if I had any questions just asked if I understood. I simply nodded my head yes. Then she went off to get another beer and I went to bed. That was the extent of my sex talk.

Danny stayed away longer than expected. With Dad and Dolores' relationship so rocky, for a while, Dolores stopped coming home. Dad would be away until late into the night. Thankfully, Michael didn't pay me any more visits. Dad bought me a bunch of TV dinners to feed myself. Sometimes I'd fall asleep on the sofa waiting for one to cook. No matter how hard I tried to stay awake, I'd fall asleep and would wake up to the smell of the dinner burning. One time, Dad came home and woke me up showing me a dinner that had completely burned. The peas looked like little black rocks. I laughed and he scolded that it wasn't funny and was very dangerous, that I could have burned the house down. He said it was just too dangerous to leave me home alone, so he told me to get my things ready because he was going to drop me off at a friend's house the next day. In rushed the same old fears. Would they hate me for wetting the bed? Would they think I was ugly and stupid? Or worst of all, would they make me do those things all the others would make me do?

The next day, after driving down a long dirt road, we pulled up in front of a beautiful, two-story white house. There were large barns with corrals and horses and dogs running all around. It felt very friendly. Before Dad turned off the truck engine, the family came out to greet us. There was a man and a woman and three boys, the Williams family. Their oldest son, Oliver, was severely mentally challenged. Although he was older than all of us, he was like a toddler in his speech and actions. The next son, Ned, was a little younger than me. The youngest son whose name I cannot remember was a toddler. Dad just left me there. He came back the next day and dropped Tuffy off. He told me that he had to work out of town but he wouldn't be gone very long before coming back to pick me up.

This place was a horse-training ranch, located in Loveland Pass, about a half an hour outside of Salida. I was able to continue attending the same school. I just had a long thirty-minute bus ride to get there. Mr. Williams was a hard worker and wasn't around much, but when he was, he was pleasant. Mrs. Williams seemed really nice most of the time. I enjoyed being there in the beginning. It was winter and the snow was still pretty deep. Mrs. Williams took the time in the morning to drive me to the bus stop. This was a first for me. I was used to being frozen before school and now, I was waiting for the bus warmed by a heater and I had a full tummy. I felt so lucky! She knew about my nighttime "accidents" and made me a special bed so I wouldn't ruin anything. My first weekend there, she took me shopping for clothes. I was so excited; I had never been shopping just for me before. I felt so special, for a little while at least. That disappeared as soon as Mrs. Williams and the store assistant started talking. I could hear them talking about me. Mrs. Williams said "I don't even have a change of panties for her, can you believe it?" The lady responded by saying, "Well, I guess you'll need a little of everything then." I wanted to disappear. I don't know why, but it made me feel so unworthy, so stupid, so much more trouble than what I was worth. While it was wonderful to have new things, warm things, such beautiful things, having them made me feel terribly guilty. I thanked her as graciously as I could, but it didn't feel like anything I could say would make me feel worthy.

Days, then weeks, went by. Spring came and it was a beautiful place to be. The snow was gone and everything was turning green. Baby horses were being born. Because they trained people how to ride horses, sometimes I got to ride one in the corral. I loved it! We went to church every Sunday. Sometimes, Mrs. Williams would let me help her cook. On sunny days, Ned and I were allowed to swim in the small creek near the house. Best of all, there wasn't any fighting, I wasn't being threatened, and I wasn't being molested.

One day, when Ned and I went down to play by the creek, I saw the baby floating face down in the water. I ran to him and I told Ned to go get his mom. I was afraid I would get into trouble for getting my clothes wet, so I found a big stick and pulled the baby close to shore with it. When I could reach him, I pulled him out of the water. He wasn't moving or breathing. I laid him down and shook him a little and somehow knew to blow into his mouth. He started coughing and I sat him up, patting his back. Ned and Mrs. Williams came running up. She was crying and scooped him into her arms. She turned to thank me and smiled. Thank God that day had a good ending.

Like so many times before, the more time I spent there, the less welcomed I felt. Ned started to become jealous of me. He would complain to his parents that they liked me more than him because I was a girl. He said they didn't yell at me as much as they did him. After that things started changing for the worse. Now, when I wet the bed, there was no more understanding. Mrs. Williams would yell and punish me and started limiting what I could drink. One morning before church, I woke up and my bed was wet again. I didn't want to be in trouble all day again, so I quietly rinsed the sheet, plugged in the iron and tried to dry the sheets by ironing them. I snuck into the bathroom to wash out my clothes and cleaned myself with a wet wash rag. I got away with it that day but no matter how hard I tried to not wet the bed, I just couldn't help it. I couldn't wake up in time.

Bad things began to happen, one right after another. Tuffy was hit by a train and died. When the Williams told me, they gave me his collar. It had spots of blood on it. They tried to make me feel better by making my favorite meal for dinner. That same evening, Ned said he was going to stab me in the back with a pencil. Thinking he wouldn't really do it, I said, "Go ahead, it won't hurt. I won't tell." I really didn't think he would do it, but he did! He stabbed me right in the back. Another thing I was wrong about. It really hurt and I screamed from the pain. As I recall, we both got in trouble, but he got a spanking.

An older boy from a nearby farm used to come over to help out with the horses. I loved when he would come over. He was really nice and used to say nice things to me like, if I was older, he would want me as his girlfriend. He would tell me that I was pretty. One day though, when Ned and I were watching him work, he was talking to us and for some reason, the conversation turned to talking about my real mom. He said he once heard the Williams talking about my parents, saying my dad had told them he and my mom used to put sleeping pills in my bottle at night so they could go out to the bar and not have to get a babysitter or worry about me. I yelled at him saying he was a liar. He said he was sorry, but it was what he heard the Williams say. I turned and ran away crying. The good feeling I had about being there was gone. This wasn't to be a beautiful place to be anymore. After learning this story, Ned used the information to his advantage every chance he had, relentlessly taunting and teasing me the rest of my time there.

From One Home to the Next

Chapter 21

I was a puzzle piece that didn't fit anywhere

It had been about four months when Dad finally came to pick me up. Although I was terrified of what was ahead of me, I was happy to see him and anxious to leave the ranch behind. It was obvious I was definitely a guest who had long overstayed their welcome. As messed up and frightening as my family was, it was still my family, and the only people in the world that would put up with me. Even though I didn't belong anywhere, I was already trained for my dysfunctional family.

We didn't go back to the trailer park. I knew better than to ask questions. I stayed quiet and just went along for the ride. We pulled up to a motel. Danny wasn't there, but Dolores, just as scary as ever, was standing in the doorway. Still, I approached her with open arms. No matter how much I was afraid of her, no matter what she had done to me, I still loved her. In my heart, I clung to those rare moments when she would put my head in her lap and stroke my face or comb my hair behind my ear with her fingers. I soon found out this was my new home. It was very small. It had two rooms; one with a bed, dresser and a television; the other was a kitchenette with a sink, refrigerator, small stove and a table and chairs. After just a few days, Dad asked me how well I knew one of the families that lived close by the Williams. I told him I knew them pretty well and they seemed nice. Then, like so many times before, he told me to get some things together because I was going to stay there. Again, I was told it would only be for a week. It ended up being quite an experience.

The place was a ranch but not like the Williams'. Instead of having horses, they raised cows. The house was very old and run down. The floors were made of wood, not like the hard polished wood that you would normally think of, but real rough, outdoor barn-type wood floors. There were big throw rugs everywhere. It had a strange odor. I guess you could say the house smelled like cows. It had more dirt than the average house, but it felt comfortable. At mealtime, everyone ate at the table and the dishes and cups were made of metal. It reminded me of the Old West days. The family was very nice and very close. They were the Harris family. There was a boy one year older than me, and a girl my age. Mr. and Mrs. Harris didn't make a big deal out of my bed-wetting. They just showed me how to make my bed with plastic and towels and instructed me how to clean up after myself in the morning. Like Mr. Thompson before, I so appreciated how they handled my problem. They didn't belittle or scold me. The kids and I played outside all day and I would help bring the cows in which was great fun. At dinner, we would have fresh cow's milk to drink. It tasted really strange, not at all like milk from the store. It was thick and had a very strong flavor. I didn't complain though, I just learned to hold my breath and drink it really fast.

One time, we went into town together. I noticed that wherever we went, we were treated like outcasts. It was probably because of how we were dressed and because their truck was old and beat up or maybe because we smelled like cows. People in the stores or those who walked by us on the street looked disgusted. It showed in their body language and the faces they would make at us. It didn't matter to me. They might have been outcasts but I was one too. That might have been why I felt so comfortable with them.

Dad actually showed up a week later like he said he would. It was unusual for him to pick me up so quickly. I thanked Mr. and Mrs. Harris for making me feel so welcome. Then I got in the car with Dad and we drove away. We returned to the motel. I never saw them again.

It was school time again and my bus stop was right on the corner. There was a line of kids that I had to stand with while waiting for the bus. I hated it! I didn't talk much and I was ready to protect myself all the time. I was so afraid of meeting new people. I felt like people were always pointing at me and whispering, making fun of, or laughing at me. Always being the new kid, I knew I was going to be picked on. My heart would race and I could feel sweat bead up on my forehead. My body and hands shook so badly that I would have to put them in my pockets. I experienced this feeling throughout my life, and now I know the feeling to be a panic attack.

I noticed a really funny looking, tall girl in the line. She must have been a troublemaker because everyone seemed to be afraid of her. At school, I saw that whenever anyone had food or candy, she would just approach them and take it right out of their hands and say "What? You got a problem?" No one ever stood up to her. One day, she took some peanut brittle from a kid and offered some of it to me on the school bus going home. Never having had it before, I smiled and said, "No thank you." She insisted that I try it, so I did, and man was it good. I don't know why but for some reason, she liked me. We became friends. Her name was Christina. Danny still wasn't living with us at the time and when my parents weren't home, sometimes I would sneak to Christina's house after school for a little while. She taught me how to make doughnuts using canned biscuits and how to pop popcorn. This would be more useful than I ever expected. I found that popcorn kernels were cheap to buy and easy to prepare. From then on, many times in my life, I used popcorn to fill my stomach.

One Saturday morning, I woke up and there was a note from Dolores that she and Dad had gone to a job together and they probably wouldn't be back until late. I was to just stay inside and watch TV for the day. I took advantage of the opportunity to go to Christina's house. She was going to go shopping and asked me to go with her. Off we went, walking to town. We went into a drugstore and she took me to the candle section. She asked me which candle I liked and I told her that I couldn't buy anything because I didn't have any money. To my surprise, she picked out some candles and put them in her pocket. She said, "You don't need any money when you have a five finger discount." She pocketed a few other things as well like a bag of chocolate chips and an assortment of candy. On our walk home, she taught me another great trick. Back in these days, restaurants used to have cigarette machines right next to the exit. She told me how to just walk up, how not to look suspicious, put money in, and then walk away with some. Then she did it and it worked.

When we got back to her house, no one else was there. Wow, were we set! She started unloading her pockets and it was party time. We smoked cigarette after cigarette and stuffed ourselves with candy. Then she asked me if I wanted to try a chocolate pizza. Chocolate pizza? She took a frozen pizza out of the freezer and put chocolate chips all over it. It smelled really great when she took it out of the oven, but when I took a bite; it was one of the most disgusting things I had ever tasted. She gave me some candy and split the rest of the cigarettes with me. It was just turning dark when I got home. Dad and Dolores weren't home yet so I quickly stashed my goodies and lay down. When the activities of the day finally caught up to me, I had one heck of a stomachache. I really enjoyed finally having a friend. I knew she wasn't a good influence, but I liked her anyway. She was nice to me. In a strange way, it made me feel special because she was so mean to everyone else. She was everything I wasn't. She was outspoken, confident, and seemed to have no remorse. I was shy, quiet, and wore my heart on my sleeve. Even though we were friends, I didn't open up to her about my life. I didn't want to tell her about the sexual abuse or any of the bad things in my life. It could disgust her and she might reject me.

It wasn't long before Dad and Dolores were fighting again. Dad wasn't coming home from work and Dolores started spending her days at the bars. I spent a lot of time alone, which was okay with me. Thanks to my new friend, I could make popcorn every night so I wasn't going to bed hungry. When Dolores would get home in the early morning hours, she would usually wake me up to talk to me. It was always the same routine, she would be upset, crying and complaining about her life and my dad.

I clearly remember one night being worse than usual. She woke me up and sat on the side of my bed putting her arms around me, her tears falling all over me. Her breath smelled strongly of alcohol. Her words were slurred and she kept asking, "What is wrong with me?" I didn't move or speak. I knew at this point I was better off not doing anything. "Why doesn't your dad love me? How come I'm not good enough for him? I'm pretty aren't I? Why aren't I woman enough for him?" She stood up and removed her shirt and then her bra saying, "What in the hell is wrong with me?" My mind went blank unable to comprehend what she was doing. "Look at me! "What's wrong with me?" She grabbed my hand and placed it on one of her breasts. I froze. This didn't seem right. She commanded me to squeeze, feel and touch her breast. "Doesn't this feel like a real woman to you?" She blurted out again, "What in the hell is wrong with me?" Personally, I could think of a few things, but I wasn't about to share them with her. "This is what a real woman looks like! This is what a real woman feels like! Your dad just doesn't seem to care."

She stood up to go get a cigarette and another beer. Relieved, I lay back down and pretended to have fallen back to sleep. I kept my eyes closed as she sat back down next to me. She tried nudging me, calling my name, but I kept pretending to be asleep. Finally she drifted off crying herself to sleep. When morning came, I quietly helped myself to some cigarettes from her pack and stashed them knowing she would never remember how much she smoked. I crept outside and had my morning smoke before she woke up. When she did wake up, just like all the times before, she didn't seem to remember a thing. There was no mention of what took place the night before and I sure wasn't going to bring anything up. After a week passed by, Dad still hadn't come home. Was he gone for good, I wondered?

Dad had been gone for a week and things were relatively quiet, but that was all about to change, again. Dolores went out for her routine bar schedule and I hung around until I fell asleep watching TV. It was early in the morning and still dark outside when Dolores shook me awake telling me to get up and get dressed. "We have to hurry," she said. My eyes were blurry and I was confused. "These are my two friends and they're here to rescue us. They're going to take us away and help us," she said. In the doorway, stood two drunk people. Dolores was loaded too. One was an old lady who looked worn down, wrinkled with gray hair. She didn't say much. The other was an old man. He walked with a limp and one side of his face hung down. His arm just dangled; he had no use of it. His words were slurred as he kept repeating, "Hurry along, we've got to get going! Hurry up and get everything loaded!" In a daze, I moved as quickly as I could. I was freezing; the air outside was cold and the wind was blowing. There was snow all around. Frantically, Dolores packed, as I carried the items she told me to take out to the old couples' rusty, beat-up old station wagon. Boxes, the TV, and shotguns were crammed into the back of the car. There was barely enough room for Dolores and me in the back seat. As we drove off, leaving Dad's things behind, the old man said, "You're going to love our house! I'll teach you how to shoot a gun. We'll go coyote hunting."

Once again, within a matter of only minutes, my life was turned upside down. We drove for hours. Finally, in the late afternoon, we pulled into a small town. The man parked the car next to the sidewalk under a sign that read, Pub. They all went inside and I waited in the car until it was dark. Finally, Dolores came out and got me. She brought me in and instructed me to sit at a small table, telling me not to move. She gave me a plate of French fries and a 7-Up. The music was loud and I just watched the man and Dolores play pool. It was interesting watching the man play because although one whole side of his body was paralyzed, he could still manipulate his pool stick really well.

There weren't very many people in the bar, so I was allowed to be inside, as long as I stayed still and quiet. We stayed in the bar until closing. Dolores and the couple were obviously drunk. They stumbled out of the bar and when we got into the car, it reeked of alcohol and cigarettes. But we were finally on our way to our new home.

We pulled off the highway onto a dirt road. It was so dark outside that all you could see was snow glistening under the moon. The conversation in the car was loud and confusing, so I just tuned everything out. I sat and looked out the window at the blackness. Suddenly, the car started fishtailing out of control, and we were spinning in circles. The car went sideways on two wheels. Everything in the car was flying around. The back door of the station wagon flew open when the car bounced back down from nearly rolling over. After a couple more fishtails, the car came to a stop. Everyone got out of the car to inspect the damage. Our things were scattered all over the road. The TV was on the side of the road with the glass broken out. For a minute, it was completely silent as we all stood staring at the scene. The man finally spoke saying, "Wow! That was a close call! Come on now, let's pick up what we can find and get home." Everyone loaded up the car and we were on our way again. We didn't drive very far before we pulled up to a large cabin-like house. "This is it," he announced. "Let's just unload when it's light. I'll build a warm fire for you and we can get some sleep."

It was roomy inside and had a strange outdoor kind of smell. The old man told us we could sleep upstairs and gave us a couple of sleeping bags. The upstairs was like an attic. The ceiling was like a triangle and kind of neat. I slept on the floor with the sleeping bag on top of me so if I had an accident in the night I wouldn't get the sleeping bag wet. When I got up in the morning, the adults were already awake and well on their way to getting drunk. I was instructed to carry our things upstairs. This was the first good look I had at the place and boy was it run down! Dolores told me to find some clothes for tomorrow because she was going to register me in school. "Oh great, here we go again," I thought to myself. I stayed upstairs all day and listened to the radio and snuck a couple of cigarettes as I unpacked a few things to try and make our room feel homey. When Dolores came upstairs to have me come down for dinner, she scolded me for unpacking the things I had unpacked and told me not to unpack anything else. She angrily said "We are not going to be staying here that long so put everything except my clothes back in the boxes." I did as she told me but at the same time, I was thinking, "If we're not staying here, then why do I have to go to school?" Too chicken to ask, I just ate my dinner and went to bed. Early the next morning, the man drove us to town to register me for school. The school was in a place called Sasquatch County. Dolores told me to not tell anyone where I was from or anything about what was going on. I nodded my head in agreement and thought to myself "Why in the hell would I want anyone to know? My life was certainly nothing to brag about."

It was a long bus ride home from school, and I was dropped off at the side of the highway. There on the dirt road was the station wagon waiting for me. It was just the old man. He was nice enough. He talked a lot and made me many promises of what we would do once the snow started melting. He said his wife was sick in bed, and Dolores had stayed home because she was waiting for a phone call from her son Justin. When we got to the house, I was relieved to find that Dolores wasn't drinking alcohol. She was drinking coffee and appeared to be sobering up. After dinner, when the old man went to bed, Dolores told me that the old lady was just pretending to be sick so she wouldn't have to get out of bed. Dolores said the couple was trying to tell her that the shotguns were thrown out of the car when we almost crashed. She went on to say that she remembered seeing them in the car the same night before we came in and that the old lady snuck them in and was hiding them under her mattress, and that's why she wouldn't leave her bed. She told me she was trying to think of a plan to get her out of the room but the couple wouldn't budge. Dolores was on the phone most of the night making collect calls trying to get her older kids to wire her some money. When I came downstairs the next morning, she was sleeping next to the phone. When the school bus dropped me off the next day, it was just the man there again to drive me home. Dolores was still sober and preparing dinner. Secretly, she told me she was trying to gain their trust so that she could get the woman out of the room and retrieve her guns. She also said she was going into town the next day to pick up some money that Justin was sending to her by Western Union. She told me not to worry, that everything was going to work out just fine.

The next morning, I had to ride the bus to school even though Dolores and the man drove into town. It was an unusual experience in school that day. I don't remember how exactly the school was set up, but I do remember that we had to walk in a line to the cafeteria which was about two blocks away. We even had to cross a street.

I made a friend. Her name was Lisa. For some reason, she decided to show me the ropes, so to speak. Lisa wore bright orange lipstick. All the schools that I had ever been to before didn't allow makeup. Before walking to lunch, we were all dismissed to go wash our hands in the bathroom. Lisa asked if I wanted to wear some of her lipstick. I told her I was not allowed to wear makeup, which was absolutely true. Dolores was adamant that I was not allowed to wear any kind of makeup, no lip-gloss, blush, eye shadow or nail polish. She said it was for religious reasons, that children should never taint themselves. She was some example with her nails always painted blood red. On our way to lunch, there was a boy curled up in a ball on the ground. He was rolling around crying in pain. The rumor was that he pissed off some girl and she kicked him in the crotch. The whole thing seems so strange because no one attended to him. Everyone just walked by him, looking at him.

When the school bus dropped me off, no one was waiting for me. It was a cold long walk home but I didn't mind. I enjoyed having my time alone. When I got there, the fireplace was warm and inviting. The old couple stayed in their room and Dolores had a drink in her hand. She instructed me to go get my things ready because we were leaving there tonight. She was upset and said that Justin would be picking us up sometime that night. She said my dad had reached Justin and told him if Dolores didn't have me back in Salida by the next afternoon at a certain location downtown, he would have Justin arrested for kidnapping. Even though this whole thing was her idea, Dad knew how to get what he wanted. Justin never fully recovered after his cancer surgery, and Dolores was

106

quick to let me know that I sure as hell wasn't worth the risk of his health. Sure enough, by the time night fell, Justin was there to pick us up. Unlike Danny, my two other stepbrothers were wonderful and I respected and loved them very much. He drove us for hours until we reached his house. We slept there for a couple of hours before we were back on the road again.

By noon, we arrived at our destination. Dolores walked me into an office where she was instructed to leave me. Dad wasn't there and it was a little scary. It was a social services office. The social worker instructed Dolores to leave me there and just go. I was left alone with a strange man telling me everything would be okay. I had only a small bag of clothes and a hairbrush to my name. I didn't ask any questions; I just watched, listened, and did as I was told. The man told me to follow him... that we were going for a ride. He asked me if I knew what a foster home was. I shook my head no. He told me that it was a place that you stay while your parents work things out. He told me not to worry, that I'd be well taken care of. To me, this was nothing out of the ordinary because I have stayed at many different places. The only difference was, instead of being called a foster home, they were called a friend's house.

We pulled up to a normal looking house, in a normal looking neighborhood. The man walked me up to the door. I could feel my legs shaking, I don't know which was worse, the cold or my nerves. A couple answered the door. They were both very large. The man handed them my small bag and instructed them to register me in school the next day. They agreed, and we went inside. I was told that their names were Mr. and Mrs. Littleton, and was introduced to their two small sons. They weren't old enough to go to school yet. I was shown to my room. It was nice! The Lord's Prayer hung on the wall across from the bed. I must have read it a thousand times during my stay there. I stayed in the room by myself most of the day until I was called for dinner. Everyone seemed nice and tried to be friendly. I just felt confused and sad. I missed my dad. Where was he? I don't know why I didn't tell the Littleton's about my bed-wetting problem. I guess it was because I just didn't know how to bring it up. Their sons slept together in the other bedroom. They had their own TV. How lucky they were, I thought. I remember wondering how it might be to live a life without being molested or not to have a bed-wetting problem, or to be smart, or loved. I thought, a lot of people don't ever realize how lucky they truly are.

The next morning, I hung my head low as I told Mrs. Littleton I had had an accident in my bed. She assured me that everything would be all right. She helped me with my bedding and let me take a shower. After I dressed, she called me into the kitchen to eat breakfast. I felt very ashamed as I sat quietly eating my pancakes. Everyone sat around the table and put peanut butter and powdered sugar on their pancakes. I had never heard of that before but I tried it and it tasted better than it sounded. I was there for about two months, and we had pancakes every single day. By the time I finally left there, I couldn't stand pancakes.

At another new school, and as usual, I wasn't doing well. I didn't understand the work, and I was made fun of because of my clothes. One week, I got really sick and they took me to the doctor. My throat hurt every time I swallowed. It ended up being strep throat. How lucky, I thought, I get to stay in bed and miss school. The family treated me really nice while I was sick. Everyone was very nice at first. Like the Williams, Mr. Littleton was nice to me but that was only because he was gone most of the time. It wasn't long before Mrs. Littleton started getting grouchy. I know it was because of my bed-wetting. It made her angry. Even though they were so much younger, her sons were jealous of me. The boys knew how to get me in trouble by starting arguments and crying for no reason. The mom would think I was making them cry so I would be scolded and sent to my room. They would sneak in and point at me and laugh. It was happening again; I began to be alienated. I tried to clean and help out around the house but instead of making her happy, Mrs. Littleton was offended, asking me why I thought she wasn't doing a good enough job. I didn't understand that at all.

Even though I wasn't going hungry anymore and I wasn't being molested, I still wanted to just disappear. Why couldn't I have gotten cancer, or any other kind of disease that would kill me? I wish that somehow I could just die, but with no pain. I didn't belong anywhere and no one really liked me or wanted me around. To me, living was torture! I had nothing to offer anyone. I was more work than I was worth. I was stupid. Why did God even put me here?

At the end of the second month, I finally got the great news that Dad was going to pick me up on Sunday to take me to church. On Saturday, my foster mom told me that my step mom had dropped off a bag for me. Excitedly, I took it into my room to open it. Inside was a new dress, shoes, and a pair of pantyhose. Wow, panty hose. I had never had a pair of those before. I didn't understand how to put them on, but the dress and shoes fit perfectly and I loved them. As promised, Dad's truck pulled up the next morning. It was Dad *and* Dolores. They obviously were getting along again, because Dolores sat next to dad, letting me have the window seat. They were both nice to me, nicer than they had ever been before. After church, we went and got something to eat. When they took me back to the foster home, I almost didn't want to say goodbye. Dad hugged me and told me they would pick me up the next weekend. Dolores swept the hair off of my face and looked at me lovingly. This was the first time I had seen them in months and looked forward to the coming weekend.

The week dragged on and on. It seemed that my relationship with my foster family just got worse and worse. I found myself craving cigarettes again but no one there smoked. I could tell it was time to move on, and could only hope that Dad and Dolores would come and get me as promised. Dolores arrived Saturday morning to pick me up. She was still being nice and brought me another pair of nylons. She actually took the time to show me how to properly put them on. It made me feel like a big girl. Could Dolores actually like me now? For real? It's funny that when you're a kid, a little bit of kindness goes such a long way. It doesn't erase the bad, but it sure makes the present a lot better. I was starving for love and approval, and was willing to hope that things might actually be different this time. Approval was given, allowing me to spend the night with my parents. I was picked up on Saturday morning and I didn't have to be returned until Sunday night. We left the house and were going to go pick up Dad and then drive to Naturita, Colorado, to visit Dolores' father.

The following pages are of a few photographs I have left from my childhood. Later in life, in a search for healing and freedom from my past, I destroyed most of the photographs I had of family, friends and myself.

My mother with me at a week old. I didn't reunite with her until after the birth of my third child in 1995.

A short-lived moment of happiness together for my mom and dad.

My dad's sister, Agnes, and my best friend, Tassey. This was taken after my dad took me from my mom and left me with her to go court Tommie, my only loving stepmother.

Someone babysitting me in a motel where we were living, let my mom visit me one time after I was taken. I am lying next to my newborn baby sister, that my mom brought with her. In the photo, I was trying to get as small as she was so my mom might want to take me with her. Later I learned that due to fear of my father, she left me behind.

I have not seen my baby sister since that day.

One of the last truly happy pictures I have of myself. This was during the time I was with my loving stepmother, Tommie, in 1969. I am three years old, and a mere year away from Satan entering my life and destroying my innocence.

1971 – Kindergarten
Already a victim of sexual and physical
abuse for a year.

1972 – 1st grade (6 years old)
The week before this school picture
was taken, my dad came home drunk
and took me to have all my hair cut
off, just to make Dolores angry. It
worked, but I was the one who
received all the punishment for it
from her.

1974 – 2nd grade
(7 years old, I had to repeat 1st grade)
The face of a child who now believes there is
no hope. Being molested daily, suffocated
without mercy, there is only shame, hiding
behind inner walls of anger, guilt, confusion,
and frustration, knowing deep down, that I was
ruined. I was worthless and not worth being
loved by anyone.

This photo was found in my dad's wallet when
his body was recovered from a plane crash in
1990.

1975 – 9 years old

These photographs were taken when I was living with my Aunt Agnes and Uncle Steve again during one of the times Dad and Dolores were separated. Below, I am dressed for church. Aunt Agnes made all of my clothes so I would properly represent her in the eyes of the church. During this time, my uncle Stevie was molesting me.

1976 – 10 years old
This was when I met Mr. Thompson, my elementary school principal. He was my guardian angel, both at school and in my life. Of all the many homes I was shuffled to during this year, I was able to spend a few weeks with him and his family. I felt safe and happy there, having a brief taste of what a real family could be. Like everyone else I encountered in my young life, I'll never know if they would have cared for me had I stayed longer.

1978 – 12 years old
Photograph taken as a Christmas present for my dad when I was at the mall with my sister, Leslie.

1979 – 13 years old
Here, just going into my teen years, I have already been damaged by years of sexual and physical abuse at the hands of my own personal Satan, my stepbrother, Danny.

115

Back Together Again

Chapter 23

Maybe it would be better this time

It was a long drive and Dad insisted he was going to drive all the way through without stopping. We had been driving all day and it was very late and dark when we reached the top of the mountains that led to Naturita when all of a sudden, out of the quietness, Dolores screamed and Dad hit the brakes. The truck went sliding across the gravel finally coming to a stop. Nobody moved or spoke. All you could see were the headlights in the blackness with dust all around. There were no trees, no roads, and no ground in sight. Dad started the engine and carefully backed up. Then he stopped the truck and we got out to look around. We were at the top of a cliff and the tire tracks came within inches of going off the edge. If we had gone over, there would have been no way we would have survived. Dad had fallen asleep while driving. This was nothing new because on most of the trips we took, Dad would always insist on driving all the way through instead of resting. We all got back into the truck. Nobody said anything for about ten minutes. By now we were all certainly wide-awake. When we neared the bottom of the mountain, the lights of Naturita were in sight. We all breathed a sigh of relief. With an uneasy laugh in his voice, Dad said "Boy that was a close one!" Neither Dolores nor I said a word. We ended up staying an extra night at Dolores' dad's house. This made me miss another day of school. That was okay with me, but my foster parents weren't very happy about it.

By the next weekend, Dad and Dolores were picking me up for good. We moved into a motel with a teepee out in front. I think it was called the Frontier Motel. We were back in Salida and this was the same motel that Dolores used to work for as a maid, so we all knew the owners. They were also heavy drinkers. The lady owner was always really nice to me and told me how she always wanted a daughter but never had one. She liked to play with my hair and give me small gifts. I could tell this aggravated Dolores because she would say mean things about the lady. Once again, I was warned to keep my mouth shut about our family and our problems. She also forbid me from going into the lady's house, even if she invited me, telling me "You know she's only being nice to you because we're renting a room here." Dolores always had a way of making sure that I couldn't trust anyone. She truly had me believing that no one would ever like me just to like me. I honestly believed that I was unlikable deep down. If anyone would get to know me, then they wouldn't want to be my friend. According to Dolores, if it wasn't for her and my Dad, I really had no reason to exist. She would tell me that she loved me and she would also explain how lucky I was for her to love me. This would lead me to believe for most of my life that if anyone ever said that they cared for me or loved me, they were either lying or they didn't know the real me.

Life at this point was good because Danny wasn't with us as often and wasn't able to be so violent or molest me as often as before. Dolores and Dad were getting along better than they usually did. Dad was coming home after work and Dolores wasn't going to the bar. Dolores bought me some yarn and a crochet needle because I told her my foster mom taught me to crochet. She taught me how to make potholders. I attempted to make a blanket but I just didn't have the patience.

I angered easily, because now, it seemed that as the days went by I hated myself more and more. This is when I really started to notice that I couldn't even look at myself in the mirror. I could look to fix my hair or wash my face, but if I ever made eye contact with myself, I would make mean faces at myself and repeat, "I hate you! You're ugly! I wish you would just die!" Sometimes I would punch the bathroom tile pretending it was my face. I felt rage boil inside. If I bumped my head, I would hit whatever my head hit. If I slammed my hand in a cabinet or drawer, I would strike the offending piece of furniture. I guess since I wasn't allowed to express myself with people, especially my parents, I took out all of my aggressions on myself. This would be a trait that I would carry with me most of my life. If my hair was tangled, I would just rip it out. If I got angry enough, I would break my things no matter how special they were to me. Afterwards, I would feel terrible and sad, but I just couldn't seem to control my anger. Every day, I prayed that God would just let me die. I didn't share this prayer with anyone because I wasn't trying to make people feel sorry for me. This was all I could think of. Dying consumed my thoughts. My problem was, I was still a big chicken!

We lived on the outskirts of town and sometimes I was allowed to go to the grocery store for Dolores. I would walk alongside the highway trying to find the courage to jump in front of a passing diesel truck or speeding car. I would be so disappointed with myself when I got home. Sometimes I would punch myself in the head and yell, "I hate you! I hate you! I hate you!"

One day, Dad was going to drop me off at the grocery store to trade in our soda bottles and then have me walk back with some more soda for Dolores. He pulled up to the front of the store and I got out, slamming the truck door on my finger. It hurt really bad and felt kind of numb and tingly at the same time. I grabbed the empty soda bottles out of the back of the truck and walked into the store. I didn't get very far past the front doors before I noticed large drops of blood on the floor. Right away I looked at my hand and noticed blood pouring from my finger. It was cut across the nail at the tip and clinging on by a scar that was left there from when the rabbit almost bit my fingertip off when I was younger. It was the same finger. I called it my bad luck finger. I ran back out of the store after Dad. He spotted me chasing him in the rearview mirror. He stopped and I jumped in, still carrying the soda bottles. By this time, there was blood everywhere, down my hand, on my clothes, and on my feet. I was crying out loud and Dad grabbed a rag from behind the seat. He told me to firmly hold my finger together. He kept asking me stupid questions like, "Did you hurt the truck? Is there a dent in the door? Did you turn the soda bottles in?" Of course, I answered no, no, no! I know he was just trying to be funny and take my mind off of my finger but it wasn't working; it just upset me more.

At this point, most people would go for medical attention, but Dad never was like most people. He took me back to our motel room and turned me over to Dolores. It was clearly cut almost all the way off but this didn't faze Dolores at all. She sent Dad to the motel owners for a first aid kit. He came back with bandages and tape. While she bandaged me up, Dad went back to the store to trade in the bottles and get more first aid supplies. I remember it hurting for days. Dolores made me soak it in warm soapy water twice a day, once in the morning and once at night. I had a really hard time with it in school since I was right-handed and it was my right index finger. It finally healed but it was crooked and looks funny to this day. The fingernail grows faster on one side than the other.

Weeks went by and delightfully, Dad and Dolores were still getting along, but it was time for me to move on again. Dad told me to get my things together, that he and Dolores had to go out of town to do some sign work. I was going to go stay with the foster family I was with previously. The foster mom was still grouchy and it was apparent that she still didn't like me much, again because of my bedwetting. The boys still didn't care for me much either. Like before, they felt I took attention away from them. Thank God I didn't have to stay there for long. The only good thing I remember from that stay was when the lady owner of the motel called to check on me and made arrangements to come visit me. When I talked to her on the phone, she told me she was going to come and pick me up and let me pick out a gift, whatever I wanted. I didn't tell anyone because I knew that I wasn't allowed to ask for anything from anyone. I knew exactly what I wanted. It was something I had wanted for the last couple of years. I wanted a sleeveless down jacket. My parents told me they were too expensive and they couldn't afford to get me one.

When the lady picked me up, I told her what I really wanted and she said, "No problem, honey. If that's what you want, then that's what we'll get you." I felt guilty and undeserving inside, but at the same time, I wanted it so badly and was excited that I would finally get one. She drove us around to several stores; we just couldn't find one that would fit me. I was too skinny. I was so upset. I had a chance to get something I wanted so much, but it just wasn't available. We finally gave up looking and she took me to the toy store and bought me a baby doll that came with bath stuff. It might not have been what I wanted, but I was still happy and very appreciative. After Dolores got rid of all my other toys, and with all the moving that I had done lately, it was really the only thing I could call mine.

119

I only had to stay with the foster family for a couple of weeks before Dad and Dolores picked me up. And what a pleasant surprise, they were still getting along and sober. We pulled up to Uncle David and Aunt Susan's house. Right away, I noticed our old camper in the driveway. It was the camper we lived in at the gas station. Once again, it was our home. It wasn't going to be as bad to live in it this time because Danny wasn't with us. We took showers inside Uncle David's house and Dolores prepared meals in there too. Dad did his sign work in their backyard. Sometimes, he would work all through the night. When it was dark, he would use very bright lights placed around the backyard. There was a chicken coup in the yard. After a week of Dad working nights and lighting up the darkness, the roosters didn't know when to crow anymore. They had their days and nights all mixed up.

For a while, things weren't so bad. Dad and Dolores were getting along better than they ever did before. For once Dolores was nice, and talking to me like a person instead of just barking orders. I didn't question why at the time or even think about it. As I look back now, the answer is simple. We were around other people all the time. Dolores never showed her true colors to others. She saved that for when we were alone.

The New Life that Would Never Happen
Chapter 24

*The news was far worse than anything I could
have imagined*

It was finally summer break, and one of Aunt Susan's nieces, Mandy, was coming to stay with her for a week. She was a couple of years older than me, but we got along really well. One day, Aunt Susan said that Mandy and I should do something productive, so we talked Dolores into dropping us off at an old folks' home. We wanted to visit and spread kindness. Dolores was to pick us up in a couple of hours. It seemed harmless enough, and it gave us a chance to get out of the house. But, it ended up being another experience I would never forget. We went from room to room visiting, talking, listening, doing some reading, and providing a polite, friendly hug. Everything went well until we were getting ready to leave. As we were walking down the hall, there was an old man yelling out from his room. He kept repeating, "Help me! Help me!" We turned around and went into his room. He was lying there, crying, with crusty snot on his nose. He was really skinny. He reached his arms out to us. I thought maybe he simply needed a hug because he was sad and lonely, so I walked up to him and leaned over his bed. He suddenly grabbed me tight and pulled me on top of him. Mandy was laughing until she heard me frantically telling her to go get help. It was so gross! I couldn't get free. For an old man, he was very strong. He made strange grunting noises. His snot and boogers were on my face and arms. I began crying too.

Two male workers came in and after struggling with him, they finally got me out of his grip. Immediately, he started yelling, "Help me! Help me!" again. The workers asked me if I was all right and if I wanted to clean up in the bathroom. I said that I was okay and that I just wanted to leave. We got out of there as quickly as we could and waited for Dolores to pick us up. I was scared, disgusted, and felt so slimy. I never wanted to go into an old folk's home again. Even as an adult, I'm still a little uncomfortable in convalescent homes.

Time with Mandy went by much too quickly and before I knew it, she had to leave. But shortly after, Dad brought home a wonderful surprise! It was a Samoyed Huskie puppy. He was so cute and fuzzy! Dad let me name him. I called him, Sam. Dad said he bought a Huskie puppy because we were going to move to Alaska. He seemed very happy about it and explained to me that we would be driving four thousand miles to get there. He bought me a pad of paper and some pens and told me it would be my job to keep track of the miles we drove. He also wanted me to keep a journal on where we were, what we saw, and how many times we had to stop for gas, how much we bought and what we spent. He thought that he was making it a fun trip. To me, it sounded complicated and like a lot of work, but I wasn't going to upset him by arguing. I just agreed and tried to share his enthusiasm. For days we packed and prepared. Finally the big day was here! Dolores would drive the car that pulled the camper and Dad would drive the pickup pulling the scaffolding. I would take turns between the two of them as the passenger. Fortunately, I got to ride with Dad the most, even though he had a real problem with falling asleep at the wheel. I wasn't a lot of help at keeping him awake, because I kept falling asleep too.

By the time we reached Grand Junction, Colorado, our trip came to an abrupt halt. I'm not sure how my parents got the news, but we pulled into the parking lot of a hospital, St. Mary's Hospital. I didn't know why we were there, but I knew something was wrong. Dolores' brother, Warren, was waiting for us with his family in their truck with a camper on the back. All of the adults went into the hospital and Sam and I were left in the care of my new cousins. There was an older teenaged girl and boy, and a younger girl and boy. The younger boy was only a year older than me and he had the same name as my dog, Sam. Even more interestingly, Sam and I shared the same birthday. We all got along really well, and I enjoyed their company. We played and talked and waited. It had been a long day and the kids were smart enough to ration the water they had in their camper. We had all complained at one point about being hungry and thirsty. It was late at night when the adults got back. When we went to a truck stop to eat, Dolores explained the situation to Dad and Warren. I was always known for being nosey, and this time was no exception.

The news was far worse than anything I could have expected. It was Justin. The cancer was back and he had a tumor the size of a football in his stomach. This meant it was too large to be operated on. Dolores said that when Justin moved back from Alaska, he was supposed to get regular monthly checkups. His real dad had convinced him that the doctors were all just trying to make money and nothing was wrong with him. So he never went in for checkups until he suddenly got very ill. By the time he went to the doctor, there was nothing they could do surgically. This was horrible news and everyone was noticeably upset as we said our goodbyes.

We drove to a small town about six miles from Grand Junction called Fruita. This was where Dad was born. We pulled into what would be our new home. The Key Court Cabins were half motel, half cabins, alongside of the freeway. Dad rented a room with a bed, and parked the camper in front of it. This worked out perfectly. I got to sleep in the motel bed and they slept in the camper with Sam. We all shared the bathroom and shower in the motel room and prepared and ate our meals in the camper. The room was very simple; it didn't even have a TV. Dolores refused to go anywhere while Justin was sick. Dad didn't argue. He got a job at the energy plant there in Fruita, which was completely unusual for him. He was usually a self-employed sign maker and painter. I spent most of my days with my dog, Sam. First thing in the morning, I would wake up and go get him from the camper. I loved him so much! He was my only friend and constant companion during this very hard and sad time.

Justin began daily chemotherapy. It made him very sick most of the time. When he didn't have to be in the hospital, he was in his camper back in Thompson, Utah, about an hour and a half from where we were staying in Fruita. Sometimes, Dolores and I would drive to visit him, bringing food and cigarettes. One day when I woke up, I went to go get Sam from the camper and there was a note from Dolores saying she and my dad were going to be gone all day, working on a sign. I couldn't find Sam anywhere. I called for him and whistled. I looked for him all day. I hoped that Dad and Dolores had taken him with them. It was dark by the time they got home. I asked them if they had Sam with him, because I couldn't find him anywhere. Dolores told me that they found him on the side of the road dead. She said it looked like someone purposefully ran him over because he was near the sidewalk. I was devastated! My friend, my companion, the only happiness in my life, was gone. I was all alone, again.

Dad was working long hours. He worked at the power plant during the day and did side jobs at night, sometimes playing saxophone at a bar too. Dolores slowly started up her drinking again. Instead of preparing meals and reading books, she started listening to Hank Williams tapes and religious music, as she painted her nails, curled her hair, and drank her beer. I tried to lay low and stay out of her sight as much as possible to avoid her argumentative discussions and her cruel temper. She became very unpredictable and said hurtful things. She hated when other people complimented me. I have always loved the sun and if I were allowed, I would bask in it all day. With light blonde hair, my dark skin stood out. Whenever I was around people, I would get complimented on what a nice tan I had. One day we were standing outside of the camper and Dolores said, "Why don't you go take a bath! You look like a pig! Look at that dirt on your arm. You don't really have a nice tan. You're just covered in dirt. You must think you're really smart accepting compliments on your dirt tan." I went in and took a shower but, of course, the deep dark tan lines on me remained, even after washing really well. "What in the hell is she talking about?" I thought to myself. It became obvious that she was just being mean. That's one thing Dolores was really good at, making sure I didn't believe anyone who said something nice to me or about me. She would make sure to remind me daily, "You're not as smart as you think you are. You're not pretty either and you have a big mouth. You're lucky to have me around to even put up with all of you and your dad's bullshit."

Fortunately, I had made friends with a girl that lived in a house next to the cabins. It was perfect timing too, because summer break was ending and it was time to start yet another new school. My new friend, Cassidy, was a lot of help showing me around the school. This time, Dad registered me for school and it was the first time that he ever did. He wanted to see the school for himself because this was the same school where he had attended second-grade, some 40 years before. He said everything looked the same as it did when he went there. It did look and feel old. This would be the first year for me to start a band class, playing the clarinet. Dad was very excited about this, because he was a very accomplished musician and he looked forward to me doing something he could relate to. Cassidy's dad let me ride to school with them in the mornings. We rode the bus home after school.

Dad finally decided to rent a one bedroom cabin. Dolores hung a big blanket across part of the room to make a divider; the smaller side being my room. Justin was in and out of the hospital a lot now, and he rented one of the small cabins there, to be closer to the hospital. I really loved him! I enjoyed any time I shared with him. He actually talked to me and listened to me. He was funny and nice. He was a good person. His looks were changing because of the chemotherapy, and he was sick to his stomach a lot. He couldn't stay up for very long or do anything strenuous, because he had very little energy.

Dolores got a surprising phone call from Danny one day. He told her that his girlfriend, Stacy, was pregnant. Stacy was one of Dolores' longtime friend's daughters. Dolores told him that the right thing to do was to marry her. Dolores also had another good friend who had two daughters. The younger one was Dolores, named after her. The older one was Denise. She had dated Justin.

Stacy and Denise had been best friends until a rumor went around that Stacy slept with Justin. Stacy always denied the rumors. Dolores always said things that led you to believe the rumors were true. She would even tell family members that she thought Stacy was pregnant with Justin's baby and not Danny's. For Danny's sake though, she accepted Stacy into the family and helped to plan their wedding.

Stacy's family came to stay with us the same week of the wedding. I was so happy because Stacy had a little sister named Tina. She was the coolest person I had ever met. I just loved having her around. While all the adults were busy, we got to spend a lot of time together alone. We hung out in the camper that Dad now had parked on the side of the cabin. We played games and talked, sharing secrets and enjoying each other's company. We smoked cigarettes together and when we ran out, we wrote a fake note saying Dolores' name and that she was sending us to the store to pick up cigarettes for her, because she wasn't able to pick them up for herself. We told the cashier that she smoked the brand Moore cigarettes, because we thought since they were longer than regular cigarettes they would last longer. We got away with it and were in smoke heaven!

On the day of the wedding, Tina, Denise and I decorated Justin's cabin so Danny and Stacy could spend their honeymoon in it. Right after the wedding, Tina had to leave with her family and I stayed in the decorated cabin listening to Elvis Presley 8-track tapes. Justin and Denise came into the cabin while I was sitting at the table playing cards. They were laughing and wrestling around being very affectionate with each other. A slow song came on and Justin asked Denise to get up and slow dance with him. I just kept playing cards and acted like I didn't notice them at all. I could see them out of the corner of my eye, no more than then five feet away from me. They were dirty dancing and I could hear Denise whisper, "What about Lorina?" Justin answered, "It's okay, she doesn't know what we're doing." I so didn't want to be there right then. How stupid did they really think I was? They both had their pants undone and Justin's penis was inside Denise's pants. I didn't move, even though it was terribly uncomfortable. When they separated from each other, I got up and went outside. What in the hell was wrong with people? Was I completely invisible, to even the people that I thought liked me? Soon the whole ordeal was over. Danny and Stacy were married. Maybe Danny wouldn't abuse me anymore, since he took a vow to be faithful to his new wife.

Within a couple of weeks, Justin took a turn for the worse. This was to be a horrible week. Justin went to the hospital and this time, he didn't come home. Danny and Stacy moved into Justin's cabin. An announcement over the radio said Elvis Presley had just died. I was devastated. Ever since I could remember, I always loved him and his music. I was one of those fans that would sit and cry at the sight of him or at the sound of his voice. His music soothed my fears and the sight of him made my heart pound. Now, it was all over. Danny was back, Elvis was dead, and Justin was dying.

Dad quit the power plant and was back to doing full-time sign work. He bought a really long, one-bedroom tow trailer that had been partially burned. He was remodeling it, so we could have a nicer trailer to live in when we were back on our journey to Alaska. Almost every day after school, I went with some family member to visit Justin at the hospital. Someone had to stay with him around the clock. Dolores was there almost constantly. Sometimes she would go home to shower or get an hour to sleep, but she was afraid that he would wake up and ask for her so she said she just needed to be there. It's sad to say, but Dolores was nicer and more humble now than I had ever known her to be. When I sat in Justin's room with her, we would read scriptures from the Bible for hours. Justin didn't wake up very much and when he did, he was usually choking or coughing up blood. The cancer had eaten away at his vital organs and was finally completely taking over his body.

This was by far one of the saddest experiences I have ever witnessed. This poor, bed-ridden human being, didn't resemble the Justin that we all knew and loved in any way anymore. All of his hair had fallen out. His skin was very yellow and his stomach was more swollen than a woman nine months pregnant. Dolores said even though he was sleeping, he wasn't peaceful or sleeping how people usually sleep. She said he was mostly just lying there, constantly in pain, trying to sleep. She would get angry with the nurses for waking him up to give him a sleeping shot. The whole thing was like a bad dream. At the time, I would have done anything to trade places with him. "Why him?" I asked God. Everyone liked him and his life was worth living. I didn't really have any reason to be here and I had nothing to offer. Even more strange, I heard Dolores praying out loud with the same similar question and statements that I had asked; only she asked God why couldn't it have been her. We prayed a lot together. I would hold his hand and hers as her other hand caressed his face. I felt so sad for Dolores. The staying up and not eating and constant crying was taking such a toll on her. That's one thing I witnessed: it doesn't matter what kind of person you are or how calloused you want the world to think you are; no parent should ever have to endure watching their own child go through so much pain.

I loved Justin so much, but I honestly didn't look forward to the hospital visits. I grew to hate hospitals. I associated them with unhappiness, horrible smells, and death. I was going to visit him one day after school. I had it all planned out. If I hurried fast enough, I would be able to grab something to eat and do my homework at the hospital. I got out of the school bus and saw this wild looking girl running towards me. She was calling my name, but I couldn't make out who it was. Cassidy was walking next to me and was looking to see who was calling my name too. I didn't recognize who it was until she was right in front of me. It was my stepsister Kelly. She grabbed me, and picked me up spinning me around. She was so happy and excited, as she told me Justin was dead. He had died that morning. My mind felt scrambled. I couldn't think straight. I forgot all about Cassidy. I don't remember walking home. I couldn't cry. I couldn't talk. I couldn't understand why she was so happy. I know she loved him but why was she so excited? She told me she was so happy because he wasn't suffering anymore, and that I should be happy too. I felt a lot of emotions, but happiness just wasn't one of them.

Eighteen years old and he was gone forever. In the next couple of days, Dolores and I bonded in a way we never had before. This time, her crying on my shoulder didn't repulse me as it did all the times before. Her heart was broken, and I felt so sad for her. I sat with her on the bed as she went through a box of Justin's belongings. The simplest of things, that had little or no value before, seemed to have so much meaning now. A pocket knife, a button, an old driver's license, all now were treasures with overwhelming sentiment. She held his Bible in her hands. We all spent a lot of time reading from that very Bible during his hospital stay. Dolores dedicated the Bible to me right under his name with the date, August 26, 1977. It is a gift that I have always treasured. I still have it with me to this day.

A lot of family showed up for the funeral, coming from all around. Everything seemed like a dream. I was being passed around to different family members, not really understanding what was going on. My Aunt Agnes and Uncle Steve (the one who used to molest me), even showed up. They told me I was to collect my things because I was going with them to Moab where the funeral was going to be held. It was still early when we arrived in Moab. We went for breakfast and Dad was there. Everyone still acted so happy. I felt as though I was outside looking in. Dad's sister showed up with her new boyfriend and they were talking about getting married. They decided the day after the funeral would be good. I don't know how you're supposed to act when someone dies, but the people around me just didn't seem right.

I rode with my aunt and uncle to the viewing home. I didn't know what to expect and no one talked with me about it. As I walked in the door, everyone's emotions were much different. There were a lot of people, and this time, everyone was obviously sad. This was how I expected people to have been acting all along. Tears, hugs, emotion, I felt Justin was worth all of it. Somebody walked up and took my hand. "Dolores is waiting for you," he said. "She's been asking for you." As I was led into another room, I couldn't have been more unprepared for what I saw. There it was, the coffin. I had never seen one before. Although I was frightened, I kept walking towards it. I took a deep breath as my body was trembling. On the inside, I was crying, but on the outside, no tears fell from my eyes. My whole face felt swollen from the previous days of nonstop crying. No matter what anyone might have said, there was no way I could have been prepared for the feeling that came over me when I saw Justin.

Dolores was sitting in a chair next to his head by the coffin. I walked up and stood next to her. I thought I didn't have any more tears. I was wrong! An endless stream poured down my face. I couldn't speak. He looked so peaceful. In my mind, it all seemed so surreal. Sometimes it even looked as though he was breathing. I was kind of expecting his eyes to just open. Dolores spoke and brought me to my senses. "Go ahead," she whispered, "touch him." My hand reached out and I put it on top of his. It was so cold and hard. Reality hit me even harder. Oh my God, this really is happening. He really is gone. He was only 18 years old. He belonged in his truck, on a horse, in his girlfriend's arms, anywhere else other than in this coffin. Dolores seemed to be handling the situation far better than I anticipated, but like me, her tears were nonstop. Every time she leaned over to kiss him, her tears would fall on his forehead. This would cause the makeup on him to separate and run over the sides of his head. Dolores was talking to me the whole time. She was telling me stories about silly things Justin did when he was younger. Some words I listened to, others I heard but didn't comprehend.

This was the saddest day I had ever experienced. It seemed as though time stood still. Even though we were surrounded by people, it felt like we were all alone and yet present in a different world. I sat with Dolores as she kissed and caressed her lifeless son. I never moved. I kept my hand on his until it was time to close the coffin and go to the graveyard. The ceremony was beautiful with wonderful prayers, words, and flowers. His favorite hymns were sung, adding even more depth to the sadness. I went back to my other stepbrother Karl's house after the service. We were going to spend the night there, because Dolores wanted to go back to the graveyard the next day to say one last goodbye before going home.

Wilderness Living
I had to learn a routine quickly in order to adapt.

Chapter 26

Dad and Dolores got along pretty well for a while, and our life at home was stable for the most part. Danny and his new wife weren't living in Fruita next to us anymore. Plans to move to Alaska had changed. Now, our destination was Salt Lake City. Dad finished remodeling the tow trailer and it looked brand new. We moved our things into it, and Dad sold the other camper. I was so glad to see it go! It held so many terrible memories for me. Like so many times before, without warning, we left in the middle of the night. No checking out of school, no goodbyes to my friend, no trace that we had even been there. It was a long drive to Salt Lake. Dad drove the truck pulling the trailer and Dolores drove the car that pulled the small trailer of scaffolding. It was only by the grace of God that we made it safely over the mountains. When we arrived, we drove to a cute two-bedroom duplex that Dad had rented for us.

Dolores registered me for school the next day. Things felt as though they may be going to be all right. We had only lived there for a week before Danny and his pregnant wife Stacy moved in with us. It turned out that Stacy was cool and I liked her. It was Danny I could do without. Fortunately, we didn't see much of him because he was working with my dad. He hadn't molested me since he got married and I always tried to steer clear of him so that we were never alone together. We stayed at the duplex for a couple of months, and celebrated Christmas and New Year's there. As I remember it, it was the best Christmas we ever had together. There weren't very many presents and I didn't get anything more exciting than bubble bath and a deck of cards, but both my parents were together and not drinking or fighting and Danny wasn't molesting me with Stacy there. That's what made it the best.

Danny and Stacy were moving back to Thompson, Utah. They asked if I would go with them to be with Stacy while she was pregnant. Even at the risk of being around Danny again, I said yes. Maybe being married, he would finally act like a good brother is supposed to act I thought. Dad and Dolores were saying that they had to move again anyway, so it would be perfect timing for me to go with them. I was warned ahead of time that the house we would be living in wasn't going to be like any other home I had ever had. There wasn't running water or an indoor bathroom and I would have to ride a school bus 35 miles to get to school. Still, I felt up to the challenge. I really enjoyed being around Stacy. She treated me like a real friend, so I was excited for the change.

Overnight, my life changed once again. I didn't check out of school. We just left and they would transfer everything after we settled into the new place. Wow, what a memory this place would end up being. Talk about primitive! It was as if we had turned back time. The house was very old on the outskirts of an old town named Thompson. The town itself had a population of only four hundred fifty. I had been to this small town many times off and on in my life, and for some reason, I had always liked it and felt at home there. Our new home was made of wood and had a small shack outside that served as a barn. There were three small corrals that were homes to a couple of pigs, a mule and a female goat. There was a canyon behind the house and halfway down there was a well. This was the real deal. A bucket tied to a rope. I was taught how to take a five gallon bucket down, fill it up and then carry it back up the hill. We didn't drink this water. It was only for the animals, baths, and dishes. Our drinking water was bought from the store.

In order to adapt, I had to learn a routine quickly. First, I had to get my homework done on the bus ride home, then as soon as I got home, I had to do my chores. I fed the animals, brought firewood into the house, and if I wanted cold milk for breakfast, I would have to milk the goat, strain the milk and put it in the cooler overnight. There was no electricity, no gas, and no propane. There was no inside bathroom, just an outhouse. It was very dark and scary at night. The coyotes would come right up onto our porch and howl at the moon and at each other. So when the evening came, we would just go to the bathroom in an old coffee can and dump it out the next day. That worked for me. Even though I was getting better about wetting the bed and I was good at taking care of my linens and wet clothes without needing to involve anyone else now, having the can right there was actually a comfort.

There wasn't a fireplace, but there was a stove in the living room, where I slept, that had bricks in it. You would make a fire and it would heat up the bricks. When the fire went out, the bricks would still put out heat. The warmth lasted only half of the night and it would be freezing in the morning. Our kitchen stove was quite an antique. It looked just like what you would see in an old western show, like <u>Gunsmoke</u>. It was large, black, and made of cast-iron. It had four burners with a detachable handle that fit into the burner. The burner was flat and round and to adjust your heat, you would remove the burner and stir the fire inside the stove. For less heat in front, you would push the wood to the back. For more heat, you just added more wood. Basically, everything came out scorched or burnt. It was not easy at all to cook meals.

When we moved in, there was already a family of skunks living under the house. The skunk smell never went away. Even the food seemed to have a skunk flavor. In the morning, I would eat Cheerios with goat's milk. It would have a slight skunk taste that was really nasty but I was hungry, so I would just hold my breath and eat as quickly as I could. When it came time to walk to the school bus, it was still dark. I would walk as quickly as I could, but it was slippery because of the snow and ice. It wasn't a very long walk to the bus, but it was kind of scary. There were lots of wild animals that I could have encountered; coyotes, mountain lions, and bears were always seen in the area. As stupid as it may sound, I was terrified of Bigfoot. No matter what anyone said, I believed it existed.

The bus driver knew everyone, being that it was such a small town. He would go out early to start the bus, and leave it running with the heater on. He would leave the door slightly cracked open so that as we got there one by one, we could get inside and be warm. There were just six of us that lived in Thompson, and it was pretty quiet for the first 25 miles until he picked up the rest of the kids. Then it was your typical school bus mayhem. School was the same to me as it always was: hard, confusing, and uncomfortable. On the way home, once all of the in-town kids were dropped off, the ride home was enjoyable. Some of the other kids would help me with my homework. I enjoyed the rhythm of the bus. It didn't take long to get into a routine. I knew what had to be done, and I knew it all had to be done before dark. I wasn't allowed to read or write by candlelight because I was told it would ruin my eyes. I cleaned the animal pens, then fed the animals, and milked the goat, before going into the house to heat up my water for my sponge bath. It wasn't the most fun way to live, but we did it. It was so cold every day that my pinky toes were always numb. That was such an irritating feeling. Sometimes the thought of chopping them off with the axe as I was cutting wood seemed almost inviting. But, my aim wasn't that good and the fear of losing my whole foot kept me from actually doing it.

It was kind of lonely there, but I had a sweet little cat to keep me company. I felt so sorry for him. He ran into walls and didn't act like a normal cat. He had a long scar on his head that went from between his eyes almost the top of his head. He got that scar from Danny. One day, Stacy made a pot roast and had it sitting on the table while she finished up in the kitchen. Danny saw the cat jump up on the table heading for the meat, so he threw a butcher knife at it. He said he was just trying to scare the cat but the knife hit the cat right between the eyes. The cat jumped and started running crazily around the house. The knife wiggled back and forth until it finally fell out. Blood shot out everywhere. Against all odds, the cat survived. Danny never showed any remorse to him; it was just a dumb animal.

We weren't living there for more than a month before Danny made his move on me. On a weekend morning, Stacy left to go do some laundry at her mother's house. I was outside feeding the animals in the barn. This time, Danny used a completely different approach. He started complaining about Stacy not understanding his needs, how the pregnancy made her not feel well, and that they argued so much she didn't care about meeting his needs. There were no threats, this time, just guilt trips. "I need you to suck me, because no one understands me like you. It's the least you can do. After all I pay for your food and give you cigarettes. Come on, it won't take me long, I promise. And you don't have to swallow." Gee, with an offer like that, how could I refuse? This was so horrible! But what could I do? I was stuck, so reluctantly, I agreed. His smell even drowned out the smell of the skunks. Afterwards, he thanked me, ignoring my feelings. He couldn't care less how this affected me; he was pleased and that was all he cared about. I went back to finishing up my chores and I tried to avoid him until Stacy got home.

As it got dark, I realized that maybe she wasn't going to make it home. We didn't have a phone and her mom's house was in Moab, thirty-five miles away. I didn't build the fire. I just curled up in the blankets trying to stay warm. Even though I was coughing and had the sniffles, Danny approached me again. "Come on, just one last time. I'll build a fire. I'll give you a whole pack of cigarettes so you can have as many as you want without asking. I won't make the cat stay outside." He got me there, I was always afraid of the cat being eaten by coyotes. Once again, I agreed. What an absolute, rotten day this had been. Thank God, Stacy came back home the next morning. I told her that I had missed her very much. I said that Danny had been really grouchy while she was away, and asked if she left again, could she please, please take me with her. She laughed a little and said, "Sure, no problem." This time, he hadn't threatened me not to tell. He knew that I couldn't. After all, look at everything they were doing for me. How could I be so disrespectful? Besides, I cared too much about Stacy to hurt her, and thought she would think it was all my fault. The safest thing to do was to just go with the flow and deal with it.

The next week, when I got home from school and finished my chores, I asked Stacy if I could go to a friend's house. She told me I could, but I would have to be home by dark. I didn't go anywhere very often, so I was very excited. I ran down the dirt road to my friend's small house. When I got there, I saw there were no cars. I thought no one was home, so I decided to try another friend's house. After all, it was still pretty light out. It was a little further away and by the time I got there, I only got to stay for a few minutes. When I left, I ran almost all the way home. When I got there, Danny and Stacy asked me where I had been. I told them that when I got to Elizabeth's house she wasn't home, so I went to my other friend's house. I didn't know I did anything wrong but they were mad. Stacy scolded me saying, "When you're told that you can go somewhere you can only go to that place. If no one is there, then you need to come straight home!" She then informed me that Danny was going to take me outside and give me a spanking. "Why?" I asked as the tears streamed down my face. "I'll never do it again. Why can't you just believe that I got the message?" Stacy was nice and soft spoken about it but still insisted that I had to be spanked. "It's our job to punish you properly. We are just doing what needs to be done. It's the right thing to do."

I followed Danny outside to the small barn. "You aren't really going to spank me are you?" I asked. "Of course I am," he replied. "Even after all the things I've had to do for you, that weren't right? After I've kept your secrets? Can't you just say you spanked me? I can pretend you did?" I pleaded. He firmly disagreed. "That's different," he said. "You were disobedient and you have to be punished." I told him that I didn't know I was doing anything wrong at the time. "Well," he said, "you'll remember the next time what's right and what's wrong!" It was inevitable; I couldn't talk my way out of it. He sat down and I bent over his lap. After a couple of hard whacks, I got up and walked away. I didn't look back. I didn't want to give him the satisfaction of seeing me upset. I spent the rest of the evening to myself, petting the cat. According to Danny and Stacy, I was just feeling sorry for myself. I remained angry and kept to myself for the next couple of days. The spanking didn't hurt; I have a very high tolerance for pain. It was my feelings that were hurt! Why couldn't Stacy have respected that I was mature enough to understand her without being punished like a child? As for Danny, he is a traitor! With as much bullshit as I have had to endure from him all these years, now he thinks he's Father Knows Best? What an asshole! I didn't have very much respect for him to begin with, but now I had absolutely none.

Everything started falling apart at that point. Danny wasn't making enough money. He and Stacy were fighting daily. The coyotes ate my only friend, the little cat. One after another, the farm animals were sold or given away. Once again life was unbearable. The more Danny and Stacy fought, the more I had to be around Danny by myself. And as usual, when I was alone with him, he demanded and expected sexual favors. Finally, great news came when I got home from school. Danny told me to pack up because Dolores and Dad were in Moab and I was going to go stay with them.

Dad and Dolores were staying at an RV Park on the outskirts of Moab, in a one-room trailer Dad rebuilt. I didn't have to change schools, for a little while anyway. Dad informed me that he had to do some sign work in Moab for a couple of weeks, and then we would be moving back to Salt Lake City. What a relief to have a break away from Danny, although I was right back in the middle of Dad and Dolores' drinking and fighting. On the weekdays, they were civil to each other and there was dinner on the table, but come Friday, Dolores was painting her nails, curling her hair, drinking while listening to her country tearjerker music, and Dad wouldn't even come home to clean up. On the weekends, he would play the saxophone in bands at various bars. When I was alone, it was kind of scary, but at the same time, when I wasn't scared, it was nice to be alone. I had to walk to the RV park bathrooms to shower and I was afraid that someone would follow me back. Thankfully, nothing ever happened and soon, we were on the road and moving again.

I scrambled to find a hiding spot. 1978

Once we were in Salt Lake, Dad had me stay at my Aunt Agnes' house for a month. I had just been registered back in school and started to settle in when I was pulled back out of school again. Dolores came to pick me up and told me that we would be staying at my Aunt Hattie's house. Hattie was Dad's other sister. We were moving into the house where she and her first husband had lived. One of her kids, Randy, who had gotten into a very bad car accident as a teenager had to have his legs amputated. He also lived in the house with them but, moved out just before we arrived. Randy was a very sweet, kind and loving person. Following his accident, he didn't really have good medical care or family help, so he wasn't able to clean or care for himself properly. His legs kept getting infected, and his flesh rotted. The reason why I'm even getting into this is to try and describe what we were moving in to. I love Randy deeply and I don't mean him any disrespect, but Dolores and I had to clean and disinfect the whole house before we could move in. It was absolutely horrible. The whole house, especially the bathroom and his bedroom, smelled like rotten meat. There were even maggots on the floor in the bathroom and around the bed in his bedroom. Even worse, his room was going to be my room. No matter how much I cleaned, or how much Pine-Sol and bleach I used, the smell never really went away.

Shortly after settling in, Danny and Stacy came, living in a small camper they moved into the backyard. Whenever Stacy wasn't there I scrambled to find a hiding spot, so Danny wouldn't find me. Now that he had his camper there, he had his perfect place of sexual torture that I wanted to avoid at any cost. Our backyard was large, with the dirty Jordan River flowing through it at the end of the property. Danny and Stacy brought their dog, Brandy. They tied her up at the end of the yard, so she could drink out of the river. There was an old, half fallen apart doghouse already there. Brandy didn't want to go inside it; instead she dug a hole under it for her shelter. Danny and Stacy didn't stay very long, but they left all of their belongings at our house, including Brandy.

Eventually we settled in, and I turned most of my attention towards music, spending as much time in my room as I was allowed. I loved all types of music. I had a small record player and would play my limited selection of music over and over. One day, I got enough guts to ask Dolores if there was any way I could earn some money to buy some records. I was shocked when she said yes. She set me up with a couple weeks of extra chores, and with hard work and trying extra hard not to argue with her, I made about fifteen dollars. She took me to the mall and we went to the music store. At eleven years old, this was my first trip to the mall and my first time in a store that sold records and tapes. It was awesome! Music was playing loudly and I was surrounded by records, cassettes, and eight tracks. I went right over to the rock and roll section. There was everything from the radio that was familiar to me, and so much more. It was unbelievable!

Suddenly, I could hear Dolores calling me from the other side of the store. I quickly went over to her and she pointed out some albums that were on sale. They were all country music albums. They were reduced to really low prices. I softly said that I really wanted to get something from the rock 'n roll section but I could tell from the look on her face that I was either going to cooperate with her or probably leave with nothing. "It would be stupid to buy those," she announced going on and on saying, "One of the albums you want costs the same as ten of these. Why don't you want to get your money's worth?" We had actually been getting along lately and I didn't want to mess that up, so I agreed to purchase what she wanted. Her face lit up. "Would you like to help me pick them out?" I asked. It was rare to see her happy these days, and she really enjoyed herself looking through the records. She would get so excited when she found one she really liked. Even though I didn't get what I wanted, it didn't matter. Seeing her happy was worth every penny. Besides, I was starting to like country music anyway, and when Dolores was happy, she was nice to me. We went home and listened to record after record.

It was one of those times when Dad and Dolores were actually getting along and had been for a while. That made for a happy home most of the time. Sometimes, I would do something that I shouldn't have done; I guess it was because I was bored, I don't know. Even if it was something harmless, I would get busted, and be in big trouble. When I would be listening to music in my room at night, I knew Dolores and Dad were messing around sexually while watching TV. There was a back door right next to my bedroom and my parents couldn't see or hear it from the living room, so I would sneak out and quietly go to the front door, ring the doorbell, and then run back to my bedroom. I did it several times and really pissed off my Dad. The madder he got, the funnier I thought it was. So much for their romantic time together I thought. They never found out that it was me.

I found that as long as I kept all of my chores done and stayed away from everyone, I would be left alone. I enjoyed being alone. I spent a lot of time sitting with Brandy, the dog Danny left behind. If it wasn't for me, she would have been completely ignored. I grew to love her. She wasn't very old and was so excited when I spent time with her. One day, when I went out to visit her, she was acting really strange. She was whimpering and pacing back and forth. I ran back to the house to get Dad explaining to him how she was acting and asked him to please come and check on her. He said he was busy painting some signs and that he would check on her later. I ran back to her and she was still running around the doghouse frantically. I could see something dangling from her mouth. It was a newborn puppy. It wasn't moving and Brandy was panicking. I ran back to get Dad and told him about the puppy. Finally, he reluctantly agreed to come and check on her. Brandy was lying on the ground, giving birth to another puppy. Dad didn't show much emotion as he told me to go to the house and get an old blanket and bring it back to him. I ran as quickly as I could, praying for Brandy and her puppies the whole time.

When I returned, I gave him the blanket and he placed it in the doghouse. Brandy was lying quietly next to the new whimpering puppy licking and cleaning it. Dad bent down and picked up the dead puppy by its back legs and instructed me to go to the house. As we walked to the house, Dad detoured over to the garbage cans and dropped the puppy into it. He acted like this was no big deal. I couldn't hold back my tears. I didn't even get to know this new puppy. I don't know if it ever got to take a breath, but I loved it just the same. I felt that it deserved more than to just be dumped in the garbage can. Dad wasn't even fazed by my tears. "Go find something to do. Make yourself useful and stay away from the dog. She'll be just fine. She doesn't need you there bothering her." As much as I didn't want to, I had no choice but to obey him, because he knew I wanted to be with her and I knew he would be keeping an eye on me.

The next day I couldn't wait to get home so I could spend time with Brandy and the puppies. When I went to feed her, she came out of the doghouse and there were five wiggling beautiful little puppies. I was so proud of Brandy and told her what a good job she had done. As I patted her back and kissed her head she seemed to understand. She looked proud as she held her head up and wagged her tail. Every day when I got up, I would have something to look forward to now. It wasn't long before she moved the puppies to the hole she dug under the doghouse but this made it more difficult for me to watch them. They started roaming around a lot before their eyes were even open and this soon became tragic. In the mornings before I went to school, I would check on Brandy to make sure she had food and water. Sadly, one morning I found a puppy floating in the still water on the edge of the river. I got a stick and pulled it on to the dry ground. As quickly as I could, I dug a small hole and buried it, saying a prayer before hurrying off to school.

I felt so sad all day. All I could think of was to get home to check on the puppies and spend time with Brandy. When I got home, I couldn't believe what I saw. There was another puppy floating in the water! I pulled it to the side and buried it next to the other puppy. That night, I told Dad what had happened. I didn't admit that I buried them because I thought he would get mad at me. He didn't even ask what I did with them. I pleaded with him to let me move them so it wouldn't happen again. He just replied saying, "Oh, they'll be just fine. Stop worrying so much!" Eventually, within a very short time, I had to bury all five puppies. They all drowned, one after another and no one cared. I never understood how they could be so cold and uncaring. It made no sense to me at all. Did the adults just not care because it was Danny's dog that he should have taken with him? Did they want the puppies to drown, so we would have fewer dogs to be bothered with? Were they really too busy to take the time to put them in a safe place? It all seemed to be so cruel, no matter what the answer. They would never have treated Dolores' poodles that way.

A New Friend   Chapter 28
The beginning of a new addiction

Danny and Stacy came back for about a week to get their belongings and picked up Brandy. Even though I was sad to see her go, I was happy she was leaving this place of bad memories behind. Things were back to what I knew as normal, soon after Danny and Stacy left. Dad would leave to do his sign work for days at a time and Dolores would get restless. She would go on her drinking binges as soon as he was gone. This was fine with me as long as I had a pack of cigarettes stashed. As long as I could smoke, I didn't need any food.

I enjoyed the freedom of no one being home. I would take off exploring after school. I would walk for blocks down streets, out into open fields or on to vacant properties; anywhere but home. Dolores always said I was just nosey, but I considered myself curious. One day, when I was walking down the street by my house, I was almost at the end where there was a field. To the right was a big house that sat back into the yard far from the street. I could see a pretty blonde girl signaling for me to come over to her. I walked over and she held out her hand. "Hi, I'm Lilly. What's your name?" she said. I shook her hand and told her my name. She asked where I lived and invited me to stay and visit with her for a while. "Sure." I answered. I got so excited. She seemed really nice and her home had a good feeling about it.

We went inside and it smelled like popcorn and sunflowers. "Your mom won't mind if I come in?" I asked. "Oh no, not at all." Lilly answered. She introduced me to her little brother. He was a handsome little brown-haired, brown-eyed boy. She said his name was Sun Prince and that he just went by S.P. When I asked her where she went to school, I was surprised when she told me that her mom didn't believe in sending her kids to school. And then, a completely naked girl with very large breasts walked by. I was shocked, especially when Lilly introduced us simply saying, "This is my sister Clara." Clara wasn't the least bit shy or embarrassed at all. Lilly explained that her family were nudists and that it was just her mom, sister, brother and her in her family. She went on to explain that her mom was outside sunbathing naked so, if I went outside and saw her, I wouldn't be surprised.

I became close to this family very quickly. They were different from anyone and anything I had ever experienced before. They didn't eat meat, and ate only organic foods. They were the friendliest and most honest people I had ever met. Any time I was left alone, I would run straight to their house. I felt so comfortable with them that I didn't even crave cigarettes when I was there. I started to stop by before school in the morning. The first time I did, Lilly's mom answered the door and said I could go up to her room and wake her up. In the front of the room, there was a big circle in the ceiling with a ladder coming down from it. I climbed up and sat next to her bed. Lilly had the coolest room I had ever seen. It was an attic space converted into a bedroom. She had chiffon curtains hanging from the ceiling surrounding the bed. I just loved her bedroom. It reminded me of the inside of a genie's bottle, like the one from I Dream of Jeannie.

I softly called her name. Her eyes opened and she smiled. I smiled back and told her that I had a little time before school started so I wanted to hang out with her if it was okay. Even though she had just woken up, she was very pleasant and said she would love to spend time with me before I had to go to school. She sat up and gathered up the curtains tying them together at the corners. She walked over and picked up her guitar and sat back on the bed. She patted the bed in front of her and asked me to sit down by her. "Let's write a song together," she said. Excitedly, I agreed. She sang the melody and I harmonized. I thought we sounded terrific together. It made me so happy when she would get excited and compliment me on how pretty my voice was and how well I could harmonize. Time sped by and when I glanced at the clock, I realized no matter how fast I ran, I couldn't make it to school on time. In a panic, I blurted out that I was going to be late to school and I needed to leave right then. Are you going to get into trouble for being late? "she asked. "Oh yeah, big trouble," I answered, already dreading what I would be facing. "Well," she said, "trouble is trouble and if you are going to be in trouble anyway, you might as well stay here instead of going at all. Your parents probably won't even know that you weren't in school. You can worry about it later! Let's just have fun for now." Lilly's response seemed logical and we were having so much fun it seemed worth getting into trouble to be able to keep our collaboration going. I decided to stay. "Won't your mom get mad?" I asked. Lilly smiled and said, "No, my mom doesn't get upset very easily and she believes people should do what makes them happy, as long as no one is getting hurt by their actions. Besides, my mom likes you and she knows that I'm always happy when we are together, so that makes her happy." I hugged her and said she was so lucky to have such a great mom. I shared that my mother was the exact opposite.

I stayed there until I was expected to be home from school. What a wonderful day we had! But, on my way home, my heart raced. I didn't know what I would be facing. I was trembling and afraid on the inside, but tried to look cool and calm on the outside. I must have done a really good job because no one noticed me, as usual. There was no call from the school, so I had gotten away with it. The next day, I did the same thing. I didn't plan on skipping school; it was just so easy to say, "Oh well, I'll already be in trouble." I loved being with Lilly, singing, playing hide-n-seek, making food and creating great adventures. With no contact made by the school, and no one asking me about school or homework; a few days turned into weeks.

Finally, the day came that I walked in the front door and there was Dolores sitting at the dining room table looking very scary. Her hair was messy and sticking out all over. Her hand was resting on her coffee cup with a cigarette smoldering between her fingers. Her other hand was clicking her long, red nails loudly on the table right next to my report card. She looked at me with her piercing dark eyes and said "Do you know why they had to mail your report to me?" I just stood there, motionless. I knew this day would come, and I was ready to accept whatever was coming to me without any argument. "Well, I'll tell you why they mailed it. Because you haven't been there to bring it home!" she screamed at me. She began to bombard me with questions, "Where have you been going? Who have you been with? Why are you doing this? Are you trying to get your dad and me thrown in jail? Who in the hell do you think you are?" Nothing she could say or do would make me get my friends in trouble. I never told anyone about them. From the beginning, I knew if Dolores discovered I had a friend, she would find a way to end the friendship, so I told her that I would just go hide in the backyard when I left. As far as she knew, I was telling the truth, because she didn't know that I had any friends. She asked me how I knew when it was time to come back to the house. I said that I just waited until I saw kids walking home. When she demanded that I give her a reason why, I simply said that I didn't feel like I fit in and the work was too hard for me to understand because I wasn't very smart." I knew she would agree, and she did. She started right in reminding me that she was right all along when she told me I was stupid and wouldn't amount to anything and my actions just proved how right she was. I responded to her question about who I thought I was saying, "It's clear in my mind who I am. I am no one. I am nothing! I have always been nothing and I would always be nothing!" She snapped back at me "Oh, boo-hoo. Quit feeling sorry for yourself, we all have problems. I'm not going to get into trouble for you because you're just not worth it! Get to your bedroom and I don't want to see or hear you until your dad gets home! I'll let him deal with you because I'm sick of you!"

It seemed like forever waiting for my dad. So many things passed through my mind as I wondered how he would punish me. It was dark when he finally got home. He came in my room, but I pretended to be asleep. He sat on the edge of the bed and softly shook me, saying my name. I timidly answered. He was uncharacteristically calm. He asked me what the problem was and told me to be honest with him. His calm and gentle approach made me immediately break down in tears. I was braced for anger and intimidation, but not love and understanding. I told him I hated school because I didn't fit in. I had no friends and everyone made fun of my clothes and me. The schoolwork was too hard and I couldn't focus. I went on to say I'd rather hide under a bush all day than to be humiliated anymore. I told him everything except the truth about my friends. Unlike ever before, he listened to what I was saying and really seemed to care. He never yelled at me or called me names. He did say I was grounded for the weekend but he also said he would try to help me get the issues resolved.

He went with me to school on Monday and I stayed in the waiting room when he went into the principal's office. I never asked him what he said to the principal, I was just happy that he cared to handle it without humiliating me, like Dolores did. Dad was so unpredictable that any support or sprinkling of love I got from him, I would soak up like a sponge. I didn't miss any more school and I was grounded through the end of the school year. The only thing I was allowed to do was to read. I read a lot of books and even got some awards for reading so many. I started getting into fist fights, but I didn't get kicked out of school.

A cousin, Andrew, moved to Salt Lake and started coming over during the day to fish in the river at the back of the property. He only lived a few blocks away, so he was able to come by often. I couldn't understand why he wanted to fish in the nasty water when all there was to catch was ugly carp and an occasional catfish. One day, I asked him, and he answered, "Because it's fun and a good place to get stoned." I soon learned that he was right. Andrew was so cool. He was mellow and good company for the few weeks I got to spend with him. I was so thankful to him for introducing me to smoking marijuana and for helping me become more of what I felt was cool.

Even though I was only twelve, I didn't feel like a stupid kid anymore. I was more aware of the differences between people. Now I knew there were the uptight and conservative people, and on the other side, there were the withdrawn, longhaired, mellow, stoner outcasts. And now, I knew exactly where I fit in.

I didn't have enough knowledge or money to purchase my own weed at the time, but whenever I got the opportunity, I smoked it. I enjoyed being high; it made me happy and helped me to not focus on my self-hatred, anger, and fears. I felt I had now truly met my best friend, Marijuana.

It was turning to spring, and Dad and Dolores were back into the same familiar routine. He was working from early in the morning to late at night. She was retaliating by going out drinking and staying away for days at a time. It wasn't as hard for me to tolerate because I was in my own world and I now had a new group of secret friends. Friends who seemed to understand how messed up my life was were compassionate enough to give me some of their weed when I needed it. I learned how to make a pipe out of a soda can. It came in handy for dealing with my parents coming home and fighting. I started to smoke before I went to bed. Now I didn't care when I was awakened late at night or early in the morning from all the yelling and things being thrown and broken. This went on for about a month, then Dad just didn't come home anymore. Dolores said that he was out of town working. But, like so many times before, she informed me that we would be moving this summer. You'd think that I would be used to moving by now, but I still hated it!

When Dad finally showed up, he announced that he had a big sign job in Moab, and that we would be traveling every weekend until it was complete. That meant I could spend time with Dolores' son, Karl, his wife Renee, and their children, because they also lived in Moab. Although getting there meant a six to seven-hour, very boring drive, I was always happy, knowing I'd be seeing Karl and Renee. I felt safe there, because Karl never did anything to hurt me. He was handsome and kind, and he always spoke softly. He was nothing at all like Danny. I adored him and thought of him as an ideal brother, husband, and father. Renee was sweet and soft spoken too. She was pretty with long beautiful, blonde hair. She was a great wife and mother. In my eyes they were the perfect couple. They had a five-year old named Jay, and a baby named Ken.

After three or four trips, Dad surprised me by asking if I wanted to stay with Karl and Renee, now that it was summer. They were getting ready to move and could use my help. I didn't even have to think about it and immediately answered yes. I was told I could stay as long as I helped them pack and watch the kids. They were moving somewhere close to Salt Lake City; I was to ride with them when they made their move, and would be dropped off at what would be my new home, also in Salt Lake City. While I was helping to pack and move Karl and Renee, Dad and Dolores would be packing and moving us. It took about two weeks before we were loaded up and on our way. Those two weeks of normalcy were wonderful! No drinking or fighting, real family meals, regular hours. I still had my cigarette stash, thanks to Karl being a smoker and snuck my occasional smoke, but I wasn't craving the weed, like I did before being there. I learned how to roll cigarettes because Karl rolled his own. I practiced over and over because I thought it was fun, and got pretty good at it.

Karl drove the moving van and the kids and I rode with Renee in their Blazer. She and I headed off to go to my new home. We drove up to a trailer park. This one was actually nice, not like the other places we had lived in the past. There was a guarded entrance, a swimming pool and a recreation hall. Maybe, just maybe, this place wouldn't be so bad, I thought. As we drove to the end of the street I could barely believe my eyes! There it was, the same mobile home, the one from my past, the one that was loaded with all my bad memories with Danny and my parent's violent fights. My heart sunk and I felt overloaded with emotion. It always seemed to show up. Why did Dad keep hanging on to this torture chamber on wheels?

As I opened the truck door, I tried to create a positive attitude by telling myself this time it would be different. Danny wasn't there, and maybe Dad and Dolores would get along. But I hated that trailer. It radiated negativity. Walking up to the door, I took a deep breath and prayed that Dolores would be in a good mood. As I opened the door, my mind was flooded with bad memory after bad memory. The smell was the same. The temperature was the same. The orange carpet overpowered the space, and everything else in the room. I looked around at the wall paneling and thought I must know every line, every spot, light and dark, on those walls. Every corner, every room, even the hallway was filled with bad memories. I froze after stepping a few feet into the room. I wanted so much to speak, to beg Renee to take me with her. I tried several times to get the words out having to tell myself, "Okay, I'll say something after my next breath." My breaths came and went with no words coming out of my mouth.

Dolores' voice broke the silence and as she approached, she actually made a nice gesture toward me. She suggested that Renee leave Jay with her for a week or two since she would have her hands full setting up her new place. Quickly, I announced that I would help watch him and that I would share everything with him, if he could stay. She thought about it while she fed the baby and, reluctantly agreed. Jay and I hugged and kissed Renee goodbye. I promised her that I would protect him with my life. Of course I wish we both had gone with her, but I was happy that Jay got to stay. He was such a cute sweet boy and I really loved him.

The week melted away. Dolores was nicer than she usually was, but when Karl arrived to pick up Jay, I knew that it wouldn't take long before Dolores would show her true colors. The soft voice she used when Jay, Karl, or Renee were with us, became sharp and abrasive. Her eyes lost their kindness and returned to the dark squinty, piercing eyes, full of hatred saved only for me. It was back to the extra chores, when I didn't stay quiet and out of sight enough for her.

The days were still quite hot, and the trailer still didn't have air-conditioning. Dolores would close the windows and send me outside to hose the outside off until she pounded on the window to let me know it had cooled down inside. Most of the time, she just sat on the couch, watching TV, drinking coffee, and painting her nails as she barked out my orders. "Now that you're finished with everything in here, go outside and wash the car and I want the inside cleaned right!" I would get so angry! When she said clean it right, it didn't just mean washing the windows and cleaning the dashboard. It meant wiping down the entire interior from top to bottom. If I didn't clean it to her complete satisfaction, she would make me start all over again. I remember one time in particular, after spending hours cleaning the car just the way she liked, I was beat! I was sweaty and dirty and my hair looked like I had been swimming.

I came into the house to announce with pride that I was finished, looking forward to cleaning up and jumping into the pool. Typically, Dolores squashed my enthusiasm saying "Well, since you're already a mess, why don't you go into the backyard and pull some weeds?" I knew it was a question I wasn't to respond to, it was just her way of giving me another command. I felt the tears well up in my eyes, but I didn't dare let her see them. I knew that would create a huge fight. I took a deep breath and tried to sound calm. "Can I please get a drink of water?" I asked. "A small one and make it quick." she barked back. My jaw tightened as I walked by her just sitting there, her cigarette smoldering, steam rising from her freshly poured coffee, her eyes focused on the TV. As I walked back past her I thought how nice it must be to just relax and do nothing.

I snuck around the shed in the back yard to enjoy a couple long cigarette butts I had found in the car ashtray and started to work pulling the weeds. I worked until my throat was so dry I could barely swallow. As I walked to the door, I looked back to admire the work I had done. The car was shiny, and at least half the yard was cleared of all the weeds. It was a big yard too. I walked through the back door and Dolores startled me, standing in the hallway. I jumped and quickly explained I was just coming in to get a drink because I was so thirsty I could hardly swallow. I actually didn't expect her response at all. She snapped at me saying, "You don't need a drink! You're just screwing around. Get your stupid ass back outside and finish what you started!" Without thinking, I seemed to have no control of what came out of my mouth. Out of anger, hurt feelings, and dehydration, I actually yelled back at her, "I have busted my stupid ass, as you call it, all day while all you have done is sit on the couch doing nothing but smoke, drink coffee and paint your nails! I have done all the chores all by myself!" Her face distorted, her eyes glazed over, and suddenly, her large hands swooped me up by the neck. I felt her hands clinch tighter and tighter around my throat. My feet were no longer touching the floor. She shook me violently; my whole body felt like a rag doll and my head kept bouncing off the wall. She shook and jerked my body to the rhythm of her scolding words saying, "Who in the hell do you think you are? If you ever talk to me like that again I will fucking kill you! You are so worthless!"

My ears were pounding like the beating of my heart and my face was throbbing. I was trying to pry her fingers off my throat but it didn't do any good, she was too strong. As I began to lose consciousness, she dropped my body to the floor. "Now get in your bedroom and don't come out! I don't want to see your ugly little face for the rest of the day! Don't bother to ask for anything to drink or eat either because you don't deserve shit!" When she walked out of sight, I crawled into my bedroom. I shut my door and buried my face in my pillow and cried and cried. I didn't blame her at all because I got exactly what I deserved! What in the hell was wrong with me? She was right! I am totally worthless! Why am I here? Why can't I just die? The world would be so much better off without me!

As I lay crying and wallowing in my own self-pity, the door opened. It was Dolores again and she was holding a handful of gifts that I had given her for various reasons, holidays, birthdays and just out of love, and coldly threw them down on the bed next to me. She said she didn't want anything from me. She didn't even want to know me. She demanded that I never tell her I loved her again. "Don't buy or make anything for me. Just stay the hell away from me!" she screamed, "I don't want anything to do with you again!" I kept my face in the pillow. I didn't want to give her the satisfaction of seeing my tear drenched face. As if I didn't feel bad enough already, now my heart was really broken. To this day, I'll never understand how I could love and hate someone so much at the same time. Why was it so important for me to seek her approval? Why was I so crushed when I heard her say that she didn't want me anymore? My throat was sore and I was still very thirsty, but I knew I didn't deserve anything to drink. When I heard her slam my bedroom door, I picked up all the cast off gifts and put them into my garbage can. I was devastated and tears began to flow again. I ran back to my bed, and cried myself to sleep.

Hours went by. When I woke up it was dark outside. I could hear Dolores' raspy voice complaining to Dad about my behavior. She was bragging about everything she had accomplished that day. I couldn't believe what I was hearing. What a liar! She told him that she cleaned the house and the car, and even talked about how tiring it was to pull all the weeds in the backyard. Unbelievable! She complained how lazy and worthless I had been and how I had smart- mouthed her when she asked for help, so she sent me to my room. She went on to tell him not to feel sorry for me because that was where I needed to stay. She should have been given an Academy Award because Dad swallowed her story, hook, line and sinker! He never came in to check on me and I thought "Now he probably doesn't want me around either!" My fragile heart was shattered. I cried myself back to sleep again and I didn't wake up until the morning.

I stayed in my room that morning and wished that Dolores would somehow forget that I was even there. I heard her heavy footsteps march down the hall. My ears followed everything she did. She made her coffee, usually my job, and I could hear her inhale as she lit her cigarette. After a while, she came into my room. "Well, you better get started on your chores." she announced. "Yes ma'am," I quickly replied trying to avoid eye contact. I straightened up my room and tried to work out a chore system, so I wouldn't be cleaning the same room she was in because when she watched me, it made me nervous and I would make stupid mistakes. No matter how simple the task I was doing, she would criticize how I did it. But, if she wasn't watching, my final work was usually satisfactory. Every time I heard her walking toward me, my hands would start to shake uncontrollably and my heart would race. I would chant a silent little prayer saying, "Please don't come near me, please don't talk to me." When she was in the front room, I moved as quickly as I could to clean her bathroom and bedroom. When she went into her bedroom to change, I would move into the kitchen or out to the front room.

When I finished my chores, I went straight to my room. She came in to tell me I could come out and strangely; she said, "By the way, I do care about you. If I didn't care, I wouldn't get so mad." I thought to myself, "Gee, if that's true, then I wish she didn't care so much." "You don't need to go sniveling to your dad either," she went on to say, "he has enough to do without listening to your bullshit." I wanted so badly to ask her why she took credit for all my hard work and why she lied about me refusing to help with chores. But after everything that had happened the day before, I was too afraid to say anything. I didn't want to come out of my room. I didn't want to be around her. As far as I was concerned, she made it quite clear how she felt about me. Even more than nearly choking me to death, I couldn't get over the hurt of her giving all my gifts back. I would have no way of knowing at the time that it would affect me the rest of my life. I have struggled with the giving and receiving of gifts to this day. Whatever it was that I had to give to anyone would never be good enough and I would always feel undeserving of anything given to me.

Kindred Souls

Chapter 30

Outcasts accepting each other just as we were.

The rest of the summer seemed to drag on. Slowly, I was starting to have nights that I didn't wet the bed. I felt so proud of myself, believing I was finally growing out of this terrible problem. Even though it was just a couple more weeks until school started, it seemed like an eternity away. Neither Delores or I could stand the sight of each other.

Finally, it was the beginning of the new school year, and it would be my first time at this school. I had the normal first-day jitters, that were overtaken by terror, because I learned that Delores wasn't going to register me in the school. I went into her bedroom to tell her I was ready and she was still in bed. Her knotted mass of black hair stuck out from the covers. In a sleepy, raspy voice, she moaned that I could get there by myself. I just stood there for a minute, afraid to speak. Having no idea what to do, I asked as softly and nicely as I could "Aren't you coming with me?" while my mind was screaming "What in the hell do you want me to do, wipe your ass for you too?" "No," she snapped. "But I don't know what to do." I replied. "That's because you're so fucking stupid! Your birth certificate and address are on the counter. Just take them to the school office and they'll tell you what to do. I can't do everything for you for your whole life, so grow up and get your ass to school before you're late!"

My body began to shake with fear, but I knew that I didn't have a choice. As I picked the papers up from off the counter, many thoughts raced through my mind. Everyone is going to laugh at me because I am so stupid. I'm never going to be able to understand what is asked of me. I'm certainly not going to be able to fill out these papers. Still, I did as I was told. I walked to the school and located the office. The halls were filled with kids laughing and joking with each other. Everyone was wearing their new school clothes and shoes. I felt so embarrassed, so ugly! A new school year was never a reason for new clothes or shoes in my world. I was lucky if I got a hand-me-down or thrift store warm coat for winter. I kept my head down, hoping my hair would cover my face so no one would notice me. When I walked up to the secretary in the office, I handed her the papers. She asked me if I had been to the school before. I shook my head no. She asked me where my parents were. "At work and at home," I told her. She looked sternly at me and said she couldn't register me without a parent present. I felt my eyes well up with tears as I took back the papers. I felt my heart begin to beat fast and my head started to throb. I tried to fold my arms tightly to keep them from shaking. I knew that I was going to be in so much trouble when I went home! If there could have been anywhere I could have disappeared to that very moment, I would have done so gladly.

Walking up the steps to the trailer door, I could hear the TV blaring. Oh great, she's up, I thought, as I opened the door. There she sat, as usual, with her cigarette in hand, coffee steaming. Her eyes glared at me with disgust. "Well, what in the hell are you doing here? You can't even do one simple thing right, can you?" My butt cheeks clinched together as I timidly responded "I did what you told me to do, but the lady in the office said I couldn't register without a parent with me." "That's a bunch of bullshit." Dolores growled as she deeply inhaled her cigarette. "Just get into your room until I'm ready to go."

By the afternoon, I was registered. When I finally walked into the classroom, I knew instantly things were going to be as they always had been before. The giggling and pointing confirmed that they were already judging me by the clothes I wore. As usual, the schoolwork was a struggle. Changing schools so many times, I never seemed to catch on to certain subjects, especially math. With no support at home, I always struggled to get through the homework. Basically, I just existed at school because it was where I was supposed to be during the day. I truly hated school. I tried to be friendly to my classmates, but I couldn't really call any of them "friends."

It wasn't until Dad and Dolores went back to their drinking binges, that I had enough freedom to meet other kids that lived around me. Eventually, I made three friends: two boys and one girl. They were all in high school. My new girlfriend's name was Amanda. She was fourteen, two years older than me. She had to watch her younger brothers a lot so, when my parents weren't home, I'd spent all of my time at her house. We had a lot in common. The greatest thing about Amanda was that she never judged me. She accepted me just the way I was. She was a little over weight and had other friends, but never got very close to them because she said they made her feel inferior. She also confided in me that she didn't feel very secure in her family. Her brothers were half-brothers and she felt like her mom and stepfather cared more about them than they did her. She knew that I was having family problems but I was too ashamed to tell her about Danny and all the years of torture I suffered because of him. I guess that's why we got along so well, we both felt like outcasts and didn't ask many questions, accepting each other just as we were.

Evan and Randy, the boys I made friends with were cool, and the same age as Amanda. Evan was cute, with long blonde hair. He was tall, thin and had a good sense of humor. He seemed interested in me, which was the first time a boy ever showed interest. Randy was kind of nerdy and tall with an English accent. He always had great ideas that were based on some type of science. He had a big crush on Amanda, but she couldn't care less. It really worked out to my advantage though, because by my being best friends with Amanda, Evan and Randy tried to win our hearts with bribes giving us cigarettes and kept us supplied with marijuana. My true motto back then was, "A friend with weed was a friend indeed." Surprisingly, Dad and Dolores approved of Amanda but I never told them about Evan and Randy.

Just as I was getting used to Dad and Dolores being gone most of the time, they decided to try and work on their problems by going to church more often. That meant I didn't get to see my friends as much, but at least home life was more tolerable. Dinner was on the table and instead of Dolores' morning coffee and cigarette, we would read the Bible together before school, and on Saturdays, we would study the Bible and pray all day. On Sunday, we would drive for hours just to get to a special church that Dad had picked out. For a brief time, we had family structure. Dolores even went out and got a job at a thrift store, down the street from the trailer park. She seemed much happier and wasn't as mean to me. Sometimes she acted as if she actually liked me.

One weekend, we drove all the way back to Moab to bring Danny's baby back to be with us, because Danny and Stacy were having problems being good parents. I know that Dolores didn't like Stacy, so I didn't listen to any of the negative things she would say about her. I felt bad for the baby, but I was also very excited at the thought of having a baby in the house. We picked up baby Dolores, (She was named after Dolores but I called her Dorie) and we took her home. Dorie was beautiful, with white skin and red hair. I could hold her for hours, staring at her sweet face. I loved to sing her lullabies. She made me think about being a mother someday, and swore to myself that I would never let my child suffer the way that I spent my life suffering.

Dolores took a week off from work to care for Dorie. I would get up early and take her out of Dolores' room so I could change and feed her. When I was at school, all I could think about was getting home to my little Dorie, to hold and love her. The week passed much too quickly. Even though I knew she wasn't meant to stay with us for very long, I secretly wished we would be able to keep her. I cried all the way to Danny and Stacy's. Danny gave us Justin's dog and bird because he didn't want to have to take care of them anymore. Danny said that ever since Justin died, the dog had been acting strangely. He would hardly eat or listen to anyone.

A bird and dog didn't make up for losing little Dorie, but it did help to fill the void. Sammy, the bird, was cranky and bit everyone who tried to hold him. I don't know why, but for some reason, he liked me. That made me happy because he had belonged to Justin and now he was mine. His dog, Bat, was a wonderful dog. He was a Corgi mix, and just as cute as could be with short pointy bat-like ears. He had a long tail, with long hair hanging from it. If he was outside when I came home from school, I would call him and he would come running to me. His tail would go around in a circle over and over like a fan instead of wagging from side to side. It was the funniest thing! He brought joy and a sense of freedom to my life. I would take him for a walk every night, allowing me the ability to have a nightly smoke and sometimes, meet up with Amanda, Evan and Randy for a little while.

For the first time in my life I was beginning to feel a sense of stability. I was finally able to say I was no longer a bed wetter. It was still in my mind and I was careful to not drink anything before bed, but all in all, a huge weight had been lifted!

I don't know why, but for the first time ever, Dolores and I were getting along much better. It really did start to feel like a genuine mother and daughter relationship. This is something that I had always wished for, to have the love of a mother. We spent more time together, praying and reading the Bible. We shared something else too. It's hard to explain, but even though the hallway was carpeted, every once in a while, you could hear someone walking there. The floor would creak a little and I would get the feeling I was going to see someone come out of the hallway, even though I knew that no one except Dolores and I were home. Dolores heard it too, because she would look at me and then we both would look to the hall. Bat would jump up and start barking and twirl his tail. He would act excited, and looked like he was following someone across the living room. This would especially happen when we read the Bible out loud or when we were praying together. There was no way to be sure, but it felt like Justin was there with us. It made us miss him even more. That might have been why we were getting along better.

Goodbye Dolores Chapter 31

I found love in my heart for her but it was too late.

Change was in the air. Dad was taking off on two and three day binges, but instead of Dolores jumping into her routine of going on her own binges, she remained strong. She kept working and focusing on God. For the first time ever, I actually respected her, and felt sorry for her for what Dad was putting her through. The closer we got, the further apart she and Dad got. One day, I came home from school and Dolores was moving her things out of the trailer and into a strange man's car. She took me by the hand and led me into my bedroom. There were pictures, clothes, and knick-knacks on my bed. She told me that these were things she brought home from the thrift store to give me on Christmas. I didn't know what to say. I just stood there and listened, like everything was a dream. "I have to go, Lorina, and quickly, before your dad gets home. You know what will happen if we start arguing. He will hit me and this guy helping me will end up getting into a fight with him. He doesn't need that because he's just a friend that I asked to help me."

She knew that I knew Dad hit her all throughout their relationship , but this was the first time she had ever come right out and said it. I just stood there, speechless. She told me to say goodbye to Bat because she was taking him with her. As she led him to the car, I bent down and hugged and kissed him goodbye. "When do you think you will be back?" I asked. "I'm not coming back again, Lorina. This time it's really over. I'm leaving Sammy the bird here with you to take care of. I love you and have always cared about you. Take care." She slipped into the car, closed the door and as I watched the car drive away, it never crossed my mind that this really could all be over. So many emotions washed over me. I was excited, sad, and definitely confused all at the same time. It had been a terribly cruel, hurtful, and at times, horrifying life, but it was all I knew. It was hard to grasp all of the thoughts that quickly flashed through my mind.

It wasn't perfect, but I had always wished for the type of love and relationship that I had just momentarily experienced with

Dolores. All I ever wanted or desired from her was love and approval and right when it seemed to be in reach, it was gone. Then suddenly, I felt a sense of freedom. My heart cried out, "What am I thinking? This is what I have always wished for!" I ran all the way to Amanda's house. When she answered the door, I hugged her and said, "It's over, at least for a while anyway." I told her everything that had just happened, and she seemed to be more in shock about it than I was. I explained to her that this wasn't the first time Dolores had left, and that she probably would be back in a couple weeks, but for now, I was free to do whatever I wanted.

We went back to the trailer and I fed the bird and fish. I left a note for Dad saying I would be at Amanda's house and to call me when he got home. Dad never called, so in the morning, I went back to the trailer to feed the animals and gathered up some clothes. Before I left, he showed up. He seemed pleasant enough and didn't even mention Dolores. It was obvious she had left with all of her things, but all he asked was how I was, and if I was okay. I told him that I had promised Amanda to help her babysit later that day and he said that was fine with him. Then he said he was going to clean up and go to a club downtown to play his saxophone. He didn't know when he would be back, so he gave me permission to stay over at Amanda's if I wanted. Cheerfully, I said "Thanks! I would love to." I went into my room to get my things ready. I was so excited! As I was pulling my clothes out of my dresser, I caught a glimpse of Dad walking down the hallway in his underwear. This shocked me. I had never seen him walk around in his underwear before, when he was sober. All of a sudden, I got really nervous. I felt my body start to shake and my heart began to pound. What was he up to walking around like this? He walked back into his bedroom and I heard him call my name. My stomach knotted up and thoughts in my mind swirled. I panicked! As quickly and quietly as I could, I ran out the front door. I didn't even take my clothes with me. I don't know if Dad was going to try anything with me, but I sure as hell wasn't going to stick around long enough to find out. He knew that Dolores wasn't coming home, he was walking around in his underwear and, he was being nice to me. All of those things, added up together, made me think if I didn't run, I could be in trouble.

I never told Amanda about what happened. I didn't think she would have understood. I spent the whole weekend with her, only going home to grab some clothes and feed my pets. On school days, I had a lot of freedom, but found that it wasn't as good a thing as it seemed. Sometimes I wouldn't even go. I didn't have any money for lunch, so I told the teacher I was supposed to go home for lunch. Sometimes kids came with me and we would just mess around, but when they found out I didn't have any food in my house, they quit coming. With no one at my house until dark, I found myself willing to do more bad things. When Dad was home, I would steal twenty or forty dollars from his wallet to support my marijuana habit. My friends would still give me some for free, but when I bought it myself, I could smoke until I passed out. Best of all, I wouldn't have to share any. I loved to smoke reality and all my thoughts away.

Not even two weeks had gone by when Dad told me to get my things together. God! Not again! "You're going to stay at a friend's house for a while until I can get everything straightened out." I didn't know exactly what he meant by that but I was too afraid to ask. Maybe he and Dolores were going to get back together. Here we go again, I thought to myself, as I sat in the car with a paper bag full of my belongings. "Don't worry, I'll take care of your bird and feed your fish for you while you are gone," he assured me. "I'll pick you up in a couple of weeks. You are going to have to go to a different school until I come and get you."

It was dark outside when we pulled up. I didn't know where we were. The door opened, and instantly I recognized the faces. It was the preacher and his wife from the church we used to drive for hours to attend. They welcomed us in and comforted my dad by telling him he was doing the right thing. "She'll be just fine, you don't have to worry. We'll take good care of her." A feeling of abandonment came over me as I kissed and hugged Dad goodbye, like I had done so, so many times before. But I thought, "I'll be comfortable here, after all, these are good loving church people. How could they be any different than they are at church?" But, my sadness overcame me and I felt so alone as soon as he was gone from sight.

"Let me show you around." the preacher said as his wife went into the kitchen. They had two sons, one was mentally disabled needing a lot of attention, but he had a very kind and gentle nature. The other son was younger than me, and seemed just like any other normal boy his age. In church, I saw this family as kind and friendly. In a very short time, however, I experienced that what you see isn't always what you get. It seems strange to say, but with all due respect to God, I think that sometimes religion can be taken too far. When I woke up the next morning, the preacher's wife, Sandra, was sitting next to the couch where I was sleeping. The familiar sight of hair rollers and fingernail polish unsettled me as she was painting her nails right next to me. The TV was loud and a religious show was on. She got up to remove the rollers and begin to style her hair. The smell of Aqua Net hairspray began to permeate the room. There was no smoking in the house, but the familiar smell of coffee from the steaming cup she had on the table in front of me blended with the hairspray and flooded my head with familiar bad memories. I could hear the disabled boy making loud noises in the bedroom. He was six or seven years old, but had the mental capacity of a two or three year old, and a very loud one. I just lay there quietly, taking it all in. Suddenly, Sandra turned to look at me and in her deep southern accent she said, "Good, you're awake. You need to get up and get ready because we need to register you in school today." How did she know I was awake? I hadn't moved. "We need to get going right now so, if you are hungry, just eat some toast." "I'm fine," I replied. "I'm not used to eating in the morning anyway." "Suit yourself," she responded. It was quite clear to me at that moment that the friendly face, the generous gestures and concern were just an emotion reserved for church or people they felt they needed to impress.

Sandra registered me for school but I didn't have to start until the next day. She introduced me to a family down the street explaining that they would be my transportation to and from school and, if we were good, then on Thursdays, we could stop for ice cream. That seemed nice and made me think this wouldn't be such a bad a place to stay." I tried to be good and stay out of trouble, but no matter how hard I tried, I kept hearing, "We don't do that, or we don't say that, in this house!" I found myself afraid to say or do anything. I became jumpy and was nervous all the time.

School was depressing. And, as was always the case, I didn't understand any of the work and I wasn't doing any good at making friends. I felt very withdrawn and didn't seem to have anything in common with any of the kids. They were all too good for me and better then I was. I was a loser; an outcast and I didn't fit in. I didn't belong anywhere.

I was going through withdrawals from cigarettes and marijuana and as if that wasn't bad enough, Sandra and the preacher felt that I needed to move and stay in a different part of the house. They didn't want me sleeping on the couch anymore, because I was taking away their living room. They made me a bedroom downstairs in an unfinished basement. In one half of the area, there was a pulpit and chairs. It was used for Bible study. In the other half of the space there was a bed, a lamp and dresser. In the day it was tolerable, but at night, it was very scary. It was so quiet down there because of the house rules. No radio, music or TV was allowed, unless it was religious At night I could see shadows moving across the walls. I could feel an energy around me. It felt cold and frightening. Occasionally when I just couldn't ignore it anymore, I would find my strength and be brave enough to speak out loud saying, "In the Name of Jesus Christ, I command all evil to leave this room and my mind, now!" I would feel a warmth come over me, and it made me feel safe enough to fall asleep. The energy always came back, though. It seemed to feed off of my fear, and it wasn't always easy to be brave.

It was almost Halloween and I made the mistake of mentioning that the sixth grade was going to have a dance in the auditorium. Sandra hit the roof! The next day, she took me to school and then she went to the office to make arrangements for me. When it came time for the dance, I was sent to the office. At first, I thought I was in trouble, but I really didn't remember doing anything bad. When I walked in the secretary's office, she told me to go take a seat until the dismissal bell rang. I was too afraid to say anything, so I just sat there until the bell rang. When I got home, Sandra asked me if I went to the dance. "No," I said, "For some reason I had to sit in the office." "Good!" she replied, "That's where you were supposed to be."

"Why, what did I do wrong?" I inquired.

"You didn't do anything wrong. In our family we follow the teachings of God. It is improper behavior to be listening to that type of music, and furthermore, boys and girls should not behave in such an ungodly, sinful manner. It's just what we believe in, and when you are staying in our home, you will follow our rules." She proceeded to lecture me on the do's and don'ts. "There will be no improper TV or music. There will be absolutely no dancing or going to the movies. No telling jokes, no makeup or nail polish, and no caffeine." I guess the rules didn't pertain to her, as she sat painting her nails and drinking coffee in the morning. I knew it wouldn't do any good to say anything, so I just stood there silently.

I tried to explain that I wasn't getting very good sleep in the basement, because I was scared down there by myself. Even though it was supposed to be a holy, religious atmosphere, it was creepy and filled with dark shadows. I explained that I called on the protection of Jesus, but still felt that unseen eyes were always watching me. Sandra and Allen both told me that I was being ridiculous, and that I was perfectly safe. All I needed to do was to pray and my fear would go away. I told them that I always prayed, that I believed in God, but I was still frightened at night and could not find a way to sleep. They completely dismissed my fears and just told me to deal with it. Sometimes at night, I would sneak up to the top of the stairs to sleep, or, if I was really scared, I would sneak all the way to the living room couch. I don't know why this made them so mad. I guess they thought I was trying to defy them. I really wasn't, I just couldn't stand to be alone. They wouldn't listen and just gave me direct orders not to come upstairs during the night. "You have to learn to deal with your fears." they would tell me.

I found a way to deal with them alright. Not wanting to lay down there in the basement, frozen in fear, I would sneak upstairs and right out of the house! I went down to the house of the neighbor, who would give me rides to school in the morning. I explained my situation to her and begged her not to tell on me. I was desperate. She just had to know how scared I was and that I wasn't making anything up. It wasn't about wanting to come over and play. I just wanted a warm safe place to sleep. She was very nice and seemed to understand. She made me a bed on the couch and then woke me up really early in the morning, before the sun came up. I would sneak back home, so no one would know I was gone. This only lasted for a week before the lady told me I couldn't keep doing it. "You need to face your fears and be honest with them." she suggested. I thought she understood. I couldn't understand how such religious, church-going, God fearing people could be so cruel. Talking to her did no good. I just remained afraid and dealt with my fear as best I could.

One Friday, after school, I was told that my dad was coming to take me to dinner. I was so excited to see him! I missed him so much and hoped that he would be telling me I could leave that place with him. I waited next to the window for what seemed like forever. When he finally pulled up, I jumped up and started for the door when Sandra stopped me and informed me that even though I was going to be with my father their rules still applied. I was to be back no later than ten o'clock. "Don't worry," I told her, "I'll tell my dad." I'll never forget the night we had. It was amazing! We went downtown, where it was big, busy, and beautiful. We walked into a restaurant called The Polynesian. I'd never seen anything like it! It had a huge salt-water aquarium, full of bright colored fish. The menu had exotic dishes, with one of my favorites, prawns. While we were waiting for our order, I told Dad about the rules of the house. I told him I had to be home by ten, or I would be in serious trouble. I also told him about my bed down in the basement... how I dreaded the nights and couldn't sleep, because I was so afraid. "These people aren't what they seem to be, Dad." I told him. "I miss you and I want to come home. I'll be good and not skip school, I promise. I just can't stand living where I am anymore."

The focus of the conversation suddenly changed when the lights started flickering off and on, and the sound of wind, rain, and thunder filled the room. The atmosphere was transformed into a Pacific storm. Somehow they made the restaurant appear as though there was rain on the windows and falling right outside the walls. When the thunder and rain stopped, Hawaiian music started to play and Tahitian dancers came out onto a stage and started dancing. It was all so exciting! As we watched the beautiful dancers put on their show, Dad announced, "I have been dating a woman that I want you to meet, and I have another surprise for you. How would you like to meet your half-sister?" he asked. My half-sister? I knew nothing about any other family members. I smiled and said, "Yes, please." "Great!" he replied, "Then I'll pick you up next weekend." I could hardly eat or pay attention to anything else he said, or what was happening around me. Wow, a potential new mom *and* a sister!

When I walked in the door, it was around eleven. Allen and Sandra were waiting up for me and they were angry. They had me sit at the table with them as they scolded me about ignoring their curfew. I tried to explain how magical my evening was and how wonderful it felt to spend time with my dad, but it meant nothing to them. They were harsh and cold. Soon I was crying hysterically and couldn't even lift my head up to look at them. It was the most amazing time I had ever had in my whole life with my dad, and they were ruining it by tearing me apart for being late. It wasn't like I was out with a stranger, but they let me know that wasn't the point. "You're disrespecting our rules and our home, and that means you're disrespecting God. Everything we do is based on how God wants us to live and we won't sacrifice our beliefs for anyone." I was so worried that they wouldn't let me leave with Dad to go meet my sister, that I stressed out about it all week. I never told them that my dad wanted me to go away with him, because I was too scared that they would forbid me from going.

When I got home from school on Friday I was relieved that Dad was there. I was already excited about seeing him, but even happier when he said that I wouldn't be returning. He instructed me to make sure I grabbed everything. Sandra had on her fake smile, acting out her church character, as she hugged me saying, "God bless you, thank you for being part of our home." It wasn't what I truly wanted to say, but I closed another chapter of my life by saying, "Thanks for your hospitality and allowing me into your home."

As we drove away, I felt a new sense of hope as Dad explained that we would be leaving for Denver the next day to visit his long lost daughter, Leslie, my half-sister. I was also told that we would be stopping in Mapleton, Utah, which was about an hour away from our home in West Valley City, Utah. We were going to pick up Dad's new girlfriend (and potential new mom for me), Sheryl, who would be traveling with us. When he told me that, it made me feel good about the trip, because it would take the fear and awkwardness out of being alone with him. My dad never did anything to me, but by now, deep down, I didn't trust any man.

We pulled up to a mobile home and I got into the back seat. I don't remember feeling excited as much as I felt curious. Would she be mean or loud or fake? This wasn't my first time to be introduced to a potential mother. Then they both walked out of the front door. She looked nothing like I imagined. She was very small in stature, probably around 5 feet tall, with short, tightly curled black hair. She was large breasted and seemed very proud of her figure. She constantly giggled and looked admirably at my dad.

It took us two days and a night to reach our destination. We actually stayed overnight in a motel. That was the first time that I can remember Dad didn't drive all the way through, only stopping for gas. All through the trip I would hear about Sheryl's seven daughters and how perfect most of them were. She seemed nice enough and was nothing like anyone I had ever been around. She said she didn't drink didn't like cigarettes, and she worked a full time job.

Dad was acting nothing like I was used to seeing. When he wanted to be, he could be the most charming man in the world. He was clearly on his best behavior. It was obvious that he wanted to impress her. Once when we were having dinner, he went to light a cigarette. She looked at him and said how much the smoke bothered her. He instantly put his cigarette out and announced that it would be the last cigarette he would ever smoke! Dad was 50 years old and in the eleven years I had been with him, he had always smoked. Right then and there, he quit cold turkey! There went my endless supply of cigarettes. Wow, I thought, maybe this would be a good thing. It seemed as though this may be a good match. Dad never bent or changed his ways for anyone before!

Denver was just as I remembered it, cold and snowy. We drove in circles for a while until we located the apartment where my half-sister lived. It was apparent that my dad was very excited. I don't know how long it had been since he had seen his daughter, but I knew this was important to him. When Leslie opened the door, she and my dad embraced and cried. It was very touching. I didn't know what to say or think. Then she came up to me and said, "So this is my little sister?" The she hugged me and it made me feel so happy. She had the biggest smile that I had ever seen. She was much taller than me, and I noticed that she had a limp. When we all sat down together, dad explained to me that Leslie was born too early and her knees and hips weren't joined properly, so they had to do surgery on her to correct it. She spent most of her early childhood in a body cast. She also mentioned her brothers. Brothers? Wow, I had brothers too? I was kind of blown away and wondered why Dad had never mentioned anything about her or her two brothers before.

I wanted to talk about my mother, but again, it was taboo to even bring her up. I wasn't allowed to ask or comment on any subject that wasn't already brought up by Dad. I was just a stupid kid that was expected to always use my manners, never embarrass my dad, and sit quietly unless asked a question. Most of my fear of my dad was instilled by the threats from Dolores, but I never knew if it was how Dad really wanted me to be. I didn't want to take the chance of making him not want to be with me.

As we sat visiting with Leslie, she told us how her whole life was upside down. Her boyfriend and she were fighting, she hated where she was living, and she felt so helpless. Dad came up with a grand idea! "Why don't you come and stay with us for a while, until you get back on your feet?" he asked her. "We can do some catching up, and it would be great for Lorina to have a big sister around." I couldn't believe it when she so easily agreed. Wow, a real half-blood sister! This was the best weekend that I could have ever asked for. We spent the night, and while we slept, Leslie stayed up packing. By morning, we were on our way home, to a real home this time. We loaded up the car and were on our way. Leslie and I snuggled up together in the back seat. I could tell we were going to get along great, and I felt a loving connection with her.

A Whole New Start

Chapter 32

Independence, the sweet taste of freedom.

When we got home back to West Valley City "SLC," there were a lot of adjustments to make. Leslie, who was eighteen years old, was living with us, and now Sheryl was living with us too. I felt myself starting to resent Sheryl when I would hear the stories about how she and Dad had such a wonderful time together while I was stuck in my own hell at Allen and Sandra's "the church people" house. They went to dances, clubbing, traveling, and even flew to Hawaii. I understand that Dad had to do something fun to heal the pain of his failed marriage to Dolores, but what about me? Again, I was unimportant and placed somewhere for safekeeping until Dad decided to have me around again. No matter what, I still loved him with all of my heart. He was my Daddy. Life with Leslie was beginning to get interesting and fun. She treated me like I mattered, and included me in her life. I shared my bedroom with her and she had all kinds of cool things that she shared with me, including cigarettes.

I was back in school and Leslie began waitressing at Bob's Big Boy down the road at the mall. This meant I now had a reason to walk to the mall. When she would get ready for work I would watch her put on makeup and she would talk to me about boys, life and partying. It was great! I had more independence than I ever had before. Dad and Sheryl were gone most of the time, and I guess Dad thought I was in good hands with Leslie. Boy he couldn't have been more wrong! Leslie loved to party and she was trying to heal from her broken relationship. She was allowed to come and go as she pleased, but I had a curfew. That was fine with me. For the first time in my life I got to come and go as I pleased too, as long as I stuck by the curfew rule. Even more importantly, I wasn't being sexually abused.

I was still going to school but my grades didn't matter. Dad never cared; he just wanted me to be accounted for so that he wouldn't get in trouble. I was in sixth grade now and couldn't have cared less about my education. My school days consisted entirely of avoiding fist fights and just making it through the day until I could get high with Evan, Randy and Amanda. Sometimes one of the boys would get some kind of illegal prescriptions like valium, cross tops, or beauties. At this point, I was up for anything. I had nothing to lose and didn't care if I lived or died. Sometimes I would freak my friends out by standing in the middle of the road playing chicken with cars. I always won because I had no fear of dying.

I wasn't studying the Bible anymore, and didn't care about the dark shadows that seemed to linger around and watch me. When I was alone, I would be frightened of the many noises in the mobile home. The cabinets would randomly open out of the blue. Because of my fear of these and other unexplainable things that would happen, I tried to have someone around or go to my friend's house as often as possible. My life was changing rapidly and it wasn't going in a good direction. God and Jesus still crossed my mind now and then, but I now was under the impression that because of my past actions, no matter what, I was going to hell, so what did any of it matter. Leslie came home late one night, woke me up and asked me if I wanted to go to a party. "I can't, I'm on curfew," I said. "Don't worry about that," she replied, and she showed me a trick that would work for me much more than once. She fixed the blankets and pillows to look like I was lying down and we snuck out my bedroom window. I felt so alive! It was snowy and cold and the roads were extremely slippery. I ran and slid, and acted like a kid, for once. But, I was off to go do adult things. We went to one of her friend's mobile homes. She started talking to a guy, then started making out with him on the couch. It wasn't very long before she disappeared into one of the rooms.

Music was playing loud; they were playing Chicago and Boston. There were probably fifteen to twenty people there. I went into the kitchen and joined in on the joints that were now being passed around. This was the best! I was having the time of my life! A couple of guys asked me if I wanted to do a shotgun. I had never heard of that before but I was up for anything, so I agreed. They showed me how to do it and then assisted me in doing it. They stabbed a hole in the bottom of a beer can, put the top by my mouth then popped the top. The beer shot into my mouth very quickly until the can was empty. How cool is this? I thought. We started racing each other to see who could drink the fastest. Before I knew it, I was trashed! I needed to get some air. Once outside, I puked my guts out, and fell over into the snow. I couldn't move. The whole world was spinning and I couldn't even stand up, let alone walk. Normally I couldn't stand the cold but right about now it was just what I needed. A couple of guys came out to check on me and tried to bring me in but I refused telling them to leave me there and I'd be in after a while. The next thing I knew, Leslie was standing over me trying to wake me up. I didn't care what she said or did; I wasn't going to budge from that spot! She went and got a guy friend to help her to walk "mostly carry" me home.

She kept trying to get me to act normal but it was impossible. It was even more difficult because the roads were so icy. The real task was getting me through the window. Once I was in, I didn't move from the same position until I was being wakened up to go to school. I could hear Leslie lying to Dad, telling him that I was sick and that she was taking care of me while I was up throwing up in the night. He bought it all. She was good!

Leslie was great, or so I thought from my young perspective. She taught me what to say to get by at a party, how to put on makeup, and to grow up in a different way than I had ever experienced. She was really into boys and relationships, but I didn't want to put any energy into anything that might involve sex. Here and there I would have meaningless boyfriends, but it would never go any further than kissing. All of my time now consisted of hanging out with Amanda, getting stoned as much as possible, and sneaking out at night with Leslie. Trust me; I learned my lesson that first night out with her. I never drank that much again! I learned from all my earlier experiences, and finally that night, that alcohol wasn't my drug of choice.

I kept attending school and hating it,. I hated the girls, that went to school too. Sheryl worked far away so she was gone all day, and Dad was back on his crazy non-stop work schedule. Everything seemed to be pretty normal, but that was all about to change. It was December, and the only Christmas season when Dad ever bought a tree in the middle of the month. And this was no Charlie Brown tree! It was a white-flocked tree with blue lights; It was just beautiful! Other than the tree though, it didn't feel festive. The most exciting thing that I did was to go to the mall with Leslie. Everything there was so beautiful; decorated in lights, tinsel, ornaments. And the music too. It was magical but for everyone else but me. I couldn't afford to get anything for anyone except a picture I took sitting on Santa's lap to give to my dad for a present. There weren't many presents under our tree, but it didn't matter to me. I was perfectly fine with hanging out with my friends and playing with their gifts.

Sadly, Dad's interest in Sheryl seemed to be dwindling. She wasn't handling it well and took it out on me. She showed signs of insecurity and resentment by commenting on how men would stare at her when she pumped gas or that men would approach her at the grocery store and ask her out. That was followed by how lonely she was because she left her hometown to be with my dad, and how she gave up everything for him. She would say that I needed to stop hanging out with my friends and spend more time at the house. Then she would say how much more mature, smarter, and fun her daughters were to be around. Next, she would start talking crap about my Leslie; how she didn't pay rent and how she was a bad influence and that she needed to do something with her life. The more she talked, the more I pulled away from her. There were even times when she talked about her own daughters actually letting it slip that she didn't get along with a couple of them. I thought to myself, if she can talk crap about her own kids and constantly gossip about everyone and everything, I wonder what she is saying about me?

No wonder Dad started to pull away from Sheryl. Leslie started to pull away too. It became clear that there was no love lost between them. Sheryl must have complained so much about Leslie, that Dad had to have a discussion with her. Then the bombshell was dropped! Leslie would be moving to Texas with her mother after the holidays. I felt rage flow through my veins. This was all Sheryl's fault! I tried to talk Leslie into staying. Even though she was gone a lot, I somehow knew she was holding me together. It was too late; she had made up her mind not to fight it.

For the next couple of days, Leslie filled my head with many stories about Dad and his relationship with her mom. They were all ugly and included alcohol-induced, violent rages that ended in physical abuse, including miscarriages. His uncontrollable jealous fits would end in him beating her mother. This is one of the reasons Leslie was born so early. I wish I could have said that I didn't believe her, but I had witnessed the same type of behavior throughout my past when he would come home drunk and have violent fights with Dolores.

As always, Christmas and New Year's had come and gone much too quickly. I cried when the day came for Leslie to leave. She had taught me so much, and I loved her with all my heart. Dad drove her to the airport. There was no exchange of phone numbers or addresses, just faces covered in tears and a simple wave good-bye. That would be the last time I would ever see her. I didn't sneak out to party anymore. Sometimes I would sneak out to be with my friends, or sneak a friend in, but the late night partying was over.

My inner energy was shifting again, and I decided to start going to the Mormon Church with my friend Amanda. That meant I got to have my Tuesday nights and Sunday's with her and Sheryl couldn't complain about it. After all she was Mormon! My dad was not; he was Christian, so they just didn't do anything "religious" together. Home life slowly deteriorated. Dad stopped coming home some nights, spending more time working. Such a familiar pattern. Sheryl and I couldn't really stand the sight of each other anymore, so we tried our best to avoid each other.

I really have no idea how it all started, and afterward I felt kind of bad, but it did start, and I couldn't stop it. I came home from school one day, and Sheryl was sitting on the couch listening to her favorite Kenny Rogers albums. I don't know why, but I went over and sat next to her on the couch and one thing led to another. Maybe I thought it would bring us closer if I sat and talked with her. Without even thinking it might not be the best thing, I started talking to her about Dad. I guess I assumed Dad had told her everything about his past. Boy was I wrong! I didn't tell her about the violence, or Danny, just about Dad's previous wives and how many there were. I really thought I was doing her a favor trying to tell her how much nicer she was then Dolores. I told her that she was wife number eight and gave her a brief description on what I knew about each of them. And I told her about my memories of Tommie. She obviously had to know that he was married to Leslie's mom, my mom, and his last wife. Well, that was not the case. She didn't know about any of it. She thought she was only wife number four. I had no way of knowing the big trouble I was about to be in, for spilling the beans!

When Dad got home she didn't waste any time in confronting him, "Am I your eighth wife, Del?" she asked. He just stood there looking like a deer caught in the headlights. I felt like the lowest piece of dirt on the planet when he looked at me. He didn't say anything and just went into his bedroom. Sheryl followed right behind him. I went into my room, with thoughts swirling through my mind. Why did I even say anything at all? I felt bad for Dad, but now maybe Sheryl would leave. But if she left, would I have to go somewhere else? Maybe there is someplace worse than here? My mind jumped rapidly thinking of the possibilities, none of which were good. It was too late. What was done was done; I couldn't take anything back. Time seemed to go by slowly before I finally heard the front door slam. I walked out into the living room and watched dad's truck leave the driveway. Out came Sheryl. She had a confused yet smug look on her face as she said that my dad confirmed what she thought all along. I was lying. He said he had never known a woman named Tommie and that she was wife number four. Furthermore, I should be ashamed of myself for trying to make trouble by creating such hurtful lies. I didn't respond; I just went into my bedroom and didn't come back out that evening. Why didn't Dad tell her the truth? How could he make me out to be a liar and the bad guy?

The days and weeks to follow only got worse in every way. I couldn't understand what my problem was, why couldn't I get along with Sheryl? Compared to my life before, this was a dream come true kind of life for me. It was what I had always wished for! I wasn't being molested or tortured. Even though Sheryl constantly complained and reminded me of how much better her daughters were than me, she didn't call me names or demean me like Dolores did. She didn't need to. I knew who and what I was. It was brainwashed into me for as long as I could remember. I was stupid, ugly, and worthless. Why couldn't I just be good? Even Sheryl's daughter, who was now regularly visiting on the weekends would tell me, "Mom will get you whatever you want and be nice to you, if you just treat her nice and do what she wants." I couldn't though. I was angry and full of hate, not only for her but also for myself. I didn't want love from her or anybody! I still wanted to die. The world made no sense to me! The only real thing that kept me alive now was the fear of burning in hell for committing suicide.

As if things weren't bad enough, I was now being bullied in school. It all started with one girl; the popular, big breasted, big mouth, promiscuous, two-faced girl known as Dottie. One day she would be my friend and the next day she would be confronting me in the bathroom with scissors, ready to fight. It then became a daily ritual. I had to watch my back no matter where I was. Other girls were afraid of her too, so to stay on her good side, the other girls would pick on me too. I never cried, walked away, or told on them. I fought! Fortunately, the lookouts always stopped the fight before we got busted. I still ended up with black eyes and random cuts on my body but no one ever asked what happened to me, probably because I was so accident prone. It stopped just being at recess. It was happening right in the classroom and the teacher didn't have a clue. I would be sitting at my desk when Dottie, or another girl seeking Dottie's approval, would walk up behind me and punch me in the back of the head. I wasn't afraid of the pain so much as the humiliation. The bullying and fighting was a no win battle, because if you beat up one girl, there was always another behind her that you would have to fight. They were ruthless!!

I tried to buy Dottie's friendship so that she would leave me alone. The trade or occasional bribes only worked for a little while. But during the short time Dottie was nice to me, she would pick on and bully other girls. It wouldn't be long before I was the prime target for her and her trouble-making group again. I did something that I have never been proud of even to this day. And when I had the chance, I never came clean about it. So I'm going to come clean now. Sheryl had some nice things and sometimes I would snoop through her dresser drawers. She had this wonderful bracelet from her last marriage. It was turquoise and silver. When I saw it, I thought it would be a great peacemaker between Dottie and me, so I stole it. I showed it to Dottie and told her I would trade it for her jacket, an old, beat up, sleeveless vest jacket. It worked, she took it. I knew it was wrong, but at the time, I didn't care about Sheryl's feelings at all. She had so many wonderful things and I didn't have anything new or nice. To make matters worse, some of those new things were gifts from my dad. He never bought me anything. Yes, he paid for my food and put a roof over my head and I did appreciate it, but that was it. Except for the Zebco fishing reel, he never bought me any other gift. Everything I had was given to me as a hand-me-down.

My life was a new kind of hell. I was in daily fear, desperate, but telling wasn't an option. My mind raced, searching for ways out of my situation. I came up with a temporary solution. Instead of going to school I would go out the front door and sneak back in my bedroom window and stay in my closet until it was time for school to get out. Normally, Sheryl would go to work before I left for school but I guess she was either on vacation or was laid off at this time, and stayed home all day. It didn't matter I would rather stay in a stuffy closet all day then go through another day of school.

I woke up one morning feeling as though I needed a break from the closet so I told Sheryl I was too sick to go to school and she let me stay home. I went in my room and read and slept throughout the day. This was much more comfortable than hiding out in the closet. Around the time when school let out, there was a knock at the door. I thought it might be Amanda, but I was wrong. It was a pack of girls, the "bullies," there to find out why I hadn't been in school. There were six of them. Sheryl answered the door and told them I couldn't come out because I was sick. It was clear, by their cockiness and body language, that they had no plans to leave. One of the bigger, older girls, whom I had never seen before, was obviously a new recruit of Dottie's. She was wearing the bracelet that I stole from Sheryl. I wedged my way into the doorway to distract Sheryl, hoping I could get them to leave before she saw the bracelet. They were acting up and starting to threaten Sheryl. She could tell by their tone, and what they were saying, that they weren't there to play. My mind was swirling. I was afraid that they would start trying to fight both of us. I could hardly believe it, but Sheryl was trying to stick up for me. No one had ever done that before. She told them if they didn't leave she would call the cops. I just wanted them to leave before anything bad happened or Sheryl saw that bracelet, so I quickly said that I would be in school the next day and we could talk and settle everything then. Sheryl reminded them that if they ever came back, she would call the cops. I don't know why I didn't come clean at that moment and tell her what I had been going through at school. I guess I was embarrassed and didn't want to seem like a baby. After they left, she asked why they were there and what they meant by saying I hadn't been in school. I gave her simple meaningless answers trying to avoid what I knew I would soon have to face.

From that time on, I looked at her in a little different light. It felt good to have someone act like they cared, but I was still too consumed in my own jealousy to make a connection with her. Later in my life, I wished I had made the effort. When the next day came, I had no choice but to face the music and go to school. Every day that I went to school, I had to fight. I hated my home life and even worse, I hated school. The teachers or principal couldn't have cared less about what was happening to me, because I already had the label of being a slacker. I guess they figured I didn't care about my education, so why should they put any effort into helping me with anything.

Sheryl finally discovered that her bracelet was missing. When she confronted me about it, I acted calm, cool and collected and acted really hurt that she would even think that it was me. She told me how special and expensive it was, saying that her ex-husband had given it to her, and that she loved it. Quick on my feet and ready to cover my tracks, I blamed it on my sister, Leslie. "Maybe Leslie took it; maybe she was mad for feeling so unwelcome while she was here." I said. I had no idea that they had Leslie's phone number and she and Dad had already called her asking about it. When Dad and Sheryl confronted me about it again, saying that they had called Leslie, and she didn't know what they were talking about, I still didn't crack. This would be something that would bother me most of my life. Even after all of these years that have gone by, I still feel bad for taking something away from her that she thought was so special, for blaming Leslie, and for never telling her the truth about what I had done.

Time seemed to crawl by, and no one was happier to see summer come than me. I'd survived the horrible year of school and the constant fighting and bullying that came with it. By now Dad and Sheryl were not the happy couple that they used to be, and Sheryl was really suffering from loneliness. They agreed it would be better if Sheryl's daughter, Lindsey, would come and live with us for the summer. I had mixed feelings about it, because it meant I would have to share my room. Dad bought a bunk bed and I had to move everything around to make space for her. I tried to be optimistic about her arrival. "Who knows," I would tell myself, "maybe we would get to be good friends." She was older than I, but so was my sister Leslie, and we got along great. I was almost thirteen and she was sixteen. That was a good combination, I thought.

When she arrived, I found myself feeling more excited than angry, and welcomed her with open arms. But then my feelings on the inside turned to jealousy. I felt inferior to her. She was everything I wasn't. She was beautiful with perfect white teeth. I was never taught about the importance of healthy teeth, let alone a healthy smile and I never even owned a toothbrush since my foster home in Salida. Lindsey's hair was jet black, shiny, and always fell perfectly into place. Her clothes were new and nice and accentuated her body. She was perfectly proportioned, including her breasts. I was basically flat-chested and was teased about it well into my teen years. Even though I was still a little girl, I never viewed myself as one. I had been exposed to sex and sexual judgment most of my life. I was quite aware of my physical body, as well as others'. Maybe my view of what a woman was judged on, was formed by the drunken crying nights that Dolores made me touch her breasts, asking me what was wrong with her.? I would be thirteen in two weeks and knew more about sex than most would know in their adulthood; unfortunately it was a very warped, unhealthy knowledge.

Lindsey was very popular where she was raised and when she moved in with us, she complained about being bored, and wanted to go back home. It was easy for her to find someone to stay with back home, because she had six sisters. She didn't stay home much, but her things did, and I took total advantage of it. I knew it was wrong to wear her clothes and most of them didn't fit me, but I did anyway. I tried so hard to be careful with her things, but I was such an accident-prone tomboy, that when I would crash on my skateboard, I'd tear her skirts. I ruined the bottom of her pants, and practically everything I borrowed. In a way I didn't feel bad, because it seemed to me as though she had an endless supply.

When my thirteenth birthday came I was invited to go to Provo, Utah to spend some time with some of Sheryl's daughters. While there, I got a permanent in my hair, went roller skating, laid out in the sun (my favorite thing to do), and went to a street party. I did have some fun, it was great to feel included; but I never felt like I fit in. They were all very social, smart, and beautiful. I was just this nasty, scrawny, ugly, leach, known as "Del's daughter." It was good to get back home, where I didn't feel as though I was being judged. Hell, I was basically invisible, which was okay with me.

Much to my surprise this was going to be one of my greatest summers. Dad and Sheryl weren't getting along, so she wasn't home much. Dad was a workaholic, so he wasn't home much either. Lindsey rarely made an appearance at our house. It was great! I had more freedom than I had ever had in my life. I spent most of my time with Amanda, and was going to the Mormon Church full time. Amanda and I would go to the pool, hang out and get stoned, or we would go to the mall. When we weren't babysitting her brothers we would ride bikes down to the mall, pay for a movie and sneak into other movies after the first movie was over. I was even preparing to go on a church field trip to California, to Disneyland and other tourist attractions in L.A. and in San Diego. Amanda and I did everything we could to earn money for the field trip to California. We cleaned up yards, washed cars, and made arts and crafts from materials supplied by the church, selling them around the trailer park.

The California trip was the most amazing, wonderful time I had ever had in my life! I loved the warmth and the palm trees. The energy that California offered was so different from Utah. The people seemed to be much more friendly, happy, and healthy. The ocean was beautiful and smelled like freedom mixed with excitement. The only large bodies of water that I had been around until that point were serene lakes. The difference was that the ocean made me feel alive. I was, in a sense, free. No sexual abuse, no verbal abuse, no real restrictions. I actually got to experience a taste of life as a normal kid. With the exception of my constant nightmares, poor self-image, and bouts of anger tantrums, this was the best summer of my life. I swore to myself that I would come back again one day.

Sadly that was all about to come to an end. Summer was winding down and everyone, but me, was filled with back to school excitement, getting new clothes, buying school supplies, and preparing to connect with friends again. As usual, I was not looking forward to going to school. Now I was going into Jr. High and the school was further away from my house. I was petrified! I didn't like being around large groups of people, or any groups for that matter. I already had a complex, and felt that when I walked into a room, everyone would stare at me because I was so ugly and stupid. Wherever I went, I would try to be invisible.

Lindsey decided she was going to move back to her old stomping grounds to go to school. I overheard her talking to Sheryl and complaining that her dad only gave her two hundred dollars to buy school clothes. I could hardly believe my ears. I never got new clothes or shopping money for anything. Sheryl comforted her by letting her know she would do what she could to get her more money. I walked in and said, "I need new clothes too!" Everything I had was worn out or too small, and were old hand me-downs from friends, or things that I got from the thrift store, where Dolores had worked. Sheryl responded by telling me that I should ask my dad, that I was his responsibility. Well, that ended that discussion. I waited for him to get home and nervously asked him for school clothes money. I very rarely asked Dad for anything, I always felt so unimportant and undeserving. I had worked all day on how I would approach him. I even tried to work on my body language. Dad was never an easy person to ask anything of. First, he would ignore me, even though I knew that he knew I was talking to him, then I would ask again, and he would always lash out saying, "What...? What in the hell do you want?" This time I said, "Lindsey's dad is giving her money to go buy school clothes. So that reminded me that maybe this would be a good time for me to get some clothes for school too." I was shocked when he reached into his pocket and pulled out fifty dollars and handed it to me saying, "Don't spend it all at once." I was stunned, but so grateful! Even though my feelings were hurt that I didn't get more, my happiness of him giving me anything at all, outweighed my desire to barter or ask for more.

Amanda and I had planned our day at the mall because her parents had given her school shopping money too. She told me that one of her friends, Amy, wanted to hang out with us and would be meeting us there. Once we got there and met up with Amy, we went around to a couple of different stores. Quickly it became clear that fifty dollars wasn't going to buy much. I was so bummed, until Amy came up with this great solution! It turned out that she knew how to get anything she wanted and was willing to share her secrets with me. Her famous words were, "Watch and learn," she said, and that's just what I did. She picked out some things she wanted and some things she didn't want. She put the things she wanted under some bigger shirts, so it didn't look like there were as many clothes as there really were. We went into the dressing room and she put the hidden clothes on under her own clothes. When she went back out of the dressing room she gave the ones she didn't want to the sales lady. Wow! I couldn't believe it! It seemed too easy, but it did work. Needless to say, a new bad habit was formed. I didn't get any pants but I was good with underclothes and shirts. When I went home with all of my things, I made sure that all of the tags were removed first. Sheryl asked how I got so many clothes and I just told her that my new friend Amy cleaned out her closet. She was okay with that answer, and so was I.

Suicide Pact

Chapter 34

We were going to give each other the strength to end our pain.

Lindsey moved back to her old home, and soon things in our home were getting worse and falling apart. Sheryl was fighting with dad and taking it out on me. Dad was back on his work-all-day and play his sax all-night at the bar routine. I seemed to get into trouble for everything. Some things I should have been in trouble for, but other things were ridiculous. It was clear that Sheryl just needed someone to punish. I had started school and it seemed to be a little bit better as far as being bullied, but the work was impossible for me to follow. I started leaving the school and just walking aimlessly around neighborhoods until, one day, a policeman pulled over, put me in the car and took me back to school. I was written up for truancy. That didn't go over well with dad. He made it clear that if I didn't give a shit about my education that was my problem, but he wasn't going to get in trouble for me not being in school.

Sheryl started traveling to Provo or Mapleton as often as she could. That left me with even more freedom on the weekends. Amanda and I were still into our same routine going to church on Tuesdays and Sundays, smoking, listening to music and getting high when we could. One of our secret things we loved to do was play with our Barbie dolls. We never told anyone, because we were obviously too old to be playing with dolls. I think we enjoyed the fantasy part of it. When we were pretending to be the dolls, we were beautiful, successful, popular, and invincible; basically everything opposite of what we saw and thought of ourselves. Sometimes we would talk her stepdad into taking her brothers and us down town to sneak into the hotels and swim in the heated swimming pools. That was really fun. She truly was my best friend and we had a lot in common as far as our home life, and our likes and dislikes. We used to always say we would run away together, but we never did.

Knowing that my parents rarely came home on the weekends we would ask her parents if she could spend the night at my house. We would stay up late, listening to music and playing board games.

One night, we decided to play Monopoly and listen to music all night. Around two or three in the morning, we were startled by the front door opening. It was Dad and he was hammered. We were in the kitchen playing our game when he walked over and started to talk to us. He could barely stand up straight. Wobbling around, he started talking to us about pointless things, trying to crack jokes and be funny. At first it was kind of comical, but then he walked over by Amanda and his arm kept bumping and rubbing into her breast. Amanda was now fifteen and had more of a full figure because of her weight. It was clear, by the look on her face, that his actions were making her uncomfortable, so I quickly sprang into action saying, "Wow, it's so late! We have church tomorrow so we need to get to bed." Following my queue, she instantly made a bee line for my bedroom with me right behind her. We just left Dad standing alone in the kitchen. We didn't even put the game away. Once we got into the room, as quickly and quietly as possible, we pushed the dresser and bunk bed up against the door so Dad wouldn't be able to open it.

We sat silently in the dark and just listened. Finally we heard his footsteps go down the hallway and his bedroom door shut. What we did next would physically affect me the rest of my life. There in the dark, we began to feed off of each other's misery, although I never did discuss my past concerning sexual abuse. It was too embarrassing, shameful, and disgusting to share. We decided to make a suicide pact, agreeing that we would take as many pills as we could find. For me, it was a way to end the nightmares and images of Danny flashing through my mind. I couldn't see much of a future for myself. I know that as far as Amanda was concerned, she hated her home life, wasn't very popular in school either, felt like a built-in babysitter and unappreciated for anything she did, and she had felt abandoned like me too.

So that was it, we were going to give each other the strength to finally end all of our pain and feelings of worthlessness. We moved the furniture away from the door, feeling safe to do so because we could hear Dad's loud snoring echo throughout the house. I searched the medicine cabinet in the kitchen and all I could find was a bottle of aspirin. It was a full bottle that contained five hundred tablets. I went to the medicine cabinet in my bathroom and found some birth control packs that Leslie had left behind. I knew we would find the stronger pills in my dad's bathroom, but neither one of us were willing to risk waking him up. Sitting in the dimly lit living room, each of us with a glass of water, we filled up our hand with pills and dumped them into our mouths. We gagged down handful after handful, until the bottle was empty and all of the birth control pills were popped out of their foil covered case. Looking at each other, we were waiting for something to happen. Now what? We decided to go lay down in my room. In the dark, we talked about how our parents' reactions might be when they found us and how the kids at school would feel. We both agreed that they would probably all be happy and that the world would be a much better place without us. We both started to feel really sick. Amanda wanted to go home because she felt as though she was going to throw up and would feel better being in her own bed. I didn't feel very good either and decided to just stay in my own bed.

The next day came and we both were still alive. At one point, when I went into the living room in the afternoon, to my surprise Sheryl was home. "You missed church," she said. I can't even put into words to describe what I felt. It was like someone had turned up the volume in my head so loud that I couldn't stand it. Her voice pierced though my ears and was like a sledgehammer pounding on my brain. All of the noises were amplified a thousand times. I quickly went back to my bedroom and couldn't move. I stayed there, unable to eat, drink, or do anything that made any kind of noise.

Neither of us went to school on Monday or Tuesday. Amanda finally called later in the afternoon on Tuesday and asked if I wanted to go to church. I was well enough to talk on the phone so I thought it would be a good idea to give church a try. Surprisingly even though I hadn't attended school in the last two days, Sheryl didn't give me too much of a hard time for going. She did, however, make it quite clear that if I felt good enough to go to church that I would be attending school the next day. I'll never forget how strange that whole experience was. When we walked to the church, we didn't share many of our thoughts; we didn't need to. Obviously we were both suffering. As we talked, we learned we had experienced the same exact things, how our hearing, equilibrium, appetite, and energy were so affected that we both just slept for most of the days that had followed our failed suicide attempt.

It was fall and the leaves were changing colors; there was a nip in the air. Class started around five and we arrived about fifteen minutes early. We were both so unbelievably tired. Before we went into the church we both wanted to lay on the grass and rest. We laid down in the churchyard next to a big tree and before I knew it, I fell into a deep sleep. The next thing I knew Amanda was trying to wake me. I could hardly believe my eyes, the moon was peeking between the clouds and the wind was blowing hard. Leaves were blowing all around. It felt very eerie and it seemed really late. The church parking lot was empty and the only lights that were on were the big lights in the parking lot. We had slept through class and had no idea what time it was. We felt an urgency to get home to avoid being in trouble. As we got close to our homes, Amanda went her way and I went mine. Even though I was late, I was never questioned, maybe because it was apparent that I didn't feel well.

It took days for the intense sensitive hearing to fade. The best description I can give for how bad it was, is that if someone were to eat a potato chip it would sound like the walls were crashing down. Even the noise of someone eating a banana was loud. Any truly loud or annoying noises were unbearable. That sensation has remained for most of my life. We quickly discovered during our trips with Amanda's dad and brothers to the hotel swimming pools downtown, that we could no longer swim very deep down into the water because of the pain we felt in our ears. I don't know what trying to overdose on aspirin did medically to our hearing but it would be an experience that I would never forget.

With our plan to end our lives being a failure, our big dreams turned to running away from home. We talked about making our plan of escape. At the mall, we would pick out furniture at the Sears showroom fantasizing about what our home would look like. We would make ourselves comfortable in the beautiful plush sofas and recliners and daydream about what our jobs would be and where we would live. We both agreed that California or Hawaii was where we wanted to live, but neither of us could come up with our dream job. That was okay; it was fun, and gave us something to dream about and look forward to.

One day when I was walking home from Amanda's house, there was a lady out in her yard that called me over. I had seen her, and her husband, several times because their trailer was only five trailers away from ours, and positioned in the middle of the path I took to get to and from Amanda's. The lady's name was Paula and her husband's was Tim. They had a three-year-old daughter named Kelly. I was so excited when I found out that she wanted to offer me a job. She had to leave for work early and Tim worked graveyards and didn't get home until two hours after she needed to leave. This sounded great. I could babysit for two hours and still make it on time for school. All I needed to do was get a signed paper from my parents to prove to them that they approved. I had to wait for Dad to sign it because at this point Sheryl wouldn't do anything for me. We couldn't stand the sight of each other, let alone have any kind of discussions.

Once I got the paper signed, I didn't waste any time running it over to Paula and Tim. Their daughter Kelly was clearly excited too, because she climbed all over me, squealing and hugging me. I was to start on the following Monday, so we started going over all of the rules and what my job would entail. This was so wonderful! I had my first official job, at thirteen years old. I felt it was a big step towards Amanda's and my dream of moving out. Amanda and I became friends with Paula, and would hang out at her house. She loved having us there, and would talk to us for hours, sharing stories of her high school years. She shared fond memories of boyfriends and stories of fights with other girls, going to dances, and in her words, being a bad ass. She even had all of her high school yearbooks. Even though Paula was only in her mid-twenties, Amanda and I couldn't stop giggling about the hairdos and funny glasses. The styles were straight from one of our favorite movies, Grease.

I enjoyed babysitting little Kelly. By the time Tim got home, their house was cleaned, and Kelly was fed and dressed. I also liked that I had an adult woman to talk to about Sheryl, and ask for advice on how to deal with her. My home life was getting increasingly worse. Sheryl was more resentful of me than ever, because I had new friend and she was stuck at home, lonely, with Dad either not coming home or ignoring her when he did. It was impossible for me to feel sorry for her, because all she did was yell at me.

Amanda's home life wasn't going much better either. One day after school, she came knocking at the door. When I let her in, she noticed I was there by myself and totally came unglued. "Let's go right now!" she yelled. "I hate my stepdad. I'm tired of being treated unfairly and like a slave!" Let's go now; let's run away! I just stood there and didn't know what to say. "Are you afraid?" she asked. "No, I'm not afraid. My life sucks too." I answered. "I just don't want to lose my job. Are you sure this is what you want to do?" I asked her. She looked at me with pure rage. As she stomped out, she said, "I knew you were full of shit! You're just a big chicken!" I didn't know what to do. I just sat down and waited until I thought she was home and then called to assure her I would stick by her. She calmed down and said we would need to come up with some kind of plan first. I asked her to come back over and we would work out the details. I waited around until late, but she never showed. I didn't see her again until later the next day. Strangely, all was well in her world. She changed her mind, saying her parents apologized and gave her money they owed her for babysitting. And, that was that. Life for me was tolerable at that time, but within the next two months it would turn upside down.

It was December and Dad wanted to make it official with Sheryl, so a winter wedding was planned. It was probably a step he had to take in order to keep her from leaving. It was a good plan, because it worked. Soon she was back to being bubbly again, and Dad was back to showing his face at home and acting involved. Adults made no sense to me! A week ago everything seemed to be in complete destruction mode and now there was a wedding being planned. The wedding was in Provo, at one of Sheryl's family member's home. It went off without a hitch and they really seemed to be happy.

Within a week of getting home, Dad and Sheryl picked out a flocked tree and decorated it. I didn't want to be part of any of it. I avoided being at home as much as possible, spending time with my friends. Because I was working, this year I could finally give them gifts. My most treasured gifts came from them. My favorite was a blue fluffy pair of house slippers from Randy. I loved them, and practically lived in them. Dad actually gave me a jewelry box with my name painted on it. It would have been great except that I hated my name. I hated the look and sound of my name. I hated me!

An escape to freedom or the road straight to hell? 1980

The only good thing about the holidays was that there was no school. New Years' was over and school was going to begin the following Monday. It was Friday, and I wanted to hang out with Amanda. She went to visit family out-of-town the day before, and I was waiting for her phone call. I had just gotten home from hanging out with my other friends, Randy and Evan, and needed to wash my hair. Sheryl and I were fighting, an everyday occurrence now. It seemed that ever since she and Dad got married, she became bossier and less tolerant of me, and of my behavior. As I was washing my hair, I heard the phone ring. I quickly rinsed out the shampoo, threw a towel on my head and walked over to check if the answering machine picked up the call. Sheryl walked into the room and I asked her if the phone call was for me. Instantly she snapped at me, "Isn't it always for you? I don't get any phone calls. Who the hell do you think it is for?"

"Why do you always have to be such a bitch?" I replied. This was the first time I had ever snapped and spoken to her that way, and called her a name. This sent her into a rage and she slapped me across my face, leaving a big red handprint across my cheek. I was stunned! I threw on my fluffy blue slippers and a coat and stormed out of the house.

I ran straight to Amanda's and told her I couldn't take it anymore! I was not going back! I asked her if she was ready to run away, plans or no plans. She said that things were going good for her right now so she didn't want to mess it up. She suggested that we should talk to our parents about me moving into her house. That sounded great, but I didn't think her parents would go for it since they had such limited space in their home and were always commenting on their financial status not being very good. It was worth a try though, so we approached her stepdad. I explained the situation I was in to him. It was easy for him to feel sorry for me, because of the outline of the big red handprint was still on my cheek. I assured him that all of the money I would receive from babysitting would go towards my living expenses. He actually seemed as if he would consider it and said that he would have to talk with Amanda's mom, Claire, first. In the meantime he agreed to give me a ride to Dad's workshop to talk to him about what happened. When I arrived, Dad was hard at work. I had not seen him for the last three days. Lately, he seemed to always have these big sign jobs that would keep him away from home more than usual. This wasn't anything new to me though, because it was an ongoing pattern throughout my life.

With tear stained cheeks, I told Dad that I just couldn't take it anymore. Sheryl was always on my case, and now she was becoming physical. I told him that I knew it wouldn't be right to hit her back but if I stayed, I was afraid that I would get to a point where I wouldn't be able to control myself, and I would fight her. I assured him that I loved him and that wouldn't change, but I needed to be in a different home. I asked him if he would let me move to Amanda's house. To my surprise he said that he couldn't take the constant complaining and bickering either, and that was why he stayed at the shop. Then he made light of it, and told me to just hang in there. He told me that I could not leave and that he would work on making things better. I was crushed, but my mind was made up! I would never go back! I looked him dead in the eyes and as carefully and respectfully as possible said. "It's either her or me. Who would you rather have?" He just looked at me like I had lost my mind. He simply said, "Just go home, everything will work itself out." I was completely devastated! That was it for me, not only did I not want to be around Sheryl, but I no longer had any respect for him. Why was I surprised? He never made the effort to ever protect me throughout my life so far, why would he now?

I went back to Amanda's house to make a plan. I was truthful with Phil and Claire about what my dad had said and they agreed that it wouldn't be a good idea for me to stay there. My option was gone. What can I do? My mind raced. There was no way I was going back home. Now that Sheryl had won, things would only be worse. I would be stuck with her knowing that she could control me and hit me. I dealt with that all of my life and I was not going to go through it with another woman!

I sat in Amanda's room brainstorming when I finally came up with a solution. I need to find Karl and Renee's phone number! That's where I'll go. I love being with them and I know they love me. Surely they would take me in. A surge of relief flowed through my mind. Instantly I went to the phone to dial information. It didn't take very long for me to find their number. I asked Phil if I could make the long distance call, and he said it was okay.

When I called, it was obvious that Karl was surprised to hear me on the other end. I filled him in on what was going on and he said it wouldn't be a problem for me to stay with them, but they didn't have the money or means to get me there. I told him I would work on it, and I thanked him profusely for agreeing to let me stay with them. When I got off of the phone, I was so excited! I asked Amanda to go with me to talk to Paula and Tim, so I could tell them that I needed my babysitting money, and ask if Amanda could take over for me in my absence. When we got there, only Paula was there. I told her the whole story about Sheryl slapping me earlier and explained how we hadn't been getting along for a very long time. She said that she understood but wouldn't be able to give me any money until the following Friday. I told her I could babysit for her that week but I would be leaving that weekend. She said that she would have my money then.

Now I had a plan, but I had to lay low for a week. Amanda's parents said I couldn't stay at her house because they didn't want any trouble, so Amanda let me sneak in late at night. I squeezed between the bed and the wall so her parents wouldn't see me, and in the morning, I would get up before everyone else, and go to Paula's to babysit. It worked out pretty good except that it was freezing. Their mobile home wasn't very well insulated and it was stormy off and on throughout the week with snow on the ground. There were times in the week that I wanted to sneak into my house to get some things but Sheryl was always there. Surprisingly Dad and Sheryl weren't really looking for me. They never knocked on anyone's door but I did hear that when my dad would pass by any of my friends on the street he would ask if they knew where I was. It had been six days since I spoke to my dad. I was afraid of facing him at all.

Friday was finally here. Now I needed to figure out the last of my plan. I had to wait for Paula to get home in the evening to get my money. Then I would be able to catch the bus downtown to get a Greyhound ticket to Karl and Renee in Thompson, Utah. Amanda had to go out with her parents, so I was on my own. With the money in hand, I was ready to prepare for my long awaited departure. I looked down the street where our mobile home was and I was in luck, there were no cars in the driveway. I decided to risk it. I went over to sneak in and try to go get some clothes. When I got to the bottom of the steps the door opened. It was dad! My heart pounded and I turned and ran away. I could hear him yelling for me to come back, but I never turned around, I just kept running as fast as I could. The roads were snowy and slippery, but I didn't let that slow me down. I ran up a hill and climbed the fence that surrounded the mobile home park, made it to the sidewalk and kept running. I was afraid Dad was in his truck trying to track me down so I was trying to get to a park where he would have to get out of the truck to chase me down.

I could hear my name being called from behind but it wasn't my dad, it was Randy. "Wait, wait!" he yelled. I still kept running until I made it to the top of a hill right before the park. Randy caught up with me when my stamina wore out. I stood there for a minute, looking to see if I saw my dad's truck. My little blue fluffy slippers were heavy and saturated with mud, snow and water. Telling Randy to hurry along with me, I began to fill him in on what was going on. "I can't turn back now; it's too late, and I have to keep moving," I told him. I explained how my home was no longer tolerable, I was failing in school and that Dad would never forgive me for being gone all week. What did I have to go back to? He seemed to understand, and told me that he had a friend that lived in another suburb of Salt Lake and if I could handle walking the fifteen miles to get there, he was sure I could stay there. I assured him that I was strong enough and could make it.

My feet were frozen beyond feeling; it was like I was walking on blocks. I hadn't planned to travel in my blue fluffy slippers and thin coat but since I couldn't get the appropriate clothes, I had no choice. The wind was picking up and it began to snow. My hands, feet, face, and entire body were frozen to the bone. This brought back so many bad memories from my past, etched deeply into my memory. I was now getting to the point where I feared I couldn't make it, but Randy kept reassuring me that I could.

Finally, we arrived at an apartment building. I was frozen beyond words. When he knocked on the door, there was no answer. I started to cry. It didn't matter though; the tears allowed me to release emotion in the moment. When I was done with my emotional breakdown, Randy signaled for me to sit down with him while he tried to cuddle me. I was so defeated, and in so much pain from the cold, that I didn't even think about whether he would try anything. He proved to truly be a friend, trying only to warm me and give me hope that everything would be alright. We sat on the porch and watched what was left of the light turn to dark. Soon, his cousin Cindy came up the stairs. "Boy, are we glad to see you!" he exclaimed. She looked quite startled to see him but welcomed us in and allowed me to sit in the bathroom on the edge of the tub running cold water on my frozen feet to start to defrost them. Randy filled her in on the whole situation. She agreed to help in any way that she could, as long as she would not get into trouble.

Randy called his dad and explained where he was and what was going on. He came over right away. After grilling me, Randy's dad insisted on calling my brother, Karl, to make sure that I would have somewhere safe to go, and that the arrangements that needed to be made would be done the right way. I could hardly believe that someone else's dad would go through that much trouble for me. When Randy's dad was comfortable with the answers that Karl gave him, he called the bus company and made the reservation for me. It was set. I would be leaving around four in the morning.; That would put me in Thompson around 9 a.m. with no layovers. Cindy offered to take me to the bus stop. She gave me some warm shoes and clothes since my once warm blue fluffy slippers were now an unrecognizable blob. But, they represented to me the cold painful walk that I had to endure, to get to my new life of freedom.

I asked Randy to say good-bye to Amanda for me. With tears of gratitude, I thanked him and his dad, from the bottom of my heart for helping me. I didn't sleep very well that night, because I was so excited to see Karl, Renee, and their kids. I loved them so much, and thoughts of what was to come swirled around in my head.

What have I done?

Chapter 36

Satan stole the only thing I had left.

It was dark outside when we left for the bus station. I felt butterflies in my stomach, knowing that my life would never be the same. From this moment on, I would be surrounded by people who loved me. I gave Cindy a long hug, thanked her for everything she had done for me, and stepped onto the bus. I remember sitting on the front seat next to the bus driver, watching his every move. I was so excited and felt so free. The bus window was the largest window I had ever seen, and the blades moved in such a gentle motion. I sat watching the millions of snowflakes that disappeared on impact. It looked and felt almost magical. Although it was mesmerizing, it didn't put me to sleep. Soon I was carrying on a conversation with the bus driver, but I was careful not to divulge any personal information. Now, I was an official runaway. He told me all about his family and how he got to be a bus driver. The conversation went on until the sun started to make its appearance. The earlier feeling of magic had now evaporated and was replaced with daydreams about how my new life would be, and the excitement of being reunited with the family I had always loved.

The bus came to a stop at a little gas station that sat in the middle of nowhere next to the highway. I thanked the bus driver for talking with me and for getting me there safe. Since I had no luggage, my good bye was quick. When I stepped off the warm bus, the crisp morning air reminded me of how much I despised the winter, even though the ground was covered with snow and everything was glistening. Karl welcomed me with a loving hug and asked me how the trip was, as he opened my door and tucked me into his warm truck. I was tired, but filled with so much excitement that I could barely stop talking the whole way to their trailer. When we arrived, we went in through the back door. There, Renee met me with a big hug, and I could feel that her tummy had a bump. She was going to have another baby! I congratulated her and hugged her tight. I was overcome by emotion, crying for the first time from happiness.

As I walked down the hall, I could hardly believe who I saw sitting in the chair. Dolores! There she was with her steaming cup of black coffee and a big smile. She sat her cup down and welcomed me into her arms. Even though we shared such terrible times together, and she so often destroyed my feelings, will, and self-esteem, she was still the woman that I had called "mommy" for most of my life. I didn't understand it, but in my heart, I felt love and warmth. Her arms felt good around me. I felt something inside that I can't put into words. Maybe it was a sense of being back with what was familiar to me, I don't know. How can you love and hate someone at the same time? I was confused, but for some reason, ready to forgive. Maybe it was Dad that made her act so crazy and mean. Maybe we could have a relationship now. I remembered how we were finally starting to get along before she left. Maybe she really did change.

I sat down by her feet and shared with all of them what had been happening in my life since we were apart. Much to my surprise, Dolores offered me a cigarette. She looked at me and said, "Go ahead. I've known for a long time that you smoke." I was shocked, but gladly accepted it and quickly lit up. I hadn't had a cigarette since Dad chased me down the road the day before. It tasted so good, especially with the nice hot cup of coffee Renee gave me. Dolores said she specifically came here to visit with me. This made me feel special. I looked up at her sitting there. It felt strange but comforting at the same time.

Dolores was only there for a couple of days because she was living with the ex-husband she had before my dad. They were staying in a little camper in Moab, thirty miles away. They didn't have a permanent residence lined up yet. As the days went by, I didn't leave the house much because I was still a runaway and didn't want to draw the attention of the few people who lived in their little town. I didn't mind though. I loved helping Renee with housework and playing with their kids, Jay and Ken. This was a house of love, with family game nights, dinner together, laughter and communication. I could have stayed inside forever. What I didn't know was that soon it would come crashing down around me.

One day, there was a knock on the door and then it opened. It was Danny! I felt my heart in my throat and I was frozen with fear. He stepped inside saying he was there to talk to Dolores, who was visiting again. When he saw me, he quickly came towards me reaching out his arms, saying with a big smile, "Don't you have a hug for your big brother?" I didn't know what to do. Like a robot, I got up and hugged him. The feeling I experienced with Dolores was not there with him. The thought of forgiveness never crossed my mind or my heart. When we all sat back down, I couldn't take my eyes off of him. My mind flashed with all the terrible pictures engraved into my memories. I could even smell the odor that the memories carried with them.

After putting the kids to bed, we all gathered in the living room. Karl and Renee began to share their fears concerning the circumstances of my being there. They were worried about me not being in school and didn't want to get into trouble for harboring me away from my dad. They said they wanted to contact my dad and arrange for me to stay with them legally. My heart shattered, my mind immediately screamed, what if he won't say yes? But I understood. Danny just sat there and listened acting concerned and adding his two cents every once in a while. When he stood up to announce that he had to go, I felt such a relief. Suddenly, I could barely believe my ears! "Lorina, come with me to go for a ride, I want to catch up with you and I'll bet you can use the fresh air." My mind screamed, "Help me!" but I just sat there hoping for a miracle. What do I do? What can I say? I didn't want to make a big deal out of it. I was hoping that Renee would try to parent me by saying it was too late, but she didn't say anything. If Karl and Renee were already worried about me being here, there is no way I could tell them about my experiences with Danny. All I could think of saying was no, I better not, it is so late and I didn't want to wake up the kids by going in and out of the house. Karl responded, "No, go ahead, it's okay. You've been cooped up here all day. Go and get some air, it will be good for you." My heart felt as though it would beat out of my chest! My stomach felt knotted up into a ball. In all my recent visions of freedom, safety, and security, his face was never in the picture. Out of nothing less than my worst nightmare, he was there, I was going off alone with him, and no one knew to help me. I was terrified!

I put on my jacket and shoes. I wanted to tell so badly, but, like always, the words wouldn't come out. I followed Danny out the door like a zombie. He opened his truck door. What could I do? Reluctantly, I climbed in. My mind was searching for reasons and excuses to tell him I couldn't go, but I was blank. I couldn't talk or move. I sat there like a statue. He offered me his lit cigarette. I took it hoping it would help to calm my nerves. He talked the whole time, telling me how nice it was to see me, how he thought of me often, and how much Dolores had missed me. "It's good to have you back in the family." he said. "I'm glad you're here." He started talking about his relationship with Stacy and how it had fallen apart, so he was focusing on staying busy working. It seemed to me that he was hoping I would feel sorry for him. The words meant nothing to me. He meant nothing to me! "I'm surprised she stayed as long as she did," I thought to myself.

I watched the headlights dance in the darkness as we bounced down the dirt road heading toward the mountains. It was icy and cold outside, but for once instead of freezing as I usually did, I felt nothing. Physically I was numb, and mentally, I was petrified with fear! I knew what was going to happen. I tried to prepare myself for the act that I believed would follow. Sadly I was wrong. There was no way to prepare me for what I was about to experience.

The truck pulled off of the dirt road and he turned off the engine as we rolled to a stop. The sky was black with millions of bright stars shining down on the glistening snow. I was searching for anything to distract me, to help take my mind off of what was really happening. We were miles away from any houses or main roads. I had to come up with something quick. So I told him that my stomach wasn't feeling very good and that I would probably throw up if I tried to do anything. "Don't worry, I understand." he cooed. "You don't have to suck me. I want to do something else." Oh my God!! Something else? I was old enough now to know what he was referring to. He got out of the truck, walked around to the other side and opened my door. His tone changed, "Get out and take off your pants!" he ordered. There are no words for what washed over me. I was beyond terrified! I couldn't run. I couldn't scream. I was trapped. "I can't, I'm afraid! I've never had sex before." I blurted out. "If you want to go back home, go ahead be my guest," he said with a smirk, "but you'll have to find your way back down the mountain. You have no choice Lorina. This is going to happen, so the sooner you do what I say, the quicker it will be over. Now get out!" My eyes were filled with tears as I slowly pulled down my pants. "The underwear too," he said, "And hurry up its cold." This was like the most horrible nightmare imaginable! What had I gotten myself into? Why couldn't I have just been nice to Sheryl? Why did it not cross my mind that Danny might somehow enter back into my life? It didn't matter, I made my choice, and because of my actions, I am standing in the dark in cold snow, alone and terrified, about to lose my virginity to the man I know as Satan.

He turned me around to face the seat talking to me the whole time. He pushed my face down onto the vinyl truck seat and told me to place my arms over my head. While kicking my ankles to get my legs apart, he was explaining to me how lucky I was for him to be doing this to me. His exact words were, "If you would have waited for your boyfriend to have sex with you, it would ruin your relationship, because the first time hurts and it would have made you hate him." His words made no sense to me. His reasoning was stupid! My legs were weak and shaking, and the air was cold on my bare skin. I was completely vulnerable. I couldn't talk or move. I prayed for God to help me! He ripped open a condom package and started to put the condom on his penis while he said "We don't want to have any accidents now do we?" I heard him spit on his hand and then he started touching me.

This was the first time he ever really touched me. It had never been his form of sexual satisfaction. I was frozen in terror! Then he tried to put his penis inside me. I cringed and tried to pull away. It hurt so badly! Instantly, my arms flew back trying to push him away. He grabbed my arms and put them back over my head holding both of my wrists in his one hand. He shoved himself into me. The pain was so intense that I screamed and tried to pull away. It was no use; there was nothing I could do. He told me to relax, "so that it wouldn't hurt as much." "You're lucky I'm doing this for you," he repeated. "I'm doing you a favor. I have a smaller than normal sized penis so this is making it easy on you. If it would have been a boyfriend it would have been much worse." I didn't feel like he was doing me any favors. It felt like he was ripping me in half! When it was over, he told me to get dressed. There was blood everywhere and I didn't understand why. This was not a part of the drunken sex talk that Dolores had given me back in 1975. I hadn't even had a period yet. I didn't know what was happening with my body. I just knew that I was in excruciating pain. I felt sick and wanted to go home.

On the way back to Karl and Renee's, there was no need for threats or warnings. He knew there was no way I would ever tell anyone about what had just happened. I knew it; he knew it! I was dirty, disgusting and ashamed. I felt different than I ever had before. Danny reached under his seat, grabbed a carton of cigarettes and threw it onto my lap. "Don't let Renee see your clothes, or we'll both have some explaining to do." he said with a slight smile. When we pulled into the driveway he said, "I'll be by tomorrow to take you to lunch."

When the next day came, I didn't want to get out of bed. I just wanted to lie there and die. Obviously that wasn't going to happen, so I had to make the best of my situation. It was obvious that something was wrong with me but I wasn't going to share. I told Renee that I must have been out in the cold too long because I felt like I was coming down with something. She let me lay low and I snuck my bloody clothes into the bathroom and tried to wash out the blood before placing them into the clothes hamper. Fortunately Renee gave me some clothes to wear when I got there. Her things were kind of big for me. Even though Jay was seven years younger than I was, some of his clothing fit me. For once I was glad I was super skinny. While some kids were teased about being too fat, I was the one always being teased about being too skinny.

As the morning progressed, the dreaded knock on the door happened. "Where's Lorina? I'm going to take her to lunch." he belted out. Renee replied that I wasn't feeling well enough to go out and that he should check back the next day. Here we go again I thought to myself; just like in the past, I was going to have to find ways to make myself scarce. It was the only way I could keep away from Satan.

I clung to the hope that sooner or later he would have to leave.

Danny would make many appearances to take me to lunch or out for his "talks." There were no more threats, no more suffocation. He knew I had no choice but to be his sex robot. He didn't force me to have intercourse again because I would beg him to not put me through the horrible painful sexual act. The painful torment of the rape was too fresh in my mind and I couldn't take that kind of pain and humiliation again. Instead, I bartered with him to perform the other unthinkable sex act and gratify him orally. I hated any sex act. I hated him, but this was my fault; I'd put myself in this situation. Now I would sell my soul for cigarettes, and whatever else he was willing to give me, to dull the pain of my situation and to keep me silent. I clung to the hope that sooner or later he would have to leave Thompson to go find work; he always did. If I could just hang in there long enough, I would soon be safe and happy like I had originally dreamed.

I don't know why, but for some reason, Karl and Renee didn't call my parents. I had been on the run for a couple of weeks and was starting to be more trusting about leaving the house without being turned in. On a bright sunny day, I finally decided to go to Karl's half-sisters' house to see if they could play. It was the greatest day since I had been there. Karl's sisters, Cindy, Tina, and Gail, and I decided to go play at the dump. We played in the old cars doing goofy kid things all day until it started getting dark. I left them to walk home, feeling more normal than I had in as long as I could remember. When I walked in the door, Karl told me to go wash up for dinner. After we ate, we played with Jay, and Ken. When Renee went to tuck them into bed, I could tell something was happening because Renee and Karl weren't their usual selves. They sat me down to break the worst news to me. They had finally called my dad and he refused to let me stay with them. They told me that he would be there the next day to take me back to Salt Lake City. As if that wasn't devastating enough, they went on to say they weren't coming to bring me home; I was simply being taken to a shelter. I was crushed. Even though Danny was molesting me, somehow my life was better. Although I was being violated, I was also being given love, warmth, and stability on a daily basis, something that I never had in my whole life. Now, after tomorrow it was being taken away from me.

I moped around the next day like a prisoner waiting to be sentenced. I sat with Renee and cried. "Please don't make me go back." I begged. But it did no good. There really was nothing that they could do. They tried to do the right thing legally, and now it was out of their hands. They could have gone to jail if they didn't comply. I didn't have many things to take with me so I was packed to go in no time. I went in the kid's room and played with them, just waiting for Dad and Sheryl to arrive. Finally there was a knock at the door. It was them. I didn't come out of the room. I could hear the adults making small talk. Renee gave them some ice water and they used the restroom. Renee came into the room and told me it was time to go. I hugged and said goodbye to the boys.

When I went into the front room I didn't make eye contact with anyone. I went over and hugged Karl and Renee goodbye. I showed no emotion, even though my heart was breaking and I felt like crying. I had to be strong; I didn't want to show any weakness in front of Dad or Sheryl. I walked right by Dad without saying a word. I picked up my belongings and walked right out the door. I went straight to the car and got in the backseat. I was hoping that Sheryl wouldn't open her mouth, because I knew it would end up in an argument if she did. I got my wish. She ignored me completely. She tried to laugh and make conversation with my dad, but he also stayed silent. Neither one of them even acknowledged my presence. That was just fine with me. I was simply a package being delivered.

It was a long, quiet ride back. When we stopped for gas or food, I pretended to be asleep. When we got into the city, Dad took me straight to the facility. I went in with my paper bag of things and was met by a counselor right away. I didn't say goodbye or even look at Dad. To me, he was a traitor. He never kept me safe, and again, when he had the chance, he chose a woman he had only known for two years that he didn't even get along with, over me.

When he left, the counselor started to show me around my new temporary home telling me what all rules were. I was happy that, for once, it didn't take long to make a friend. Her name was Julie. She told me what to expect and what the outcome would be if I acted the way they wanted me to act. Personally, I thought the place was pretty cool. I had a bunk bed in a room that I shared with one other girl, Ashley. There was a game room that was equipped with a foosball table, pool table, and television. There were comfortable couches and chairs, and a kitchen with snacks available. The facility provided all the toiletries and even a little bit of makeup in a gift pack that was placed on my bed when I arrived. Sure the windows had bars on them, but compared to how I had grown up, this place didn't seem half bad.

After a couple of days went by, I had my first counseling appointment. I never told any of my secrets about the sexual abuse or any of the physical abuse that I had experienced in the past except for what I had suffered from Sheryl. I didn't feel that they would understand or even be able to help me out with any of it. I felt that if I told them about being raped by Danny, they would have said I deserved it because I ran away. I kept my words limited and let them think they were running the whole show the way my new friend had advised me to do. The counselor suggested that I have sessions with Dad and Sheryl, so that we could work things out to be able to go back home with them. I reluctantly agreed.

We had that meeting the next day and it didn't go well at all. I tried to be nice, but Sheryl made it impossible. Immediately she started in on me, complaining to the counselor about everything I did. She took no responsibility for herself. I couldn't take it anymore; I started to swear and call her names while Dad just sat there and said nothing. It was very clear that we were beyond repair and it would definitely take more than a few appointments to straighten this family out. The near future counseling appointments were scrapped and a new plan was formulated.

I was advised that I would be placed in what is known as a shelter home the following day. This was kind of like a foster home, except that it would be more secure and the rules would be stricter. There would be no going outside with or without family and no incoming or outgoing phone calls. The good thing though, was that I would be able to smoke, if I found a way to earn the money for the cigarettes.

The foster parents were Bob and Kelly, and they seemed nice enough. They had their hands full with two other foster children when I moved in. Another child would soon move in after me. We were labeled troubled pre-teens. They had been taking care of troubled youth for a while, and were being reimbursed by the state for doing it. I pretended to fit in. I was great at doing chores so it didn't take me long to get in their good graces. I was making an allowance; they were buying me cigarettes and we were getting along just fine. It was a great family, actually. We had meals at the table every day. Bob was kind, and helped the other kids with their homework. Kelly and I would talk during the day, while the others were in school, and eventually she brought up that I needed to be in school. So much time had gone by at this point, and I had missed so much school, that it would be pointless to start back in this year. I had another plan though. As nice as it was there, I was working on my escape.

I looked up Randy's dad's name in the phone book and when the coast was clear, I made the call. It took several attempts to reach Randy but when I did he was sure surprised to hear from me. I pleaded for his help and asked him to get his dad to take me to the bus stop. I assured him that I would pay for my ticket and that I would never ask him to do it for me again. I told him that I would call back the next night after everyone had gone to bed. He promised me that he would talk to his dad and try to help me. I woke up the next morning, hopeful that I could set a plan into motion. I lied to Kelly and told her that I wanted to earn some money to buy a nice shirt and a pair of pants. I asked if there were extra chores I could do. She lined housework jobs up for me but told me Bob wouldn't get paid until the next Friday so I would have to wait a week to get paid. I eagerly accepted the terms.

I could barely wait for everyone to finally go to bed. I snuck out of the house and made the call. Randy picked up right away. He said his dad agreed to it, but that it would be the absolute last time. It was Thursday, and that would give me eight days to come up with the money for the ticket. I asked Randy to check all of the bus times that would get me to Thompson from Salt Lake. I would have to get the late bus so I could sneak out of the house. Randy said he would do the research and that I should sneak to call him again the next night.

It felt like it was taking a long time to set everything into motion, but it was happening. I was trying to be as patient as possible. Again I was anxious for everyone to go to bed so that I could call, but now, with it being Friday, everyone wanted to stay up later. Time seemed to drag on and I was hoping that Randy wouldn't fall asleep before I could call. Finally Bob and Kelly turned the television off and I heard their bedroom door shut. I quietly snuck down the hall into the kitchen and made the call. Randy picked up the phone. "I have some bad news," he said, "They don't have any seats open for next weekend so you will have to leave next Thursday. The bus leaves at 11:00 p.m. I made your reservations because the week after that, my dad is going out of town and I didn't think you would want to wait around that long." I thanked him and told him I appreciated everything that he had done and would find a way to work it all out. I gave him my address and told him to meet me down the block by 10:15 that night.

More planning needed to be done. If Bob and Kelly weren't in bed, I would have to sneak out the window. Now I needed to find out how to get the money together. It was under twenty-five dollars. I would need to steal it somehow. I kind of felt guilty because the family had been so good to me, but at the same time my sense of urgency outweighed my values. I needed to get out of there before they tried to send me to school or even worse, send me back home. I didn't have Karl and Renee's phone number, so they would have no clue I was coming. There was no way they would turn me away, I thought. At least I could hang out there long enough to formulate another plan. I kept my eyes open and watched for ways that I could get the money. The only thing that I found was Bob was a coin collector and he had a framed collection of silver quarters, dollars, and half-dollars. That would be my back up plan if I should need it.

It was Thursday night and I had to go with my backup plan. When everyone went to bed I snuck out to the front room and grabbed the frame. There was only fifteen dollars in it but I was hoping that Randy would front me the rest. Besides, it was too late to turn back now. I packed up my things in a little suitcase that I took from Kelly's closet and quietly snuck out the window. The night air was cold but it was nearing April so at least the storms had passed. Randy's dad's car was in sight. I was free again and on my way back to the bus station. My estimated time of arrival in Thompson would be 4:00 a.m. This time I didn't sit in the front of the bus; I took a middle seat and managed to fall asleep. The ride didn't feel nearly as long as it did on my last bus ride. It felt as though I had just fallen asleep, when the bus came to a stop at that familiar old gas station in the middle of nowhere. This time Karl would not be waiting for me, only the freezing cold wind and the wild animals. It was still dark outside and the bus driver was apprehensive about leaving me there all alone. I assured him that my ride would show up at any minute, and took the lie even further, saying that my ride was always late. He had a schedule to stick to, so even though he didn't want to, he left me there, telling me to be careful and stay warm.

It was about a five mile walk to the town itself. I tried to walk quickly, listening and keeping my eyes alert. There were wild animals like bobcats, coyotes, and in my young mind, Bigfoot, out here in the open fields and deserted narrow paved roads. My hands were frozen and my tummy was grumbling from a combination of hunger and my nerves. I could only hope that Karl and Renee didn't get mad at me for showing up unannounced. I could see their trailer in the distance. I was both excited and nervous. By the time I got there, the sun was coming up. It was quiet and there was no one around but me. In that moment it felt like I was the only person on the planet.

More twists and turns in my life.

When I got to the trailer, I looked into the window. Renee was in the kitchen preparing Karl's lunch for the day. It was obvious that she was the only one up so I knocked lightly. She didn't hear me and I was kind of afraid but I had come so far that there was no turning back. I must have stood outside for at least fifteen minutes before finally getting her attention. When she opened the door, I felt so good when she greeted me with a hug. When Karl came into the front room he was equally receptive. They both told me to get some sleep and when Karl got home, they would talk to me about what the plan of action would be to help me. It felt good to be there and even better to be around the kids that I loved so much.

That evening, after the kids were tucked in their beds, we sat in the front room to have the serious discussion. Karl and Renee were concerned that Dad might press charges against them for letting me stay there. Since he knew I went there before, this would be the first place they would look. While we were talking there was a knock on the door. It was Danny. He came in, sat down and joined the discussion. How did he know I was there? I know it's a small town and news travels fast, but how did he find out? Why can't he just leave me alone? Of all people to come up with this, I could hardly believe he did. "Did your dad ever do anything to you sexually?" he asked. "No, not really," I answered, "but there was the one time with me and Amanda." I shared the story with them. Danny had this great idea. Go to Moab and talk to someone with social services and file a report. Then they won't be able to send you back home." Part of me didn't want to do it, but at the same time, I wouldn't report anything that didn't happen. I wouldn't be lying when I said that it made me feel uncomfortable. So that was the plan. The next day, we went to Moab. I filed my complaint and Karl and Renee received information on becoming foster parents and we left to go home.

Renee felt a little easier about me being there, even though nothing legally allowed it. We received a phone call from the social worker and he said that I would probably have to go back to Salt Lake to go to court. My heart dropped. Soon, another plan was set into action. Dolores was going to be moving to Las Vegas, and it was decided that once she was settled in with her ex-husband, I would join them. This sounded good to me, because we seemed to have a good relationship the last couple of times we were together and, more importantly, there would be no Danny. Karl and Renee thought it would be a good idea for me to stay with another family in Moab until I left, so that they wouldn't get in trouble for me being there. They would tell the social worker that I ran away again and didn't know where I went.

I ended up staying with Stacy's mom, Mary. Stacy's little sister Tina was there with her older brother, Doug. This was a wonderful surprise, because I had spent time with them earlier in my life. Tina was a couple of years younger than I, and Doug was a couple of years older. I always had such a crush on Doug. That used to bother Tina, because she wanted my undivided attention when we were together. Although I had not seen them since 1977, my friendship with Tina seemed to pick up right where we had left off. I will always have great memories of her. We shared our secrets, joys, hopes and dreams together, although I never shared my secrets about Danny, afraid she wouldn't want to be my friend if she knew.

Even though I wouldn't be staying long, I enjoyed my time there, and was sad knowing that I would be leaving. The day before I left, Stacy came over. She seemed happier than I had ever seen her before. She had her two daughters with her. Dorie was three now and had grown so much. She was more adorable than I had remembered. Stacy had given birth to another daughter. Sunny, who was around two, was as cute as could be. Stacy was very pregnant and looked radiant. It made me think pregnancy was the greatest gift a woman could experience and I looked forward to being a mother someday. When she asked me if I wanted to go for a ride with her, I said absolutely! Stacy was fun and I looked up to her. She asked her mom to watch the girls and we jumped into her big car. She had the Beach Boys blaring on the stereo as we flew down the highway. She asked me to light her a cigarette and told me I could have one too. I felt free and happy in that moment. It was the beginning of spring in Moab, and as Stacy pulled into her trailer court, the smell of the beautiful bright purple lilacs filled the car. The flowers were everywhere. Stepping out of the car, I just stood there taking it all in.

I followed her into the trailer and watched her as she went into the kitchen to knead some bread dough that had been rising. She ran a towel under the faucet, wrung it out, and placed it back onto the large silver bowl. "There we go," she said, "all done now. We'll have fresh baked bread for dinner." Wow, I thought to myself, she makes a good mother. She was taking care of babies, pregnant, and still making fresh bread for dinner. We left the trailer and got back into the car. "You know, if this Vegas trip doesn't work out, you can always come and stay with me. I could always use your help with the girls and the new baby. I'm sure Danny won't mind." I wanted so much to tell her of all the horrible things her Danny had done to me, but no matter how I tried, I couldn't make the words come out of my mouth. I just lit us both another cigarette and listened to the music. She made a quick stop at the store, came back out and handed me a couple packs of cigarettes. "Here you're going to need these for the trip," she said. "Wow, thank you!" I responded, "but you don't have to do this." She just looked at me and smiled.

When we got back to Mary's house, I went in and played with Dorie and Sunny. They were so cute and full of life. Dorie had a head full of blazing red hair and a huge smile. Sunny looked just like her name. She had shiny blonde hair with rosy cheeks and kind of a button nose. It was so easy to fall in love with them, even if their father was pure evil. When it was time for Stacy to leave, I hugged her goodbye and told her that I loved her and how happy I was for her. In my mind I didn't know if I would ever be back, believing I was embarking on a whole new life of freedom and happiness.

For the rest of the evening I hung out with Tina and Doug. I had to think of a whole new alias. I don't know how we came up with the name Marci. We played games, smoked cigarettes, and talked about everything from school to religion. I was always preaching about Jesus and the Bible for as long as I could remember, putting the scriptures into simplified form. Mary came into the room and told us we needed to get to sleep because I had a bus to catch really early in the morning. Doug left saying "Goodnight Marci." Tina and I lay in bed talking and giggling until we drifted off to sleep.

When it was time to leave, tears and addresses were exchanged. Mary gave me a hug and a twenty dollar bill, saying it was from Dolores in case of an emergency. It was five a.m. "Why do buses have to leave so early?" I thought to myself as I stepped up into the bus. I traveled forty-five miles to Green River, Utah, where I had a two hour layover. The bus stopped at a restaurant that also served as the bus stop. I found my way to a table and ordered a cup of coffee to settle into a long wait. I was only there for thirty minutes when an older lady approached me and said that Dolores had called her and asked her to pick me up. She said that Dolores was concerned about me sitting by myself for so long. I gathered up my things and went with her to her trailer. This whole situation seemed very awkward to me, but I just politely went along with it.

There wasn't much of a conversation because I already knew anything that involved Dolores meant giving out no information, especially now that I was officially a runaway. I didn't know what the lady knew, and thought I should just keep it all to myself. We just sat there drinking coffee. After a few polite comments back and forth, there was nothing left to do other than just sit. There was no television or radio there to fill the emptiness . I think we were both happy when it was time to go back to the bus station. I thanked her for staying with me, and happily got back on the bus. It was a long six hours away. Fortunately I was able to sleep most of the way. When the bus pulled into Las Vegas my heart was filled with hope and excitement.

Everything was so big and amazing! Dolores greeted me with open arms and a loving heart. Bill had a smile and was excited that it was my first time there. He seemed eager to be my guide. The first thing we did was go to a buffet. There was more food than I had ever seen before. I ate until I could hardly move. After we went home to the trailer, I was shown where I would

213

sleep. Then we sat down and I had the rules explained to me. They seemed simple enough, and I understood that my identity could never be revealed, even more so now, because Bill and Dolores would be in really bad trouble for helping me to get across state lines. I said that I understood. This was great. Dolores seemed happy and I felt like I was home.

When the sun started to set, we jumped into the truck and headed for the Strip. It was magical. The lights of the casinos were the most amazing things I had ever seen. Everything was so big and bold and bright. There were people everywhere. It was breathtaking and brought tears to my eyes. After Bill got his fill of showing me around, we headed back to our little trailer. I was so excited for the next day to come, because we would be meeting with some of Bill's friends who owned a nice expensive home. Then we were going to follow them out to Lake Mead and go boating for the day. I couldn't have imagined how much fun I would have.

It was the best day ever! I felt special. I loved the hot Nevada sun. The water was too cold to swim in, but it was beautiful to look at. The adults were all laughing, drinking and having a great time. Only two days into my new life and it was awesome!

Six weeks passed, and in that time, there was no turmoil, no being molested, and no alcohol. I made friends with a couple of older girls. Susan lived in a doublewide across the street and had a trampoline. I would find myself wishing that I was her many times. She was sixteen, beautiful, and spoiled. She also smoked pot, which was a perk for me. She was still in school, because it was the end of May and it wasn't summer break yet. During the day while Bill was at work and Dolores watched TV, I laid outside in the sun working on my tan while listening to Donna Summer on an eight track. This was the life, or so I thought.

Bill worked in construction, and sometimes Dolores would go with him to help in any way she could. On one particular day, I wanted to do something special for them since they had been so kind to me, so I set the table nice and made fried chicken with mashed potatoes. Everything sat on the table as I watched the time tick by. It was quite late when I saw the headlights pull in. They sounded like a herd of elephants as they came into the trailer. They had been drinking and were yelling at each other. The smell of alcohol was strong and the smell of disaster was even stronger. Bill was ready to sit down and eat but Dolores wasn't going to let it go of whatever they were fighting about. It quickly got out of control. Dolores was throwing things around and calling him names. Finally, Bill jumped up and started lashing back. Before I knew it, Dolores and I were packing to leave. I didn't know what to say or do; I just did what Dolores told me to do. I didn't want to leave, but I had no choice. Soon our blue Ford pickup was loaded and ready to go; we didn't have many things to pack, just a few of the boxes that Dolores always traveled with. All I had was a small suitcase of clothes.

As we drove away, I was hoping we wouldn't get pulled over by the cops. Dolores was clearly drunk and slurring her words. The first thing she did was drive to her uncle's house but no one was there. She drove to another part of town that looked dirty and creepy. She turned down an alley and up to the back of a bar. "Stay here." she ordered. "I'm going to see if they'll let me use their phone." It must have been a really long line waiting for the phone, because she didn't return for what seemed like hours. When she got in the truck we cuddled up together on the seat and went to sleep. The next morning we went to a casino and had a cheap buffet meal, which was delicious, and used the bathroom to freshen up. That was one thing Dolores always preached about. "I don't care how poor you are, it's no excuse to be dirty!" she would say.

After leaving the casino, she seemed hopeful. Sadly though, instead of following through on a reasonable plan, she headed straight back to the alley where we had spent the night. She told me not to worry that she wouldn't be long and would be right back. She said she met someone the night before who was willing to help us out, but she needed to meet with him this afternoon. It was a little before the noon hour when she went in and, once again, it was well into the dark night before she came back out. I was already well conditioned to sit and wait quietly for hours, from my childhood. Many times I would sit in our van for hours and hours, waiting for Dad and Dolores to finish a sign. I knew better then to ask for food or even a bathroom. When Dolores was drunk, it was dangerous to make any waves. I just cuddled up to her and listened to her complain about how the men in her life had always been worthless, while she cried herself to sleep.

The next day we repeated the casino bathroom ritual minus the buffet; because she had spent all the money she had on her. It isn't cheap to sit in a bar all day. We went back to her uncle's house and they agreed we could stay there for a couple of days as long as we were out by the end of the week. I don't know how she did it but somehow she found a job cleaning houses and got us a little furnished duplex studio by that time. She worked during the day and sometimes came home at night. I was never allowed to go outside and we had no TV, so I spent my days inside listening to the radio and abusing myself. I was full of anger and hatred and, since I had no one to take it out on, I punished myself. I would look into the mirror and yell at myself punching myself in the head. I hated myself and reminded myself that I deserved everything bad that ever happened to me. Sometimes the lady who owned the apartments would hear me yelling and knocked on the door asking if I was okay. I would open the door and lie to her that I had the radio up too loud. She would try to peek her head inside and ask where my mom was, and I would just say, "Oh, she is working and won't be back for a while." I never said anything to her about my situation, but she must have been keeping an eye on me. Once in a while she would bring over a breakfast to me in the morning. It was always so delicious and I devoured every bit of it, because sometimes there would be no food or Dolores, for days.

One late night, I was lying in our foldout couch bed and heard Dolores stumble in drunk and laughing. There was a man with her who was also drunk. She woke me up and told me to go make a bed on the other side of the room. I put the kitchen chairs together and grabbed a blanket. "Come and say hi to my friend, Snake." she slurred. Wow, I thought, when I looked at him, she scraped the bottom of the barrel for this one, yikes! He was really skinny and looked like a street bum with long scraggly hair that was pulled into a rubber band. "He's going to help us," she announced. "He's a sales man. Now, go to sleep." Thoughts raced through my head! This guy really gave me the creeps. I just lay on the chairs pretending to be asleep. In no time at all, the sounds of sex were coming from the bed that I was just laying on, no more than twenty minutes ago.

It was so disgusting. I couldn't believe that they didn't even care that I was right there. When they were finished, I could hear Snake asking Dolores if she thought I was awake. "No," she replied. "She is a heavy sleeper." I just laid there trying to place other thoughts in my head to clear out what I just experienced. When morning came, he was still there and more than willing to brag about his business. He sold fake social security and identification cards, a very profitable profession in Vegas according to him. He and Dolores had this plan. He would make me a fake social security card with her number on it so I could go to work and whatever I made would later go towards benefitting her. Sounded good to me; I liked the thought of me being able to go to work. That meant freedom and independence from the life I was living.

After a while, Dolores said, "Get dressed. We're going to go meet some of Snake's friends." They went in and showered together. I hurried and got dressed, while they were out of the room. Once they were ready, we were on our way, in Snake's van. It was his home and office. It all seemed very strange to me but if it meant I would get out of the box we were staying in, and get to eat, then I was game. At his friend's apartment, I was even more surprised that Dolores would associate with those kinds of people. As soon as we sat down, a joint was passed around. Dolores said it was her first time to smoke, and it looked like it too. When the joint came to me I toked it right up, leaving Dolores shocked that I wasn't coughing or choking. She lectured me on how this would be the only time that we would smoke, and how she didn't want me to grow up to be a druggie. We left the apartment and Snake took us out to eat at the Golden Nugget buffet. Maybe this guy isn't so bad after all, I thought to myself.

Snake ended up staying with us most of the time, but was never left alone with me. When he wasn't with Dolores, he was off hustling. He looked rough around the edges, but he was nice and actually, somewhat considerate. One night, while we were at the buffet, I thought it would be a good time to drop the bomb that my fourteenth birthday was in two days. I don't know what I expected, because I should just be happy that they were taking care of me at all. Is it right to get recognition for a birthday? Snake said "Cool! We'll take you out for an ice cream." Dolores agreed that that was a good idea. The big day came, and off we went to McDonald's for my ice cream cone. Dolores also gave me a small pair of fake pearl earrings and a deck of cards. I can't say it was the best birthday ever, but then again, it must have been, because now that I look back, I don't even remember my other birthdays.

It wasn't long before Dolores chased off our meal ticket by her drunken angry tantrums. I was back into the routine of being alone, for days, in our little box-like studio. At least I had the cards Dolores had given me that helped to fill in the boredom. Sometimes I would sneak off to the landlady's house to play cards with her and her husband. They were an elderly couple that seemed to enjoy my company, and were more than happy to feed me when I was there. I had to be very careful to not let Dolores know that I was ever there or she would have flipped out. She ordered that I stay completely out of sight when she wasn't around.

One day Dolores came by with a lady that she introduced as her second cousin, Susan. She seemed nice enough, but struck me as being rather strange. She was very overweight, sweated profusely, carried a milk gallon jug full of water, and had a dirty kind of smell to her. She dropped off a small bag of food and seemed glad to be in contact with Dolores. Sometimes Dolores would randomly go through the white pages to search for any relatives that might live around us, and this was how she had found Susan. Susan only stayed a short time. After she left, Dolores got herself all dolled up and said that she had been working so hard, she was going to treat herself to a night out. I kissed her good night and told her that she looked beautiful. Three days came and went, and no Dolores. I was starting to think that maybe something had happened to her, but there was nothing I could do. I couldn't report her missing and I had no phone or money to reach out to family for help.

I was sitting at the table playing solitaire when there was a knock at the door. I opened the door and to my surprise, it was Susan. "Hi! Where's Dolores?" she asked. I really didn't know what to say. Even though she was family, I thought I had better mind Dolores' very strict rule about sharing her business with anyone. I decided to spill the beans, though, because I was genuinely worried about her. I said that I hadn't seen her in three days and that I was scared something had happened to her. "Come with me," Susan demanded. "I'm going to Death Valley and I don't want to leave you here alone."

"I can't," I replied. "If I'm not here when Dolores gets home, she'll be furious."

"What if something did happen to her? Are you willing to sit here until you get thrown out?" Susan responded. "Besides we will leave her a note. If everything is okay, she'll understand. And if it isn't, you'll be safe with me."

That sounded logical to me, so I grabbed a couple of things, wrote a note and we were off. When I got out into her car, I was kind of grossed out. It was a big old station wagon that looked like it had never been cleaned. There were emptied-out milk gallon jugs, , newspapers, pieces of trash, and dirty clothes strewn about. Our first stop was the gas station, where she had me get out and pump the gas for her. Next to me there, was a young girl wearing a t-shirt that read "Itty-bitty Titty Committee." I remember that seeming so bizarre to me. Why would someone announce their breast size on their shirt? I was small chested and hated it, always teased about looking like a boy. I got into the car and asked Susan why someone would wear something like that and she said, "To bring more attention to herself." That made absolutely no sense to me. How could anyone want to draw attention to their body, especially when they were flat chested?

Well, we were finally on the road. It was sweltering hot. We drove all the way to a town called Tecopa in Death Valley, California. On the outskirts of the town, there were natural spring pools inside a building with no doors. Susan told me we were going to be stopping there to go into the pools because they had healing properties that helped her with her health issues. When we got out of the car, I noticed that all the roaming hills around had white crosses on them. I asked her what they were there for, and she told me that she wasn't sure but it had something to do with the Manson gang who was known for hanging around the area. She warned me not to bring it up to anyone, because people around there didn't like to talk about it. When we went inside the small brick building, you could smell the sulfur of the hot spring water. "Put your hair up and take off all of your clothes," she said. She must have been able to tell that her statement shocked me because she quickly started to tell me that the water would strip away anything with color. It didn't matter to me what color my underwear and shirt were; I was not going to take them off. This was a public place with no doors. I put my hair in a rubber band and got into the water. It felt amazing. It was very warm and felt soft. She took her clothes right off, like it was nothing. I turned around to face the wall and felt very uncomfortable.

After getting out and showering, she pulled out the empty gallon jugs and filled them in a sink. She warned me there would be no running water in the camper where she lived. That explained all the empty jugs. We loaded up the jugs and were on our way again. We drove a few more miles, until we got to a town called Shoshone. It was not what I expected at all. The trailer court was small, with campers and old converted busses. Her camper was very small and made out of tin and aluminum. I don't know if it was hotter inside or outside. There was no air conditioning. She was hooked up to a butane tank for cooking, which it was way too hot to do. I was amazed that someone could live like this, even more so being so overweight. I was never one to sweat much, but there I was, always drenched. Across the street there was a small public hot spring pool. Warm water on a hot day, sounds strange but I have to admit it was my favorite place to be especially, when the sun was just coming up.

Aside from the heat, I loved the desert. It is full of life. There is a down side to being so close to the hot springs though. Strange flying insects must have come from a hundred miles away to be in the water. These little critters stung like crazy. Once you were in the water it was best to try and stay under it or be sure to be completely out it and as far away as possible to avoid being stung. The pool would be packed in the afternoon because everyone who had kids was searching for a way to stay cool. I don't remember the actual temperature when I was there, but I'd spent most of my life going barefoot, but it was impossible to do it there. In fact, if sand went on top of my foot when I was wearing thongs, it would blister my foot.

We were supposed to stay for a week but we ended up only being there for four days, when Susan decided we better go back and check on Dolores. We loaded up the car and prepared to trek across the hot Death Valley desert in July. When we finally reached the apartments, I was relieved to see her truck in the parking lot. I didn't have a key, so if she wasn't there, there was no telling how long I would have to wait for her. The door was locked but when I knocked on it, thankfully, she quickly answered. I was not expecting the kind of welcome that I received. She looked at me with her dark cold eyes. They were filled with anger and hate. "What in the hell do you want?" she snarled. "I'm back," I answered. "I'm so glad you're alright," I said, as I tried to hug her. She pulled away from me and told me I was full of shit. "You couldn't care less about me! Get the hell away from me! You made your choice when you went traipsing off with Susan." "She's your problem now." she snapped at Susan. Susan and I tried to explain, but Dolores wasn't going to hear it. "I'm done taking care of your sorry unappreciative ass. You abandoned me, so now you can get out and stay out." She handed Susan some money and told her to take me to the bus stop. "I don't want to see either of you again!" she said, as she slammed the door. Once again, my heart was crushed. And as always, I believed that I deserved it. I should have never gone with Susan.

"I had no idea she would react that way. I was just trying to help." Susan kept apologizing. "Do you have somewhere you can go? Will you be okay?" she asked. She wanted to make sure that if she got me on a bus to somewhere I would be taken care of on the other end. I didn't have any phone numbers. All I knew was I would be safe with Karl and Renee. Convincing her I would be fine, she got me to the bus station and soon, I was back on my way to Thompson.

When I arrived at their house, as usual they were surprised to see me, but welcomed me with love. I explained all that had happened in Vegas and Death Valley. They were understanding and promised they wouldn't be attempting to contact my dad this time. Renee's brother Shaun was now living with them. He was very kind and never made me feel weird; in fact he was like a brother and friend all rolled up into one. We would smoke cigarettes and share other things together. He would tell me his thoughts and dreams, as I did with him. I kind of developed a crush on him, because of his kindness and warmth. Nothing would ever come of it. I wasn't interested in boys that way, in fact, when it came to anything sexual, I was terrified.

Life was good at the moment, mostly because Danny wasn't around. He had some kind of job out of town. Life was simple and enjoyable. I would help Renee with the kids or the chores, which was easy, and a pleasure because she was always so kind to me. Her tummy was really big now. Her due date was getting closer and she was glowing with beauty. Sometimes we would play board games or Yahtzee, while drinking fresh sun tea. I admired her as a mother and a friend. I really liked how Karl and she communicated. I always found myself wishing that I would have had parents like that as I grew up. The reality was that I didn't; I'm sure that's why I was able to be even more appreciative of them.

It was moving into the end of July and in Thompson, the best way to beat the heat was to go to the Reservoir. This was the swimming hole, the party place, and my favorite place to be when I could get there. It was a long walk up an old dirt road, so it was important to pay attention to anyone who might be heading up that way to catch a ride. One day when I went to the little town café to get a Coke and listen to the jukebox, I met a girl named Janet. Her mom owned the café. She seemed to be very independent. I would watch her and find myself wishing I was her. She was only fifteen but looked like she was around eighteen. The more I got to know her, I found myself becoming envious of her. She had long very blonde hair and a much larger chest than I had. She was in control of her own decisions. Later I found that she was really flat-chested but her mom was thoughtful enough of her feelings that she made her customized bras to enhance her self esteem. She had horses, ribbons, nice clothes, and could come and go as she pleased. She soon became my role model. Renee didn't like this very much, because she didn't care for the changes it was creating in me. This was a new form of independence for me and I seemed to run with it.

I didn't want anything to do with boys sexually, but I found myself seeking the approval of the opposite sex. I had a never-ending need to be liked. I felt so ugly inside that I was constantly reaching out to replace my warped self image with others' fake opinions and empty compliments. Janet was great at demanding attention. I was shy and didn't know how to act. I felt I could learn how to be a more outgoing person and feel like I fit in, if I hung around her. She was known as a "prick tease" among other things. I saw it as the game that it was, but others thought she was just being a tramp. Maybe she needed the fake attention as well; after all she was adopted and had no dad in her life. Who knows, maybe this was her way of filling that void. I stuck up for her whenever someone badmouthed her. Regardless of what most people thought, she was my friend. Even more important, she came to like me, and that made me feel important.

Back to School
Another new home and a fresh a start.

Instead of enjoying the family and hanging out in the mornings, I now found myself rushing through my chores to go hang out with Janet. Sometimes we would go horseback riding, hang out at her mom's café, or play foosball. Most of the time, we would search for a way to get to the Reservoir. Occasionally, there would be different companies that would come into town bringing workers to fix the roads or be affiliated with the railroad. Janet loved this, because she was always looking for any kind of male attention. One of the men that she soon became friends with, was a guy named Brodie. She used him for everything… a place to party, rides, cigarettes and weed. I would just tag along and watch her in action. I found myself becoming less respectful of people like she was. This was not my nature. Even though I had lived a life of great turmoil, struggle and disappointment, I was still polite, considerate and caring. One evening when we were at Brodie's house, he was playing the guitar and the three of us were drinking beer, singing and having a good time.

There was a knock at the door. Janet opened it. It was Danny! Oh my God, I thought to myself, what was he doing here? I didn't even think he was in town. Danny came in and Brodie offered him a beer. I acted like I wasn't drinking because I didn't want Danny to know. I was afraid he would have something to hold over my head by threatening to tell Karl and Renee. A fear filled my whole body. I was already searching my thoughts for ways to avoid being around him. As always, the pictures of his torture, the smells, and the feelings from when he raped me flashed through my mind. I tried to look calm on the outside, but inside I was trembling, terrified to think what he would do to me if I didn't do whatever he demanded.

He just sat there watching all of us and not saying much. I was careful to never make eye contact with him. I was just praying he would go away. I didn't want to sing anymore, I just sat quietly letting Janet entertain us all. "Well I guess I better get going; I have a busy day tomorrow," he announced. "Come on, Lorina."

"No!" I instantly replied. I lied, and told him that I promised Janet's mom I would stay with her until she went back home; we were on the buddy system. "Come outside then, I need to tell you something." I slowly followed him with no intentions of letting him put his hands on me. When I got to the door, I froze and wouldn't go down the porch steps. I kept my hand on the door jam, and one leg inside the trailer. "What do you need?" I asked, showing him I wasn't going to go any further. "You better watch that guy!" Danny warned me. "If I find out that anything happened between you two, I'll take care of him." Imagine that, Danny was warning me about being careful around another man. What a joke!

I assured him that I wasn't that kind of girl, and that he had nothing to worry about. Again, I reminded him I was just there to be with Janet, not Brodie. He lashed back in an angry tone, "Well, the town knows what kind of girl Janet is, and if your hanging out with her, then the town is going to think you're the same way."

"Well, I don't care what the town thinks. I know differently, and like I said, I'm not that kind of girl." I snapped back.

"I just want you to know," Danny went on, "that I have friends that will tell me what you're doing, and they will be keeping an eye on you, so you better keep your nose clean." I thought, oh my God, that must be true, he seemed to always know where I was and would pop up out of the blue. This was the first time I was ever able to stand my ground and refuse to go with him and have him accept it. As he walked away I was washed over with relief! I didn't let my guard down though. I was afraid that he would come back, so I went back in and told Janet I had to go home. Brodie offered to give us a ride and I accepted immediately.

We agreed to meet up the next morning to go to the Reservoir and spend a day sunning and swimming. After my chores were finished, Renee let me go to Janet's knowing that we would spend the day swimming. We couldn't get a ride so we decided to walk. It was a long walk and such a hot day, that by the time we got there, we were ready to just float in the water. There were inner tubes that were always left up there for anyone to use. We had just run out of drinking water and were regretting the long walk back when suddenly, an old Chevy pulled up. They were a couple of cowboys that Janet knew. She seemed to know everyone, especially the men. She went up and greeted them with a hug asking them where there beer was. They pointed out a cooler and told us to help ourselves. We sat there and drank with them for hours. Janet started asking them if she could shoot their rifles. "Sure," they replied and went to retrieve them off the gun racks. One of the guys took some empty cans and went up the hill to place them on the rocks to be used for targets. Janet looked like she was having fun so I thought I would give it a try. I placed the rifle on my shoulder scoped out the can and, when I fired, the gun jerked and the scope hit me right in the middle of the forehead, leaving a perfect circular mark and bruise. Anyone who knows anything about guns knows that's the mark of stupid. I would clearly carry that mark around on my forehead for at least a week. While I was distracted with the shooting event more people were showing up to swim.

Much to my surprise, Stacy pulled up to go swimming with her new boyfriend David, the two girls and the new baby. This was a real treat and surprise, because they lived thirty miles away in Moab. I was so excited that I completely forgot about Janet and her cowboy friends. I played with the girls and didn't want to leave the new baby's side. He was so cute and so little. He was only two months old. Stacy had named him Kent. After Stacy and David were done swimming, Stacy brought up a great idea. "Why don't you come on back to Moab with us and stay for a couple of days?" she suggested. "I could use your help with the kids and it will get you out of this boring place for a while." That sounded great to me because it would be fun. It also put distance between Danny and me. I didn't think twice before saying yes and was ready to go with them right away. Janet didn't want me to go because she said she would be so bored without me. I told her I would only be gone for a couple of days, and promised we would be back to being inseparable. I asked her if she wanted us to give her a ride back home, but she wanted to stay and party. She hugged me and said, "Don't be gone long and have fun."

On the way back home I was thinking of what I might say to ask Renee if I could go with Stacy. I was kind of nervous to ask if

I could go, because Renee had been so good to me and I promised her I would help her with the boys, especially while she was in the final stages of her pregnancy. It didn't help matters that Stacy and Renee once where sisters'-in-law and even friends at one time, but now there was no love lost between them. I got up my courage and decided to go in alone while Stacy waited in the car. I was only going to ask if I could go for a week, thinking that she probably wouldn't mind me being gone such a short amount of time. Boy, was I wrong. I totally did not expect the reaction I got from Renee. She told me I could go if I wanted too but I wouldn't be able to come back. "This isn't a hotel where you can just come and go as you please. This is our home," she scolded. I was shocked by her reply but I couldn't blame her or even be upset with her because of all they had done for me.

I shouldn't have been so disrespectful, but I quickly went out to share Renee's ultimatum with Stacy. "That's okay," Stacy replied, "you can stay at my mom's house. I'm sure she won't mind if you stay with her, as long as you help out around the house." She told me that Mary had just moved into her dream home; a two-story house on a little street that circled around. There was a small park in the middle, right across the street. It all sounded great to me, so it was final; I was moving out. I ran into the trailer and packed up my things before Renee changed her mind. I would miss them all so much but I was finally getting away from Danny. I watched the trailer get smaller and smaller as we drove down the road. I thought about the boys and all of the promises I had made to Renee about helping her out with the new baby. I took in a deep breath and pushed the sad thoughts out of my mind. I had to think this was going to be a fun adventure and I was ready to make the best of it.

On the way to Moab, David was driving. He must have been tired from the couple of beers he drank, and the swimming, because we almost crashed. He swerved for some reason and then over-corrected the car, and we started to fish tale. My body slammed into poor little Sunny pushing her into something hard. It ended up giving her a big goose egg on her head. I felt terrible. We were all very much awake after that, and fortunately made it home to Stacy and David's trailer in one piece.

David was nothing like Danny. He was playful but not in a creepy way. He seemed to really enjoy being around Stacy and her babies. I spent a lot of time at their mobile home babysitting, and when I wasn't there, I was with Mary at her house, which I also loved. Stacy's youngest sister Tina and I soon became inseparable. Wherever I went, she was right there with me. Even though we would have little squabbles, she was my best friend in the world. We babysat, listened to music, smoked cigarettes, and just hung out together all the time. When we would come home from the public swimming pool, we would have fresh vine tomatoes with mayonnaise and toast. They were delicious! We had so many good times together. Tina was nothing like Janet. She had different interests like playing, and roller-skating. She enjoyed being young, not wanting to grow up too soon. She was great with children and liked to hang out at home, instead of looking for boys and adventure. There was nothing wrong with Janet really; I just resonated more with Tina. Tina's older sister Valerie and her brother Doug lived there too. It was so very kind of Mary to take me on too and I was very grateful.

Mary wanted to have guardianship of me from the state so that she could get some kind of financial help for me. She was on disability and had a family to feed. So, it was back to the social services office to make everything official. Surprisingly, things went well with social services, better than it ever had before. At first I was worried about the social worker sending me back to Salt Lake, but Dad had given up his search for me and with no one looking for me. I was, in a sense, property of Grand County and no longer considered to be a runaway. Stacy worked different jobs here and there and helped out her mom with getting us girls some new school clothes. I felt like I fit in, I actually belonged, and for once, I was kind of excited to be going to school. Now we just had to figure out what school and what grade I would be accepted into.

I only went to the first three months of the seventh grade when I lived in Salt Lake with my dad. I had been held back in grade school, so I didn't know what grade to sign up for. I was fourteen now and should have been in the ninth grade. It was all very confusing but after Mary met with the principal of the high school, she somehow arranged for me to start the ninth grade, where I belonged according to my age. That meant I had completely skipped junior high school. I was kind of sad that Tina wouldn't be there with me, because she was younger than I was and would be going into seventh grade. But that was okay because I got to see her every day at home.

I'll never forget the first day of school. For once, I was excited about going to school. It was nothing like I ever imagined it would be! The High School Mascot was a devil and the Drill team was called the Devilette's. The School's motto was the Red Devils. The first day we had an early assembly and the Devilette's made their first appearance. They came out dancing to "Funky Town." I had never seen anything like it before. It was great! They looked so cute in their little red shorts, tux with tails and white gloves. Wow, I thought, if I would have ever got the chance, I would have love to be a Devilette! I often dreamed about what my life would have been like if I had the opportunity to have a stable education, or anything stable in my life. But that would always be just a dream; it was never to be a reality meant for me.

School was exciting for about two weeks, and then it crumbled quickly from there. It was hopeless, I had missed so much school in my life that I couldn't even get the hang of how to manage my work schedule, let alone understand the work. No matter how much I wanted to learn or how good my intentions were, the struggle to be studious, or even fit in, was pointless. Dolores was right; her words would always haunt me, no matter how much I tried to push her and everyone else in my life out of my mind, the voices of my past echoed loud and clear. The reality of my brainwashed truth was inevitable. I was stupid and worthless and would never amount to anything. I never found anyone to hang out with from school, and the other students were picking on me. Sure I didn't have the best clothes or social capabilities at school, but at least I was happy at home, for the moment.

A Real Family Life

So this is what it's like to laugh and have fun

I'm not sure what the story was or how it happened, but one day Stacy and the babies were moving into Mary's house, because David and she broke up. The relationship was over and there would be no reconciliation. Stacy had just gotten a job, surveying land. It seemed to be a difficult physical job with long hours. That meant we all had to pitch in together to watch the babies more. When Stacy got her first paycheck it must have been pretty good because it made it possible for her to look for a place for her, the babies, and me to move into. By the later part of October, we moved into a small one-bedroom trailer. I loved it! It felt like a huge move toward independence. It was great living at Mary's house, but as with most large household circumstances, there were many rules and often bubbling tension.

We had our schedule worked out. Stacy would take the babies to her mom's while I went to school during the day. Then I would watch the babies when I got out of school. This gave me freedom in the mornings and I quickly found a way to fill it in with things I shouldn't have been doing. Stacy tried to be supportive of my education, but I think that she just had so much on her plate that it was hard for her to really keep an eye on me.

I met a girl who was staying at her brother's house so she could to go to school in Moab. Her parents lived in Grand Junction, Colorado, about two hours away. Her name was Mindy, and she and I quickly became best friends. She came over in the mornings to hang out before school. On our way to school, we smoked pot. That's when I was introduced into the cool, stoner crowd. We would get to school to be there for the head count but right after that, we split. Neither of us had any real interest in getting an education. Because Stacy worked so hard in the day, by the evening, she was so exhausted that she couldn't hear Kent crying for his milk or his wet diapers during the night. I had no trouble hearing him, so I would be up and down all night taking care of him. By morning, I felt like a zombie. I never complained though, because I was grateful that she took me in and treated me so nicely. There were times when she would go out partying on the weekend. Whenever she had her mom watch the kids on those nights, I was free to do what I wanted too.

Mindy's brother was in a band. He and his girlfriend were partiers and would often be away doing their own thing on the weekends. That left us with a house to have our own parties in. We didn't need money, because when you provide the home, everyone else brings the weed and alcohol. It didn't bother me that I was hanging around the wrong crowd, because to me, it just felt good to be liked and to fit in. Mindy was cool and everyone liked her. That meant I was automatically in.

Stacy would hang out with us sometimes and would even take us to the drive-in. I remember one time at school it was "Hairlarious Day." Stacy and Mindy decided to do my hair in a really crazy style. They braided my hair in a bunch of tiny braids and somehow, they made them stand straight up. Then they took green food coloring and put it on my hair. Not a good idea! I ended up having green hair for months! No matter what I did to it, from dying to stripping it, my hair always had a tint of green.

One day Stacy decided to load us all up into the car and go down the old river road to have a picnic. When we returned later that afternoon, our little trailer was a disaster. Someone had broken in and ransacked it. It was such a terrible feeling to know that someone could break in that easy. Nothing was missing, but the clothes, dishes and everything else were torn apart and strewn across the floor and furniture. This must have really scared Stacy, because shortly after that, we moved back in with Mary.

In November, I had one of the best Thanksgivings I ever had to this point of my life. The house smelled of delicious food and the special dining room table was used. It felt so comforting because the home was full of love. I ate until I couldn't move, and when I could move again, I ate some more. Now that we were at Mary's, Stacy came home less and less. She worked so much that she wanted to let off steam on the weekends. She still needed to enjoy her youth. I didn't get to hang out with Mindy as often, so that meant I wasn't partying as much. Tina and I were back into the close friend groove, and when Mindy could come over, we all got along really well.

Soon it was Christmas time. Stacy had been working so much that she had enough money to provide us all with the best Christmas ever. The babies got toys and clothes; Stacy bought matching silk jogging suits for herself, Tina and me! She bought me new clothes that were cute and that I loved. I was so happy!

Tina was pretty happy too, because she got a new motorcycle from her mom. Mindy, Tina and I had a lot of fun on that motorcycle! We would go out to the field and all three of us would get on. We took turns changing positions. One would sit on the handlebars while the other two sat on the seat. We started getting brave and going off the jumps like that too. Sometimes we would crash and get pretty scraped up, but we couldn't tell anyone because we knew we weren't supposed to be riding three at a time. I'll never forget those days. They were probably the best I ever had as a kid. It was all just good clean fun, no drugs involved, yet we were always laughing… something I hadn't experienced much in my life.

I decided that I would make a real effort to focus on school. I had made friends with Mary's neighbor, Alice, an older woman with two children in elementary school. She had been a schoolteacher and she offered to help me with my math when I needed it. I went to her house after school every day, for an hour, and would sit at the table trying my best to focus on what she was teaching me. She was so patient, but no matter how hard I tried, I just couldn't seem to get it. Finally I simply gave up and fell back into the same routine of just accepting that Dolores was right… I was stupid and would never amount to anything. All of my grades were at their lowest point and it seemed completely hopeless to even try to improve them. I didn't sit around expecting anyone to feel sorry for me; and I didn't reach out and ask for help. I just accepted whatever consequences that would come for failing my classes.

Stacy continued to be away from home most of the time and I was about to find out why. It was a cold Saturday morning and Stacy asked me to come into her room to talk. I couldn't have imagined in my wildest dreams what she was about to ask me. "Would you like to move to Colorado with me? I'm going to move to a little town called Paradox that's close to Naturita. Danny and I have been seeing each other again, and for the children's sake, we've decided to give it another shot. We could really use your help and would like you to come with us." I was stunned. I didn't know how to respond. I couldn't find any words. My first thought was "Hell no!" For the first time in my life I finally had a taste of what it's like to be a kid and live without being in the constant fear of being a disgusting sex toy. Sure I was struggling in school, but I would get through it somehow. I felt, however, that I owed Stacy for taking me in and helping me, and I couldn't let her down. In my heart, I wanted to tell her why I didn't want to go, but I was terrified! What if she turned around and told him what I said? I just couldn't risk that. Why did this evil keep showing up in my life? Why does God allow him to even be here on this earth? I just could never understand how He could allow it.

"Come on Lorina, it will be fun. I'll teach you how to make bread, and I'll be able to spend all of my time with you, because I won't have to work. Danny will be making enough money to provide for all of us. He will be out herding animals, so he will hardly ever be home. It will be nice to have you there with me to help me with the kids. And, Danny won't have to worry about me being alone with them on the farm while he's gone. I'll even let you drive my car around, since it is so far out in the middle of nowhere. You won't even get in trouble for driving. If I need something from the store you can just drive over and pick it up. It'll be fun. You'll get a new start in school with fewer kids. That might be easier for you. I'll help you with your school work."

"What about the friends I have now?" I asked.

She answered, "Mindy can come and stay with us whenever she wants too." It was obvious that she really wanted me to go, and wanted an answer right away.

"Can Tina come with us?" I asked. "She loves the country and the animals." "No," she answered. "Mom would never allow that. Besides, mom needs her here to help out with the house and she wouldn't want her to change schools." I felt stuck. How could I tell her no? Immediately, I started reasoning with myself. Things could be alright. Maybe Danny would be gone all of the time. Maybe this time he really would try to make his marriage work and want to have a real family. On the surface it seemed almost possible, but something deep inside me knew that there was an evil that lurked inside of him. Reluctantly I told her yes. She was so excited! She hugged me and said, "Just watch. It's going to be so much fun!"

No matter what kind of lies I told myself to bring myself to grips with what I had just agreed to, I just couldn't bring myself to feel the same excitement as Stacy. I shared the news with Mindy and asked if she might be able to come with me. She said her mom wouldn't let her move there, but she thought she would be able to stay for the weekend if I could bring her back, so she didn't miss school. I was trying to come up with ways to avoid being alone with Danny. I regretted my answer, but there was no way out of it. It was decided that we would be leaving the following Friday. Unfortunately, the week passed much too quickly. Too soon, we were loaded up to go. Danny pulled up into Mary's driveway. He had his evil horrible dog, Sissy, with him. I remembered that dog from his dad's house in Thompson. I was terrified of her. She was a biter and hated everyone. She was a good herding dog though, and that's why Danny had her with him.

Seeing Danny made my nightmare a reality. He got out of the truck, walked over to Stacy and gave her a big hug and kiss. "Well, are you ready to go?" he asked. The sound of his voice and his body language made me sick. I didn't trust him! I just kept thinking, I'm doing this for Stacy and the babies, it'll be okay. I quickly jumped into Stacy's car to avoid having to come in contact with Danny. The kids were excited to be moving. Stacy had built up the excitement in their minds. I loved seeing them happy and truly enjoyed being a part of their lives. Even filled with all the fear of being within Danny's reach again, the thought of being with them brought me joy.

Stacy got into the car and looked at all of us with happiness and hope in her eyes. She excitedly said, "Well, were moving to our own home. You're going to love it!" Dorie, Sunny and baby Kent squealed, giggled, and clapped their little hands. It was a long drive, so their excitement finally faded and the backseat was filled with sleeping angels. Although I was afraid to ask, I got the courage to ask her why Danny was going with us right now. "I thought he would be gone most of the time," I said.

"Oh, he'll be leaving on Monday. He just wants to make sure that we are all set up and taken care of first." That knowledge gave me a little reassurance and helped me to feel a more relaxed. I'm not exactly sure of the month, but to the best of my memory, it was around the end of January or the first of February 1981. I was fourteen years old.

"There it is, Paradox, Colorado!" Stacy announced as she pointed to what looked like a small patch of trees off in the distance. It was such a small town that the only professional businesses were a post office, a small convenience store, and a gas station, which were all one building. She told me she would give me a tour of the area after we unpacked. I don't remember having a lot of feelings about it, one way or another. The best way to describe how I felt was ambivalent, but that was about to change. We turned off of the main road and followed a dirt road down a past a bunch of old abandoned looking barns. They were actually large wooden buildings with tin roofs. There were six of them, and Stacy commented that they all were ours, meaning they were our responsibility. She may have interpreted them as barns, but I saw them as potential sexual hiding spots for Danny to attack and torture me. We kept driving down the road until we reached the end. There was an old beaten down looking house on the right where we would live. Directly across from it was another barn, full of straw.

There was a goat running around in the yard. Stacy said it was one of many pets that we would acquire. "No way!" I squealed. "Really? He's ours?" I was so excited. I loved goats. When the car pulled into the driveway, my eyes were surveying all that they could take in. I could see our closest neighbor, a mobile home, off in the distance. On the side of the house was a clothesline, and on the other side, a dark looking hole with cracked cement stairs leading down to a padlocked, small wooden door. I thought to myself, "If it looks this creepy in the daytime, it must be really scary at night."

Danny got out and started unloading the things he had in his truck. He let Sissy out to pee. I refused to get out until Sissy was put away. She looked so scary to me with one white eye. She was crazy and couldn't be trusted, just like her owner. After Danny put her back into the cab of the truck, I got out and started to help Stacy unload the kids. It was a lot of work to take care of the babies. Kent was around eight months old, and the two girls were very active toddlers. Just watching them was a big chore. Stacy finished unloading the car and started making dinner. Danny was busy making a fire for the evening and bringing in more firewood. To let the kids have a little excitement, Stacy said we could let the goat inside. The kids loved it and to make it even better, the goat pooped and the little round poops rolled across the wooden floor. Stacy laughed along with us but Danny didn't think it was so funny. He told us to get the goat back outside.

The living room had an old wooden floor with a couple of round braided throw rugs. The kitchen, connected to the living room, had the usual appliances and a linoleum floor. To the left was a hallway that led to three bedrooms and a bathroom. I could have had my own room but I preferred sleeping with the girls. Danny and Stacy kept Kent with them in their room. The house smelled old.; I thought it would take a long time to get used to it, but soon Stacy had it feeling like home. I stayed as close to Stacy's side as possible, making sure Danny didn't have a chance to make a move on me. Luckily, it worked. When Monday arrived he and Sissy were gone before the sun came up.

Stacy and I loaded up the kids and went to Naturita to enroll me into school. I didn't want to go to school, but I didn't want Stacy to get in trouble, so I tried to have a good attitude about it. She arranged for me to start the next day so that I could help her with the kids as she ran errands while we were in Naturita. The little store in Paradox didn't much in the way of household items, just emergency type stuff. I was shocked while in one of the grocery stores and saw Denise, the girlfriend of my brother Justin, who had died of cancer. She was just as surprised to see us and gave us her phone number so if anything ever happened when I was in school, she could come to help out, since she lived there in Naturita. I knew that she and Stacy used to be friends, but it didn't seem that they were very friendly any more. In fact, that would be the one and only time I would see her. Her phone number seemed to instantly disappear too.

After getting everything we needed, Stacy took us home. On the way, she pointed out were I would be catching the bus in the morning. It was still fairly early when we got home, and she laid the babies down for a nap. She said I could take the car out for a drive. I could hardly believe my ears. "Really?" I asked in disbelief. "Sure," she said, "just be careful and stay off the paved roads." I didn't hesitate. It was great! I drove around on the roads until I got brave enough to get on the highway. Yep, I was told not to and knew better, but I wanted to go fast. From one exit to another, I pushed that big old family car to speeds of eighty and eighty five miles an hour. The windows were down and the wind felt great, I loved it! When I got home I never mentioned my disobedience, I just thanked her for the experience.

When I caught the bus the next morning it seemed like such a boring ride. It took forty-five minutes for us to get to the school. I was really nervous, but soon I began to feel calm. The kids were pretty mellow and the teachers seemed nice. I distinctly remember one teacher teaching us about the stock market and I actually understood it! The energy was much different there from what it was in Moab; maybe because there were fewer kids in the classrooms and everyone seemed to know each other more. I just know that for the first time, I felt that I might actually be able to be myself and fit in at school. And, I might even be able to learn.

The bus ride home was much better, because the bus driver let us listen to music. He would play The Cars and had it turned up really loud. Danny did come home on the weekends, but as long as I stayed close to Stacy and the babies , it was impossible for him to get me alone. Living the country life was hard work, but it felt good. Stacy taught me how to use the scrub board and do the laundry by hand. Together we would ring each piece and hang it up to dry. One time it snowed for two days. It was so cold that it didn't make any sense to me how the laundry could dry in the freezing cold. But Stacy said, "Trust me, it will work." We had no other options; we needed clean pants. So, together we washed the jeans and hung them out. The clothesline was made of a thick wire and when we placed the pants on the wire they stuck. By the time we were finished hanging up all the clothes, our hands were frozen.

That evening, when the fire in the wood stove made the house all toasty and warm, Stacy asked me to come help her bring the clothes in. I'll never forget it. It was the funniest thing ever. The clothes were frozen solid! We brought them into the house to put near the wood stove. I couldn't believe my eyes. The pants stood up all on their own. We watched as they got warm enough to fall over. With no television, we had to find ways to keep ourselves entertained. Sometimes it was really boring, but it made us even closer. It was great for the babies, because they got all of the attention.

When I got home from school on Monday, Stacy surprised me saying that we would be going to Moab for the weekend, leaving when I got home from school. She said that she was so happy with how helpful I had been, that she thought that it would be a good reward if she picked up my friend Mindy to come and stay over for the weekend; we would take her back on Sunday. I was thrilled by the idea of seeing Mindy again. The week seemed to drag on, and I prayed every day that she would be able to come back with us. It ended up being well worth the wait. When we got to Moab, I went straight to Mindy's brother's place and she was there. I asked her if she could come with us, and she said she could. Greatest day ever! I missed Mindy so much, and now she was coming to be with me at my house.

Danny was at the house when we got home but I wasn't frightened. With Mindy there, he really wouldn't have a chance to get me alone. First thing in the morning, we decided to go exploring, something that I hadn't done before she was there. Mindy was great with coming up with cool ideas for adventures, and we were about to embark on one of them! The dried straw in the barn across from the house was stacked, leaving big holes so that it wouldn't mildew. We played hide and seek in there for at least an hour, before Mindy had an even better plan. Next to the barn was a great big oak tree. Its branches towered over the top of the barn. "Look," she said, "if we can pull enough bails of straw out, cut them lose and spread it around, we can slide off of the tin roof and into the straw. And that's just what we did. We didn't have a knife to cut the black nylon string that banded the straw, so we lit matches and used them to break it. We had such a great time but we were very lucky we didn't set the whole barn on fire. The only bad thing that happened was that we both ripped up our clothes getting snagged on the nails on the way down. Afterward, we went and took turns riding the goat, which was also very fun.

That night Danny said he wanted to talk to us, and we thought we were going to get in trouble for pulling out all of the straw. It wasn't that though. He had seen all of the burned matches that we left lying around and was concerned about our lack of fire safety knowledge. We swore to him that it would never happen again. Stacy was making spud nut donuts for an after-dinner treat and suddenly, she turned and threw some potato dough at Danny. It hit him in the side of the head and we laughed. This would be the only time I can remember having fun playtime with Danny. Everyone was grabbing hands of dough and throwing it at each other. We had a blast! Afterward we all pitched in to clean up the mess. It made me think that maybe Danny had a good side to him; he just wouldn't ever let it come out.

The weekend was over much too quickly and when it came time to take Mindy home, even the babies were sad to see her go and were crying. "Don't cry," Stacy said, "maybe in a couple of weeks Aunt Tina can come stay with us." We all cheered at the idea.

I endured another week of school, while everyone else was getting excited about the big school dance coming soon. It was going to be a dance contest. The couple that could dance the longest would win some sort of prize. I was shocked when a boy actually asked me to be his partner. I was a freshman and he was a sophomore, who already had a driver's license. He was a very polite, nerdy kind of boy, named George. He didn't give me the creeps at all. I said that I didn't know if I would be able to go because I wasn't allowed to date and I lived so far away. He told me to go ahead and ask, because he didn't mind picking me up and taking me back home. He told me he would have to know by Friday morning, because the dance was that Friday night.

I didn't think I would get to go, but it meant the world to me that he asked. When I got home and told Stacy about it she said she would talk to Danny. It really surprised me that she would even consider it. When Friday came, Danny and Stacy talked to me at breakfast. They agreed to let me go, as long as they got to meet George and, he had to have me home by one a.m. The reason they were even letting me stay out that late was the school flier said the dance wouldn't end until midnight. Stacy said that she would lend me a dress and help me get ready. This would be my first dance ever. I couldn't believe I could tell George I could go. Everything was going so nicely! Danny was actually being nice and not creepy for once. It almost seemed too good to be true.

It was the big day. I got home from school, had dinner and played with the kids. Stacy helped me to get dressed up. Danny read me the riot act. "No kissing, no drinking, and you better be home no later than one or you will never be trusted again," he warned. "No problem," I said. I even gave him a hug for letting me go. George arrived. He held himself very respectfully as he introduced himself. He promised to have me home on time. This was amazing, I thought to myself. He wasn't a loud-mouthed jock after all. I was, as they say, over the moon. I wasn't in love or anything; I was just so happy to have a taste of what a normal girl my age might experience. We got to the dance, picked up our numbers right away, and immediately went out onto the floor. I could have danced all night even if it wasn't a contest. Half way through the night they let us have a bathroom and fresh air break.

When George and I stepped outside, he brought me over to introduce me to his friends. Right away I was handed a little brown bag. George said, "Go ahead and take a big drink. It will make you dance better." I took a big long drink. I didn't want them to think I was a light weight. It was tequila, and my first time drinking it. They all made a comment on how cool they thought it was that I could just toss it back. I took one more shot before going back in. George was right. It really did make me dance better. My head was tingling and I was warm all over. I felt great and was no longer shy or inhibited. The tequila was like liquid courage and kept me rockin' all night. Before we knew it, it was midnight and there were only two other couples on the floor beside us. It was a three-way tie. I don't even remember what we won. What I do remember is that it was an amazing night, one of the best nights of my entire youth. George got me home safe and on time. Maybe I could like him, I thought to myself. We'll see.

Life was actually good for the moment. I was starting to do better in school for the first time in my life. I was even making friends. It seemed that Danny might just behave himself. To make things even better, Stacy was making good on her promise. When I got home from school on Friday, we were on our way to Moab to pick up Tina.

I was so excited to be seeing Tina again! I enjoyed Mindy too, but out of all my friends, I had known Tina the longest. It always felt good to be with her. Back at home we kept ourselves busy and enjoyed reading, singing, and playing with the kids. We loved to take them outside and hold them on the goat, letting them pretend they were riding him. We had named him Billy. Danny and Stacy spent a lot of time in the bedroom having loud discussions. It made us all feel uncomfortable, so Tina and I would try to keep the music up and dance with the kids. After all the screaming and fighting I had experienced in the past, I didn't deal well with it now, at all. It filled me with a great sense of anxiety. When the time came for Tina to leave, I really didn't want her to go. I wished I had the courage to ask Stacy if I could stay with Tina in Moab. On the other hand, I couldn't desert Stacy. I had promised to help her with the babies, so I knew I would just have to just suck it up, be brave, and act happy for the kids' sake. When we got home, I was relieved that Danny wasn't there. Maybe now things would get back to normal, since there would be no more arguing. I was soon to learn I couldn't have been more wrong.

It was Monday and when I got home from school, I saw Danny's truck in the driveway. I walked over to the barn to see if Stacy was outside before I went into the house. Oh my God! I could hardly believe what I saw! It was Billy hanging upside down from the doorway of the barn with his throat cut and a bucket underneath to catch the blood. His eyes were open, black and empty. His lifeless body just hung helplessly. I have been around farm animals and I know that sometimes the animals are used for food, but this was different. I wasn't warned to not get close to him.

Billy was our pet. He was our friend and we loved him. The kids and I rode him, and we let him into the house and played with him. We dressed him up. He was part of the family, and now he was dead. As I stood there in disbelief, Danny stood next to his lifeless body and glared at me. I got the message loud and clear. This wasn't about killing an animal for food. This was a warning that he was in charge and in control of us all. He had no compassion whatsoever for animals or people. I ran into the house crying, but tried not to let the kids see me upset. Billy was never cut up or cooked; he was simply thrown away. The whole act of killing and bleeding him out was nothing less than a cruel act to intimidate not only me, but Stacy.

The week got even worse because our electricity was turned off. What was happening to my life, I thought to myself. Why did everything always have to fall apart? It was Wednesday before Danny went back to work. We were all relieved that he was gone. None of us were happy to see Danny when he was home on his visits. Everyone walked on eggshells, scared of his unpredictable behavior. Even though it was now the end of March, it sure didn't feel like it. This week there was a terrible snowstorm and everything was covered in a blanket of snow. Stacy was really good about keeping enough firewood in the house so that we wouldn't run out of dry wood to burn. Even though we had no electricity and things were tough at the moment, Stacy made the best of it. She was good at managing country living and a good mom, when she wanted to be. I was happy when it was just her at home with us; she made us all feel safe and loved. By the end of the week the snow was finally starting to melt. The sun was out and shining. When I walked to the bus stop on Friday morning, the air was cold and crisp. It looked like it might be a nice weekend and we were all looking forward to being able to go outside again, after being all cooped up in the house for so long.

It was a regular normal day, just the same as the rest, but my greatest fear was just about to become a reality. The school bus pulled up to its regular place where I always got off. When I stepped down from the bus I could see our home off in the distance. As I started to walk down the dirt road, I realized that Stacy's big white car wasn't there. When I arrived at the house, there was no

Stacy, no babies, nothing, but an empty house. My mind started to racing with thoughts of why she wasn't there. Maybe she went into town to fix our electricity? Would she be back before Danny? Please God, I thought to myself, don't let Stacy be gone for long! Time went by and it started to get dark. I started to panic. I didn't want to be in the house if Danny came home and she wasn't there. I ran to the neighbor's house and knocked on the door. I told them that no one was at my house and that I was cold. I asked if I could stay with them until someone came home. Silently, I was desperately praying that someone would be Stacy. The lady welcomed me in and told me to take off my coat and get comfortable.

She noticed how dirty my coat was and offered to throw it in the wash for me. She called me into the kitchen and gave me some hot soup. Although it was delicious and made me feel warm and good inside, I still couldn't make my mind settle down from the anxiety and panic that was consuming me. When I was finished eating, she invited me to watch TV with her. This was a real treat for me for two different reasons. One, I was able to be warm and comfortable sitting on the couch with her heater on, not like at home, where we had to sit close to the fire in the stove to keep warm. Two, we didn't have TV.

As my coat was being dried, I began to feel comfortable, thinking that maybe I would get to spend the night there. I was jolted back to reality when there was a sudden knock on the door. When the lady opened it, terror overwhelmed me. It was Danny and he looked angry. The lady invited him in but he told her "No thanks. Just send Lorina out here now, it's time for her to come home." The lady said that my coat was almost dry if he just could wait a little bit longer. "No thank you ma'am." he replied. "She can hang it to dry at home." "Is Stacy home?" I blurted out. "No!" he scolded, and he commanded me to hurry up. "I have things that need to get done. I don't have time to stand around waiting on you." I wanted to cry out to the lady, "Please don't make me go!" I wanted to ask for help. I thought about running once I got out the door, but where would I go? What would I do? It was freezing outside, and what if Stacy was gone for the whole weekend? My mind went in many different directions, but my body just obeyed. I felt like a robot that had no control, and just did as I was told. Like all the times before, my fear of Danny left me paralyzed. I hugged and thanked the lady for her kindness and put on my mostly dry coat. The sleeves were still wet but overall it felt nice, warmed by the dryer.

I went outside and followed Danny like a motionless zombie. Immediately he began to drill me. "Why were you there? What did you say to them?" I assured him that I was just cold and afraid, so I went were I could get warm and wait for someone to come home. It was obvious that he was angry and not in the mood for any games, as he called it. His steps were heavy and quick. His whole body seemed to display his emotion. His hands were shaking and his chest moved in and out quickly. It was easy to see his breath in the cold night air. I asked no questions and made sure to keep up and do as I was told. When we got to the porch he turned around and faced me. "Stacy went to Moab." he snapped at me. "She told me that Kent wasn't my son." I didn't say anything. I didn't know how to react. I just stood there and looked at him. "She's a lying bitch just like all of you females!" He opened the door and ordered me inside. He had a scowling look on his face. His voice was mean and demanding. "Get your ass inside, and go sit in the front room."

I did as I was told; it was clear there was no chance for me to go anywhere else. He lit a lantern and made a fire. He was throwing wood around like a child throwing a tantrum, only he was a grown man who I felt would snap at any second. He disappeared down the hallway and then returned with a sleeping bag. I sat quietly and just watched him. I could hardly breath as I watched him unroll and unzip the sleeping bag, lay it on the floor. My heart raced and my mind flashed back to the memories of when I was younger and he would hold a sleeping bag over my face to suffocate me, when I refused to give him oral sex. I was frightened and knew what he would be soon asking of me. Today would be much different than the times before because now he was filled with rage!

He didn't seem like himself. He was very combative and ordering me around. He walked over and sat the lantern on an end table, and then he turned to me and said get your clothes off now. Get your ass on the sleeping bag. I just sat there petrified with fear. I started begging him, "Please don't make me do this, I don't feel good. I think I'm coming down with something." I had to choose my words wisely and be careful not to make him angrier, but I was desperately trying to get out of whatever he had planned. He went back down the hall towards the bedroom and for a moment, I was dared to hope that he would leave me alone. But I saw his shadow coming back towards me. I was careful to not make eye contact with him even though I watched his every move. I thought my heart would beat right out of my chest. He pointed to the sleeping bag and commanded "Now!" I wanted to run, but I had nowhere to go. We were so far away from the next mobile home that if I screamed, no one would hear me. As he walked up to me, he placed a small jar of Vaseline on the coffee table.

Oh my God, no, he wants to have sex with me! I started pleading and begging for him not to do this. I told him that it hurts so much; I'd do anything but that! "You'll do what I want you to do! I'm sick of all the lies! Now get your clothes off and get on the sleeping bag before I take them off of you myself." I slowly did, as he demanded, complaining of the cold. "You can leave your shirt on," he told me. "Don't worry, you'll be warm soon enough." I sat in the middle of the sleeping bag, shaking more from nerves than the cold. Tears were pouring from my eyes. I felt completely repulsed as I heard his belt buckle unclip and then, the sound of his pants hitting the floor. I wanted to die! I could smell his disgusting odor as he moved around to stand in front of me. He ordered me to suck him.

As he forced himself into my mouth, I gagged and tried to keep from throwing up. He was so repulsive! After he was fully erect, he pushed my forehead back and ordered me to turn around and get on my hands and knees. He made a comment that I would be fine if I just followed his orders. He warned me that it was going to hurt and that I needed to relax. I felt so helpless and frightened. I thought about the goat hanging in the doorway of the barn and tried to think of something else. I searched for something to focus my attention on. I watched the shadow of the flame from the lantern dancing on the wall. There was no sound other than his breathing. Then I heard him open the jar of Vaseline. He pulled my butt cheeks apart and began to rub gel onto my anal area. What is he going to do, I thought? I could hear him rip open the condom wrapper and place it on his penis. Then to my horror, I felt the tip of his penis try to enter into my anus. The pain was beyond description! My legs collapsed as I jerked away. "Get back up here now!" he ordered furiously.

"No! No! Please don't do this!" I pleaded. No matter what he said I couldn't raise myself back up. He grabbed me by my mid -section and pulled me towards him. With his other hand he held me firmly. "Just hold still!" he growled. "The more you try to fight it, the more it will hurt." My face was planted firmly into the sleeping bag. My arms were flailing trying to push him off. He was too strong. He thrust his penis into me. I screamed! My body went limp. As I cried, I brought my hands forward grabbing handfuls of the sleeping bag. I could no longer fight. I lost all control of my actions. My gut was cramped up but my body was limp. My eyes were squeezed shut. I couldn't catch my breath. The pain was unbearable! I prayed for God to just let me die!! My body was not my own; I was Danny's rag doll.

When he finished, he let me go, letting my body to fall to the floor. My backside was throbbing. I just lay there whimpering with my with my eyes still closed. I heard him get up. I heard his every move. When he left the room I quickly searched for my panties and put them on. My butt hurt so much so I tried to gently rub the area to make the pain go away. I felt something wet and pulled my hand up to see if it was blood like when raped me. It was dark and hard to see but sure enough. I was bleeding. I didn't get up to go to the bathroom or wash myself. My legs were weak and felt wobbly; I was afraid to move. I was stuck in the house of hell with the devil himself. I just lay there in a ball, shaking until I fell asleep.

It was still dark outside when I woke up to him pulling my panties off again. I started to cry begging him to not hurt me anymore. He said "Don't worry, I'm not going to hurt you again. Just get on your knees! Now! This is Stacy's favorite position," he said. He opened the Vaseline jar again. Then there was that familiar sound of ripping open the condom wrapper. He rubbed the Vaseline on my vagina and raped me again. Even though he penetrated me in a different area, the pain was still excruciating. When he was finally finished, he told me to get comfortable and go back to sleep as he began to build up the fire. Hate pulsed through my veins, as it never had before. The only thing I could think of was getting away from him forever. I was exhausted and somehow, drifted off to sleep again for a while.

The sun was up but it was still cold when Danny told me to wake up. He was lying next to me with his penis erect. "Suck me!" he commanded. "I can't, my butt hurts too much for me to move," I replied. "Quit complaining. If you want to go back to Moab, you'll do what I want." I didn't believe him, and I didn't want to comply to his disgusting demands either. He knew how to get what he wanted though... once again, he got what he demanded by making it clear that if I wasn't willing to suck him, he would satisfy himself using me in another way. I couldn't let him do that again. After performing the oral act, he told me to go get ready to head out for Moab. I was so relieved to know we really were going. I went into the bathroom. When I went to pee, the pain was excruciating; everything burned. I wanted to die, I felt so worthless and helpless. I was a fourteen year old whore. The events of what happened played over and over in my mind.

Danny ordered me to stay in the house until it was time to leave. I sat in silence, praying that he wouldn't molest me again before we left. I wanted nothing from him. Not water, not food, not even his cigarettes. I felt sick to my stomach and just wanted to get out of this house, and away from him! I didn't grab too many things. I had made up my mind, I didn't care how much Stacy needed me, I would never allow myself to be in the same house with him again, let alone the same room.

On the way to Moab, I could barely move. Sitting was unbearable. I was bruised everywhere. Danny tried to strike up a conversation with me as though everything was fine. All I could do was stare out the window. "I love you Lorina and I'm sorry I was so rough with you, but if you would've just listened to me, it wouldn't have hurt so bad. You shouldn't have tried to fight me.

If you and Stacy come back home, we'll get everything all worked out." The only thoughts going through my head were how much I hated him and how I would rather be dead than to ever let him touch me again.

I promised myself from that moment on, I would never let that animal touch me again! But could that ever be? Could I ever really get away from him? How was it that when I least expected it, he always seemed to slither back into my life?

We pulled into Mary's driveway. Stacy's car wasn't there. I didn't wait for him to say stay or go; I got out of the truck and went into the house. I just needed to be alone in a safe place. Hearing the TV downstairs, I went upstairs into Tina's room, and collapsed onto her bed, and cried my heart out. I just needed to be alone in a safe place. At that moment, as I sought safety and solace in my isolation, I had no way of knowing he would not only be a horrible memory of my past, but a lurking shadow that would control my nightmares, my thoughts and tragically, my life, for decades to come.

My Invitation to You

I want to thank you for reading the story of my early life, leading to my becoming 'Damaged. This is the first of a trilogy. In my second book, Ripples, I will share with you the unbelievable journey of my life's choices based on the incorrect perception of who and what I thought I was, instead of the reality of who I really was. This created and fueled the fire of pure self-destruction. Decisions that I made as an adult were based on my young life experiences and how it caused me to have a warped sense of reality. Healthy relationships were impossible. I had no self-esteem and placed no value on my life.

For most of my life, I would be repulsed by my own reflection , because I was so full of self-hate. The center of my being was pure rage, and I trusted no one. I suffered from PTSD and was a prisoner of my own emotions and tortuous thoughts. I would be raped and tortured over and over in my nightmares, and haunted with flashbacks. This, in turn, left me hateful, depressed and angry. All I really wanted was to have a family and be a mother and have someone to love. Even when that opportunity was in my life, I still couldn't find any happiness or love within my own self, because I was pre-conditioned by the brainwashing of my youth, believing that no one could ever truly love me.

Without self-love, I was unable to truly nurture the children I was blessed with, though certainly I've always loved them with all my heart. I honestly tried to escape the control of my past, for their sake, but it proved to be impossible. I hated life and myself. I made many unusual choices as I desperately searched for self-worth, healing, independence and freedom from my pain. These choices would lead to a great sense of guilt and regret, creating even more self-hate. Some of my choices and experiences would be more damaging than helpful to my psyche, but at the time, I was too broken to recognize it. I lived in the moment, because I didn't have any faith in tomorrow. I was unable to visualize a happy life ahead and prayed that I wouldn't live long enough to be part of the future.

My three oldest children had to experience, first hand, my self-loathing and constant struggle with self-destruction. In the next book, my children share their independent feelings and how they coped through the madness. They will describe the damage it created in their own lives. There was a part of me that tried desperately to be normal, clinging to my desire to be a good person and mother. I never gave up on prayer or God, even though I felt that God had given up on me a long time ago. So many times I would feel completely defeated and discouraged. But, I survived the destruction from drugs, the world of exotic dancing, bondage, and a trail of broken relationships, as well as numerous suicide attempts.

I was not able to accept the thought of having to take prescription drugs and seek psychiatric help for the rest of my life just to be somewhat normal or be able to barely function on a daily basis. This is when I started to study the art of meditation and self-hypnosis, which, in turn, led me into even deeper spiritual studies. My never- ending search for strength and healing would be far more rewarding than I could ever hope for, but I had to literally go through hell to get there. I will share that journey in the final book of this series. I hope you will want to follow my journey to see how I came out of the depths of hell into a world of love, real love, for me from other people, but most important, the unconditional love I found for myself.

59691125R00159

Made in the USA
Columbia, SC
08 June 2019